AMONG THE HIMALAYAS

AMONG THE HIMALAYAS

BY

Major L. A. Waddell
L.L.D. F.L.S., etc., Indian Army Medical Corps,
Author of "The Buddhism of Tibet"

*With numerous Illustrations by A.D. McCormick
the Author and others, and from Photographs.*

GYAN

Published by

GYAN

Gyan Publishing House
5, Ansari Road
Daryaganj, New Delhi-110002
Phone: 011-47034999, 9811692060
E-mail: books@gyanbooks.com

Distribution Network
gyanbooks.com
India, USA, Canada, UK, Australia, France

ISBN : 978-81-212-2927-2 (PB)
First Published, 1899

2nd Impression 2021

Printed at: Gyan Press, Delhi.

Among The Himalayas
Author: Major L. A. Waddell

AMONG THE HIMALAYAS

By Major L. A. WADDELL

L.L.D., F.L.S., etc., Indian Army Medical Corps,
Author of "The Buddhism of Tibet"

SINIOLCHU PEAK

With numerous Illustrations by A. D. McCormick the Author and others, and from Photographs.

WESTMINSTER
ARCHIBALD CONSTABLE & Co.
2 WHITEHALL GARDENS
1899

CROSSING A TORRENT BY A RICKETY CANE-BRIDGE.

TO

MY WIFE,

THE BRIGHT COMPANION OF SOME OF THE JOURNEYS
HEREIN DESCRIBED, THESE PAGES ARE
AFFECTIONATELY DEDICATED.

PREFACE

THE grandest part of the grandest mountains on the globe has, strange to say, no book devoted to it, except one that was written about half a century ago. Since that time, however, these lofty regions, on the rugged borders of Tibet, have become much more accessible. Roads have penetrated the mountain fastnesses in nearly every direction in the state of Sikhim, a Switzerland of the East, situated in the heart of the Himalayas, within sight of the culminating pinnacle of the world, Mount Everest. The worst torrents have been bridged, and travellers' staging-houses have been erected along some of the chief routes, thus facilitating the exploration of these mighty mountains, and creating a desire for further and more general information in regard to them and their quaint Tartar tribes, than is to be found in Hooker's *Journals*.[1]

Having visited many of the less frequented parts, and possessing an intimate knowledge of the social and political state of most of the primitive tribes, I venture to hope that some account of my travels may contribute to the supply of this want. During the past fourteen years I have traversed portions of this region nearly every year, sketching, shooting, collecting, and especially exploring the customs of the people on the frontiers of Tibet, and of Nepal—the land of the warlike Goorkhas—where I lived in tents for four or five months of several successive years. In regard to the more interesting tribes, such as the Lepchas, who are fast dying out or losing their ancient customs, I have endeavoured to rescue some of the curious practices of these wild and primitive people; and I have simplified, as far as possible, most of the uncouth native names which, while they add to the mystery of these Tibetan borderlands, are so repellant to the general reader. [2]

To render the narrative more complete, I have added in respect to some glaciers and peaks, which were not reached by Hooker or myself, a summary of the descriptions of these by Sherwill, Graham, White, and Hoffman, and also some geological notes by W. T. Blanford, mostly from reports that are buried away in more or less inaccessible journals. Mount Everest I approached somewhat nearer than any European except Hooker; and I here record some new research respecting it and other peaks alleged to be still higher.

The commercial possibilities of Tibet are also referred to. This mysterious land has at the present time a very special interest for us, in view of the imminent disintegration of China. Its gold-mines, which are probably the richest in the world, should alone make it of commercial importance, though most of this riches lies in regions almost as inhospitable as Klondyke. Much of the country. however, is habitable and has many promising resources undeveloped. And with an English protectorate over Tibet, replacing the shadowy Chinese suzerainty over that country, and the rich valley of the Yangtse up to the border of Eastern Tibet secured within the English "sphere of interest", England would not only prevent a possible Russian wedge being interposed between her Indian, Burmese and Chinese possessions, but she would consolidate her position from the Indian Ocean to the Northern Pacific, and gain thereby the paramount position throughout Asia.

The illustrations are specially numerous, and it is hoped that they will bring vividly before the eyes of the reader truthful pictures of the scenery and people. As most of them are photographs, and these as well as the careful sketches by Colonel Tanner and myself and others, done on the spot, and the sympathetic drawings by that Himalayan artist, Mr. McCormick, based on my photographs, have all been reproduced by photo-mechanical processes, they are not open to the objections offered to the illustrations in Hooker's Journals, that they "do not convey by any means a correct impression; like most lithographs of foreign scenes printed in England the characteristic features are lost.., everything is Europeanised."[3] For several of the photographs I am indebted to the kindness of Mr. Hoffmann, and especially for the splendid one on the title page—an icy horn that lifts its glittering pinnacle about 7,000 feet higher than Mont Blanc, and surpasses the Weisshorn in boldness and grace.

These attractive regions, still to a large extent unexplored, should arrest the attention of travellers and climbers thirsting for fresh fields of adventure. Their valleys vie with the Andes of Brazil and Peru as the paradise of the butterfly and orchid-hunter. And, above all, there is the varied ever-present human interest of the many Tartar tribes, with their wild picturesque characters, customs, and idyllic surroundings; and the awe at once forbidding and alluring of the strange inhospitable land beyond the mountains.

The facilities for travel, in the way of roads and rest-huts, are increasing every year since the recent war with Tibet, detailed in these passages, which has brought Sikhim more closely under British suzerainty. Thanks to the energy of the British agent, Mr. White, most of the objectionable cane-bridges that beset our path have now mostly been replaced by substantial iron structures. The attractive valley of Choombi, if ever it shall become British territory, as it might have done, will surpass most parts of Cashmere. And already, is it not a great deal to find that the new roads bring the glaciers of Kanchen-junga, itself one of the most magnificent mountains in the world and almost the highest, within five or six days of Darjeeling, which is under one day's journey from Calcutta, which is less than three weeks from England.

This illustrated narrative of my journeyings I hope may reflect, in some measure, the keen enjoyment of travel in these regions, may awaken further interest in a fascinating though little known land, may assist in guiding the traveller to those features that are of greatest general interest, and bring home to the reader a whiff of the bracing breezes of the Himalayas.

L. A. WADDELL.

London, December 1898.

CONTENTS

Page

CHAPTER VII

Through British Bhotan to Darjeeling.

CHAPTER VIII

To the Eastern Pass of the Jelep, and the Scene of the late War.

CHAPTER IX

Along the Nepal Frontier towards Everest, etc. to Sandook-phu and Faloot.

CHAPTER X

The Southern Peaks and Glaciers of the Kanchen-junga Group.

CHAPTER XI

The Kang Pass for the Western Glaciers of Kanchen-junga and for Jannu—Nepalese jealous exclusiveness.

LIST OF ILLUSTRATIONS

MAPS

CHAPTER I

TO DARJEELING AND THE PREPARATIONS FOR OUR JOURNEY

"In a hundred ages of the Gods I could not tell you of all the glories of the Himâlaya."—*Old Sanskrit Poem.*

THE long cherished dream of years is about to be realized! To-morrow we plunge into the wilds of the mightiest alps in the world to explore their little-known regions, to camp among their breezy heights and thundering torrents, and to live among their semi-savage Tartar tribes.

We are starting from Darjeeling, on the threshold of the mountains, and famous for its view of those distant peaks with which we are now going to make closer acquaintance. Let us then invite the reader to accompany us to Darjeeling to look at our preparations for the journey, to see some of the strange people who are to be our companions, and enjoy the magnificent scenery by the way.

The journey from India to Darjeeling can now-a-days be done comfortably within twenty-four hours from Calcutta, thanks to the railway. Vividly do I remember my first journey to that mountain health-resort.

How refreshing it was to escape from the vegetative artificial existence and steamy heat of Calcutta, and after speeding along on the leaden wings of the Northern Bengal express, to emerge one April morning from the train at the comparatively cool station of Siligoori. We now could see looming high above the quivering haze that smothered the dusty plains, the soaring peaks of the cool "hills," as Anglo-Indians are wont to call these loftiest summits of the earth. In the distance they looked as if they belonged to another world. Their lower ranges were hid in the grey haze and rosy morning mist, above which towered the purple spurs of the higher ranges, rising above the clouds in long lines, tier over tier, up to the snows, which were topped by the dazzling white peaks of the mighty Kanchenjunga,

"Whose head in wintry grandeur towers,
And whitens with eternal sleet;
While summer in a vale of flowers
Is sleeping rosy at his feet."

When we had fortified ourselves against the anticipated cold of our sudden ascent into these high regions, by putting

THE HIMALAYAS OF SIKHIM RISING ABOVE THE CLOUDS.

on warmer clothing and snatching a hasty breakfast, we entered the little toy-like train that was to carry us up the mountains, and ensconced in arm-chairs in one of the open cars, we were soon rattling gaily across that dreaded belt of fever-laden forest—the *Terai*, which separates the plains from the foot of the hills. Passing the Tibet-Pekin trade-road on our right, and crossing "The Bent-going River" (Mahaldi,

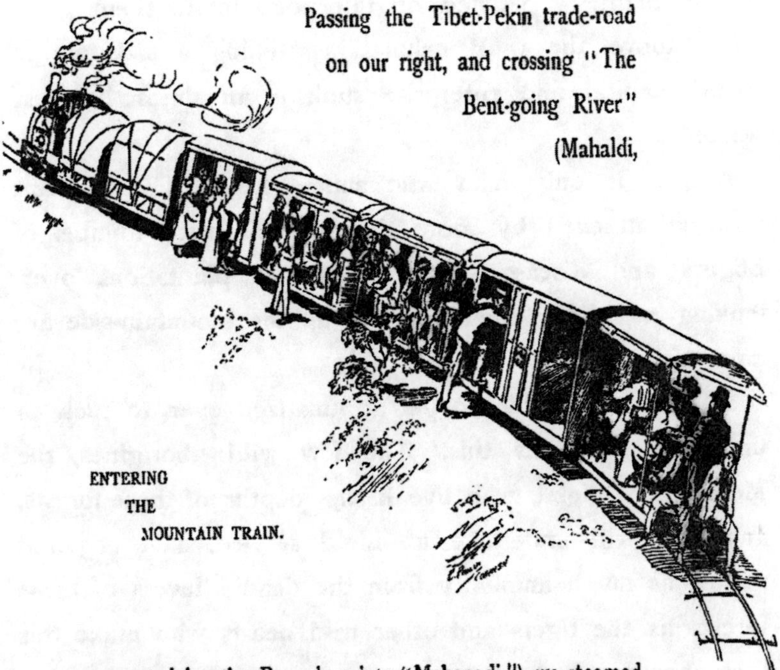

ENTERING THE MOUNTAIN TRAIN.

corrupted by the Bengalees into "Mahanadi"), we steamed through some deserted tea-plantations in clearings in this deadly forest. For in this poisonous atmosphere no labourers can be induced to settle. Each fresh batch of imported coolies soon flees panic-struck before the "Black-Death" (*Kala-asar*), "Black-water Fever" and other malarial pestilences which lurk in every brake and lay their avenging hands on every intruder who invades their reeking solitude. And they claim their victims also from the highest. Here it was that a former English vice-queen of India caught fatal fever when halting to sketch by the wayside in returning from a visit to Darjeeling. Amidst this desolate tangle of grass-grown tea-bushes are to be seen a few ruined huts of the planters, perched on tall posts to lift them somewhat above the rank exhalations, telling a sad tale of British capital and enterprise sunk in an almost hopeless waste.

Nor is it only man who suffers here. The tea-plant itself is attacked by more than the ordinary number of blights and diseases, from which the plantations overlooking us a few thousand feet up the mountain-side are comparatively free.

Still it is possible to get acclimatized even to such an unhealthy place as this. The few wild aborigines, the Mech and Dhimal, who live in the depths of these forests, and who will undertake no hired service, have acquired almost as much immunity from the deadly fevers of these forests as the tigers and other wild beasts who make this their home. And as we steam along past clumps of upstanding Sal trees, which look like pines in the distance, you may see in the clearings on the banks of the streams that deeply score the plain, some of the black aborigines[1] fishing in the shallows with long push-nets of Chinese pattern.

Further on we passed through a bit of real "jungle"

FISHING IN THE TERAI WITH PUSH-NETS OF CHINESE PATTERN.

or primeval forest, with a wild luxuriance of vegetation as rank as any in the heart of Brazil. Its tangled thickets of sensitive Mimosa and dark greenery between the tall tufts of giant grass twenty feet in height, are still the haunt of the tiger and of the herds of deer and boars on which he preys, also of wild elephants, rhinoceros, buffalo and other big game. And here, under the figs and the stalwart cotton-trees with their fiery crimson blossoms, clusters of fern and clumps of moss carry the cool influence of the snowy mountains far out into the dust beclouded plains.

The ascent begins quite suddenly. The Himalayas here shoot up abruptly from the Indian plains like giant cliffs from the sea-shore, so that here, at their base, notwithstanding we were about 300 miles inland from Calcutta, we are yet scarcely more than 300 feet above the sea-level, though in the next thirty-five miles or so of railway we rise over 7,000 feet, and pass within a few hours up through all the gradations of climate, ranging from tropical to temperate and sub-Alpine. We can see here, from this deep base, at one glance, the striking differences in the foliage that sharply demarcate the different climatic zones as detailed by Hooker, and which give such magnificent and varied scenic effects as are to be seen in no other part of the world. Not even in this very same range further to the north, can the like contrast be seen. For in the north-western and Panjab Himalayas the mountains do not rise so suddenly. The outlying sandstone range of the Siwaliks, famous for their mammoth fossils, intervenes; and owing to the much less rainfall there and the greater heat and drought of spring, and greater cold of winter, the vegetation is not only very much less luxuriant and varied than here, but many of the lower slopes there are almost burned up and bare of trees.

This part of the Himalayas that we are now entering is called "Sikhim", which seems to mean "The Land of Mountain Crests".[6] It may be viewed as a stupendous stairway hewn out of the western border of the Tibetan plateau by glaciers and great rivers and leading down to the Indian plains, with a fall of about 17,000 feet in a hundred miles. The face of this vast incline is roughly cut up into countless peaks and ridges of stupendous height, and valleys of corresponding depth, adown which dash the glacial streams and thundering torrents of water precipitated by the excessive rainfall of this rainiest section of the Himalayas, for it faces the Bay of Bengal and receives the full force of the heavy summer rains or "monsoon". And the deep gorges of the rivers so interpenetrate the mountains as to carry a hot climate far along their banks, till the semi-tropic vegetation becomes almost overhung by snowy peaks, thus giving endless variety of climate and scenery, from the torrid heat of the tropics up to the bleak arctic cold of Tibet and its everlasting snows. Zoologically, Sikhim is situated on the borderland between the Palæarctic and Oriental regions, and at the junction of the Chinese, Malayan and Indian sections of the latter region. Thus its

OUTER HIMALAYAS IN NORTH-WEST PROVINCES.
(Kumaon, about 6,000 feet.)

animal life is representative of all these. The Palæarctic animals of Tibet enter from the north and the others from the east and south—the oriental animals ascend no higher than about 8,000 to 10,000 feet; and a few Ethiopian animals also have wandered from Africa thus far eastwards.

It is peculiarly isolated from the Himalayas on either side, shut in as it is, by two great wall-like ridges that run out into the plains, the so-called "Singalela" and Chola ranges.

We now ascend a low gravelly spur of the former or western ridge, at Sookna, or "The Dry Site," proceeding at the exhilarating rate of nine or ten miles an hour; for this miniature railway, quite a curiosity of engineering, runs with its two-feet gauge, for the most part along the carriage-road that winds by long zig-zags up the mountain. The powerful little engine, weighing only from ten to fifteen tons, drags the train of ten to fifteen laden carriages up the gradient of about 1 in 28 at that rapid rate; but as the cars are mostly open trollies and there is no plunging into tunnels, this journey is made more like a drive in an open carriage, and you see the scenery to advantage.

As we advance up this gravelly spur, which is clothed with a forest of stately Sal trees, our narrow path seems like an avenue festooned with ferns, pepper-vines and ropes of many-hued climbers, through whose thick foliage the sunbeams filter in broken flecks of dancing light. One of the ferns that encircle these tall trunks, crowns them with massive coronets of stiff feathery fronds that stand up like the head-dress of a red Indian chief, and many of the trees have six to ten of these coronets, one over the other.

Emerging from this forest at a red clayey ridge about one thousand feet above the sea, we rose through the haze, and then the hills passed from grey indefiniteness into bright masses of form and colour. The twisting train curved in and out of shaggy ravines, carrying us through a swift succession of ever-changing scenery. We catch glimpses now of the blue hills and curling clouds above us, and now of the rich green masses of the woods and gorges through which we were passing, or again of the fast dwindling dusty plains below, which stretched out to the far-off horizon like a great dark restful sea. And we get

HILL PEDESTRIANS.

picturesque peeps at groups of the bright-eyed little Mon-

STEAMING UP THROUGH AN AVENUE IN THE *SAL* FOREST.

goloid people of these hills, sturdily trudging along the winding forest path, some of the women carrying their

GIRL CARRYING A CHILD.

children in a basket slung over their back, and the men with their loads in baskets similarly strapped over their foreheads; and all occasionally waking the echoes with snatches of some high-pitched Tartar melody. The refrain of one of these songs runs:

> Travelling with a pretty maid
> The road seems very short and charming,
> And so seems life with a lovely wife.

The landscape has hitherto presented the appearance of the truly tropical evergreen forest with its rank growth of gingers, calladium and other broad-leaved herbs and shrubs, its wild confusion of fallen trunks and decomposing leaves, matted with thorny twiners and bamboo thicket, through which the tall trees struggle in the choking embrace of giant creepers; while others shoot aloft like tall masts, tied down by countless climbers which creep along the ground, cling to every trunk and fling themselves from tree to tree, making the jungle quite impenetrable.

Now, however, the forest began rapidly to change its character. The undergrowth, which was almost a forest in itself, thinned perceptibly, and the landscape got more smiling. Birds and gaudy butterflies and other insect-life became more numerous amongst the many-hued wild weeds, including velvety Begonias, tall Cannas, and others which are prized hot-house plants at home. A startled deer or monkey might be seen where the wild plantains waved their broad shiny plumes against the warm slopes and the Sikhim screw-pine bore itself aloft like a giant mop. A few large-leaved oaks and chestnuts also showed themselves as stragglers from the temperate zone above. The greatest straggler of all, however, was a lowly little weed, like a blue-flowered groundsel *(Ageratum conyzoides)*. It had travelled all the way from Mexico, and seems only recently to have been introduced here, probably as accidental tares

A CLEARING IN THE FOREST.

amongst the American Indian corn which is extensively grown higher up. But it is rapidly overrunning the hill sides, springing up everywhere and fast displacing the native weeds on all the fresh landslips and clearings; even the hardy worm-wood is disappearing before it.

Steep paths struck down the hill side to clearings in the forest; and here and there in these clearings amidst the fragrant white blossoms of the orange trees and the pink of the peaches, and the bright yellow patches of mustard beside the fresh green of the maize, we passed several huts of the hardy highlanders. Wretched hovels they are, meaner even than the poorest Irish shanties, but the cheery inmates with flowers in their hair and the bright splashes of colour in the dress of the women and children make a pleasing picture in spite of the squalor of their dwellings.

Our thirsty little engine, toiling up the mountain, stopped frequently in the ravines for water, and thus enabled us to get out, as from a coach when changing horses, for some minutes now and then, to pick a few wild flowers, or "gold" and "silver" ferns, where cascades tumble down cliffs of gneiss with mica-schist glistening in the sun. And we got time to glance at our fellow-passengers.

The fresh faces and robust figures of the planters who have joined us by the way attest the healthiness of their exile in these hills, and contrast strikingly with the pale pinched faces of the tired workers whose lot is cast in the plains, and who are now hurrying to the cool hills to restore their lost strength. There are a few soldiers proceeding to their batteries or detachments in the mountains, British and Indian; the latter including some Afghans or Pathans and Sikhs (pronounced somewhat like "Seeks"), but whom the British soldier (Tommy Atkins) perversely calls "Pythons" and "Sykes!" Then there are several of the perky hill peasantry, the women loaded with jewelry and the men carrying ugly knives stuck in their girdles. There are a few boisterous young Bengalees venturing to visit these mountains under the *pax Britannica.* They are clad unromantically in European ulsters and patent-leather shoes, and their warlike eyes flash under their aniline-dyed turbans as they clutch a Birmingham umbrella in their "National" grasp. And there are a few belated stragglers from the flock of cold-weather tourists, or "globe-trotters" as they

NEPALESE VILLAGERS.

are irreverently called, on their way to Darjeeling to try to get a peep at Everest, the highest point in the world; and they are now seeing these mountains to greater advantage than their fellows who flock here in the dry dusty winter months, when the lower atmosphere is laden with dust haze.

The chance reference by one of them to a mutual friend at home makes us realize how small the world is after all.

The geological formation of the rocks was also noticeable. About 2,000 feet up, we passed in the cuttings at Choonabuti (or "The Kime-kiln"), strata of lime-stone, russet veins of iron ore, and shaly outcrops of coal, dipping down at the most acute angles. But these seams of coal were so contorted by the enormous crushing force which threw up the Himalayas that they are not profitable for mining. Further on we passed through shiny layers of mica-schist up into stratified gneiss, which was often crumpled into wavy folds and ripple-like markings. Much of the soil of this part of the outer Himalayas, and that which is most preferred for tea-growing, is a stiff reddish clay of the kind called "laterite."

Still higher up, on rounding the shoulder of a spur, we got a whiff of the deliciously fresh breeze from the cooler region above; and we commanded bird's-eye views of the lower hills and plains, such as are got from balloons. Far below us we saw the circling kites and eagles; and the rivers from the ravines that we have crossed threaded their way like streaks of silver across the plains that stretched out as in a map. Our train then boldly skirted the top of precipitous valleys, alarmingly near the edge at times. To circumvent these precipices and the dangerous water-courses which threatened disaster, demands many an ingenious engineering device of spirals, reversing stations and deep masonry embankments. One of the most dangerous of these torrents is the Pagla Jhora, or "The Mad Stream," so called from its being subject in its freshets to fits of fury, during which it swells up suddenly into a raging torrent that tears madly down the hill side and hurls great rocks headlong down the valley. In such places the roadway has to be supported by deep buttresses built up from over a hundred feet below.

The clearings get larger and more numerous. The less steep slopes are shorn of their forests for tea-cultivation, which with its trim cabbage-like rows of tea bushes does not enhance the beauty of the landscape. The white villas of the hospitable planters dot the mountain sides, and villages become more frequent. At one of the largest and busiest of these marts, Kurseong, about 5,000 feet above the sea-level, where we stopped for a few minutes, we notice some Tibetans, conspicuous amongst the many divers races which thronged the street. They are lounging about, or acting as porters: big, grimy, deep-chested men and women, with unkempt pigtails, and clad uncouthly in greasy sheep-skins or blankets, and decked with massive turquoise trinkets.

Now we are in a fresh temperate climate. The vegetation has completely changed, and we recognise the bramble and raspberry—of which there are fourteen kinds here, the strawberry, maple, chestnut, cherry, willow, sorrel, stag-moss, and many other common trees, shrubs and weeds of temperate Europe. The undergrowth has got more open and grassy; and almost the only feature of the landscape which suggests the tropics is the feathery frond of the tall tree-ferns, which lift their graceful heads like stately palms.

Further up, towards Sonada, or "The Bears' Den", suggestive of the bruins which frequent this neighbourhood, we passed above the clouds, which were seen hugging the mountain side far beneath us. And the prevailing dampness showed itself in the moist dripping forest and frequent moss-covered grottoes. In this chilly shade, the colours grow more sombre, the foliage loses its warm olive tints and gets a greenish blue. Magnificent parasitic orchids cling to the moist moss which thickly clothes the dripping bark of the tall oaks, ilex and magnolias, and long tufts of stringy lichens hang from the branches in fantastic shapes, and stream in the wind like hoary beards.

In this rapid ascent of over 6,000 feet in a few hours I had been watching the quick revolution of the index of my aneroid. Now I experienced one of the effects of this rapid ascent by a slight explosion in the ear, followed by the instant relief of a feeling of tension in the temples. This is one of the ways in which Nature adjusts our physiology to the diminished pressure of the atmosphere at such elevations. The air in the inner chamber of the ear behind the "drum" expands with the diminished atmospheric pressure, and so causes a feeling of tension, but the excess in this volume of air is ultimately expelled through that passage into the throat, called by anatomists the Eustachian tube, and then equilibrium is restored.

Still ascending, ere we gain the elevation of 7,470 feet

at Ghoom, on the bare bleak ridge of Jala-páhar, or "The Burned Hill", which a forest fire has shorn of its timber, the chill air has compelled us to don our thickest ulsters and wraps. It is indeed delicious to feel really cold again! This village of Ghoom is the first large outpost of the Tibetans,

TIBETAN TWIRLING A PRAYING-WHEEL.

or "Bhootiyas" as they are here called. Here we see them shod in snow-shoes, busily plying their prayer-wheels and counting their beads and mumbling their mystic legend—"*Om manee pad-me Hoong*", "Hail to the Jewel in the Lotus-flower"—the mere utterance of which sentence gains them sure entrance into heaven. Their huts, most of which are built of empty Kerosine-oil boxes and tins, are gay with many-coloured bunting, streaming from poles topped by yaks' tails and bearing various symbolic devices to ward off devils. And from tall bamboos inscribed prayer-flags flutter in the breeze, wafting their petitions to the countless demons who infest

"BAKSHEESH!"

the air and springs and hillsides in the neighbourhood. Among the many beggars here who clamour for ***baksheesh***, is one very ancient wrinkled dame commonly called "the old witch of Ghoom". She is dirtier even than most of her fellows, and her coat, worn into tatters and a greasy polish, seems more ancient than herself. Few Tibetans are conspicuous for personal cleanliness, most of them wear constantly the same suit day and night for months without changing, and often till it is a thing of shreds and patches. Needless to say a Tibetan garment is always a zoological preserve; and both here and along the road it is no uncommon sight to see, as in India, both men and women seated on the ground reciprocating kind and necessary attentions to each other's hair.

Leaving Ghoom we glide down the grassy northern slopes of this ridge, which now shuts out the view of the Indian plains, and after about four miles of curving road, each bend of which reveals enchanting views, we sweep round a corner, and with a cheery whistle our plucky little engine runs home and lands us in the station of Darjeeling.

When we have rescued our luggage from the group of eager porters, men, women and children, who vigorously fight over it, we are free to look about us and see that Darjeeling stands, not in a valley like ordinary Alpine towns, but perched high on the summit and shoulders of a spur which runs out into a great gulf of valleys of stupendous depth, beyond which rises a vast amphitheatre of dark shaggy mountains, rising range over range up to the snows.

The snowy peaks which were visible in the morning are not now to be seen, so late in the afternoon. They are hidden by a great bank of cloud, below which, however, the snow showed itself in silvery streaks, fingering away down the higher gorges in delicate traceries.

But the first thing that strikes the traveller, on his arrival from the plains, is the surprising and complete change in climate, and in the country and its inhabitants. And how sudden it all has been! We have shot up directly from the burning plains of India into a European climate in about four hours; and into a country which is not physically a part of India at all, but a Tartar land, judging from the oblique Mongoloid eyes of the people, their pig-tails, Chinese hats and dress, and strange non-Indian speech, and the freedom of the women whose bright and happy faces, hidden by no jealous veil, recall in many ways the Japanese, though lacking the culture and refinement of the latter. It is refreshing too to see the manly independent bearing of these boisterous good-humoured mountaineers after the mercenary obsequiousness of the fawning plains-people. Indians also are here, as servants and followers of their European masters, but their lanky legs and flabby shivering figures are strangely out of keeping with their surroundings.

It is also pleasant to be once more in the midst of a real spring, to breath its freshness, and feast the eye, fatigued by the monotonous evergreen of the Indian plains, on its budding blossoms. For the gradations of seasons that mark the opening and course of the natural year in temperate Europe are almost entirely absent in India; and this contrast increases the delight of the traveller to Darjeeling, when he meets again the glad season which "hangs her infant-blossoms on the trees", and hears the cuckoo's plaintive note that recalls sweet memories of home.

Such were my impressions whilst following my sturdy Tibetan porters up a steep path to one of the villa-like houses perched on the hillside, where I found awaiting me a cozy room with its blazing fire, a comfort to which I had long been stranger.

To see the famous sunrise on the snows, I was up next morning long before daybreak, and rode up to Senchal, a peak about 1,500 feet, higher than Darjeeling, and commanding a finer view, weather permitting. And I was soon rewarded with a sight of the grandest snowy landscape in the world. Far away in the yet dusky sky, and at an amazing height, a rosy peak flashed forth for an instant and vanished into the darkness. This was the summit of Kanchen-junga. It reappeared almost immediately, and brighter than before, in the rising glow of dawn, which, reflected from peak to peak, streamed down the lower pinnacles, bathing them in a soft rosy light that faded quickly away into cold bluish grey, and left the snowy ranges a sea of dull sapphire peaks. Then, as the sun shot up with its first long low beams glinting on the highest and then in quick succession on the lower peaks, these dim blue crests and crags leaped forward tipped with ruddy gold and splashed with fire, which, as the sun rose higher and higher, melted away in the distance into amber and frosted silver against a turquoise sky. In the full flood of sunlight these snows lost most of their broad details of light and shade, and presented an almost uniform chalky whiteness through the pearly haze.

SNOWS FROM SENCHAL.

Not a cloud obscured the view. Snowy mountains stretched round almost half the horizon, culminating in the mighty

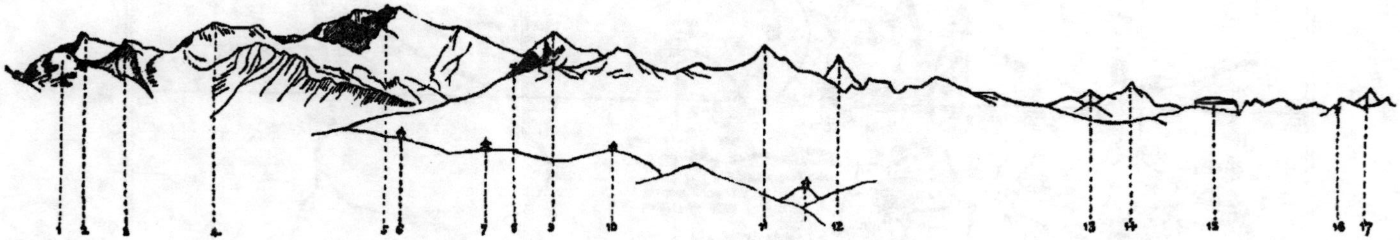

KEY to SNOWY RANGES, ETC., seen from SENCHAL.

1. Kangla peak, 18,300 ft.
2. Jannu, 25,300 ft.
3. Kang-tsen, 21,970 ft.
4. Kabru, 24,015 ft.
5. Kanchen-junga, 28,150 ft.
6. Sangacheling monastery.
7. Dubde monastery.
8. Guicha pass, 16,430 ft.
9. Pandim, 22,020 ft.
10. Pemiongchi monastery, 6,922 ft.
11. Narseng, 18,145 ft.
12. D[2] or Siniolchu, 22,520 ft.
13. Chomiomo, 22,385 ft.
14. D[3] or Jakcham, 19,200 ft.
15. Kanchen-jow, 22,550 ft.
16. Dongkia pass, 18,100 ft.
17. Dongkia peak, 23,136 ft.

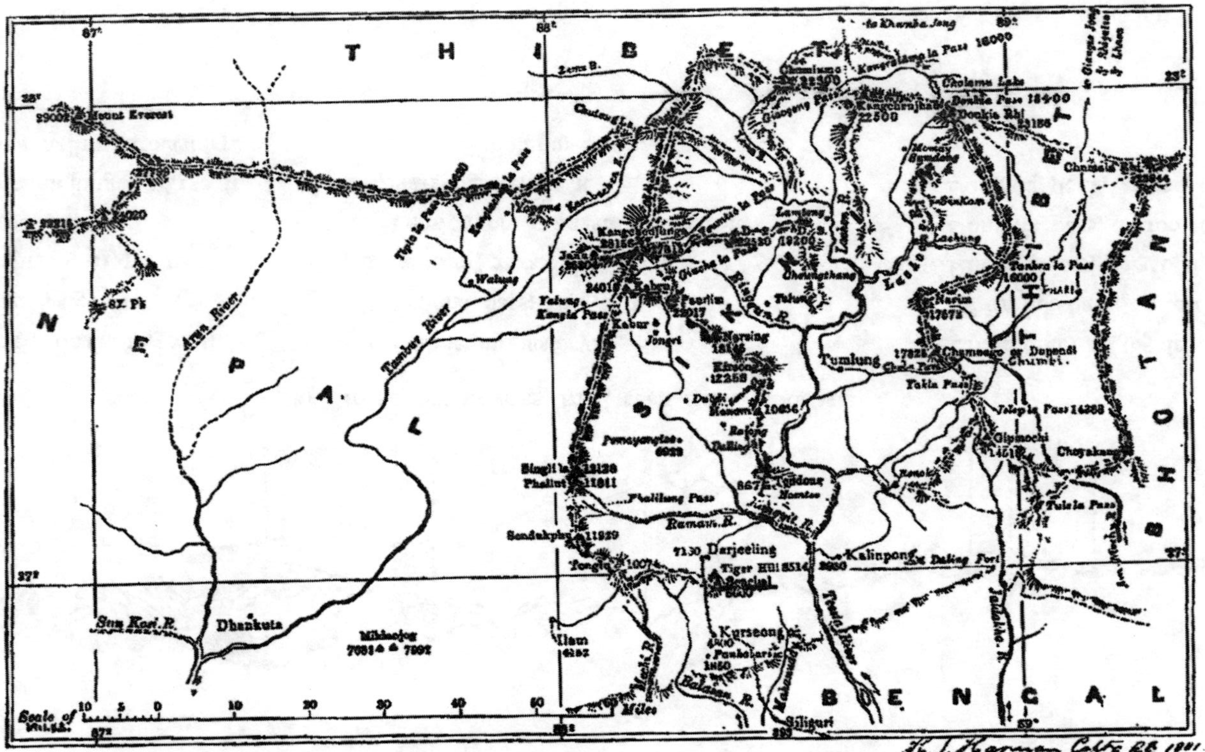

SKETCH-MAP of PEAKS and RANGES seen from SENCHAL, DARJEELING.

mass of Kanchen-junga (or "Kinchinjinga") with its 13,000 feet of everlasting snow, and Everest in the background. From this latter peak, rising on our left over the dark shoulder of Sandook-phu, the crowded range of snowy pyramids extends almost continuously eastwards to Jannoo and Kabroo (25,000 and 24,015 ft. respectively) on the flanks of Kanchen-junga (28,150 ft.), and thence far away to the silvery cone of the

EVEREST FROM SENCHAL.

Tibetan Choomo-lha-ri (23,940 ft.), and sinks in the eastern snows of Bhotan, on the extreme right. It was sublime!—

> "Northwards soared
> The stainless ramps of huge Himâla's wall
> Ranged in white ranks against the blue—untrod,
> Infinite, wonderful—whose uplands vast,
> And lifted universe of crest and crag,
> Shoulder and shelf, green slope and icy horn,
> Riven ravine, and splintered precipice
> Led climbing thought higher and higher, until
> It seemed to stand in heaven and speak with God.
> Beneath the snows, dark forests spread, sharp laced
> With leaping cataracts and veiled with clouds:
> Lower grew rose-oaks and the great fir groves
> Where echoed pheasants' call and panthers' cry,
> Clatter of wild sheep on the stones and scream
> Of circling eagles: under these, the plain
> Gleamed like a praying-carpet at the foot
> Of these divinest altars." [7]

The vastness of this view, vast beyond that of any other spot of earth perhaps, is almost oppressive. In every direction the eye as it sweeps the horizon traverses some hundreds of miles of the earth's surface; and from the deep gulf of the silvery Rang-eet river, flowing 7,000 feet beneath our feet, great masses of dark forest-clad mountains rise, tier over tier, carrying the eye up to the majestic snows with the graceful Kanchen-junga towering up 27,000 feet above the river in the foreground. Thus, at one glance, we see an elevation of the earth's surface of considerably over five miles in vertical height. As if we were to imagine Mont Blanc rearing its full height abruptly from the seashore, bearing on its summit Ben Nevis, the highest mountain in Great Britain, and above all that, two Snowdons, one on the top of the other, and were able with one glance to take in all these four superposed mountains.

The surpassing height of these Himalayas may be realized by comparison with the peaks of the Alps of Europe. None of the latter peaks exceed 15,784 feet, and only six or seven are above 14,000 feet. While the Himalayas have several peaks over 28,000 feet, and more than 1,100 which have been measured exceed 20,000 feet.

So enormous, indeed, is this great projecting mass of the Himalayas that physicists have shown, not only that it draws the plumb-line considerably towards it, but that it so attracts the sea as to pull the latter several hundred feet up its sides.[8] Yet this fact is so little generally known that most sea-captains would stare were you to tell them that in coming from Ceylon to Calcutta they had been actually sailing up-hill! Nothing perhaps gives a better idea of the enormous size of the Himalayas than this, that they pull the very sea so far up their sides.

In this unique view of snowy mountain scenery from Senchal, it takes time and reflection to adequately conceive the dimensions of the panorama extended before one. The height from which they are viewed together with the peculiar atmospheric conditions modifying the perspective, tend to dwarf their actual extent, both in horizontal and vertical directions. It is difficult for instance, to realise that the summit of Kanchen-junga is nearly forty miles distant as the crow flies, from the Rang-eet river in our foreground. But the longer we look the more the true proportions of the scene grow upon us, till we begin to gain some sense of its stupendousness, and then it holds us spell-bound.

Such a view, and to get it you must be favoured with a clear day, spoils you in a measure for vastness in scenery ever after. Its only defect is the want of variety and boldness in the great swelling mountains in the foreground and middle distance, owing to the relative absence of cliffs in the outer ranges. For very bold and rugged scenery we require to go further in amongst the mountains, nearer to the snows.

I was much amused at my Indian servant's estimate of this grand scenery. It was his first visit to the mountains, and I had taken him with me to carry my field-glasses and camera. While I was sitting on the summit, enjoying the view, feasting my eyes on the elegant outline of the higher ranges, of which the detailed formation can be distinctly made out through a telescope, and drinking in the delicious mountain air, and watching the clouds creeping up the mountain side, and the swift kaleidoscopic change in colours and light and shade from the clouds which were drifting lightly over head, I asked him what he thought of it all. He replied with much feeling and tears in his eyes as he gazed again at the view: "It is a horrid country! It is so covered with forest and so steep and stony that few or no crops can grow, rice cannot grow at all, and every eatable, even milk, is so dear that it can scarcely be bought. And the people look like devils and will certainly kill us whenever they get a chance. I beseech your honour to take me back to India soon!" His ideal of a lovely country, poor fellow, was a fever-breeding rice-swamp in Bengal. On the other hand, the sprightly highland lad who had come to look after my pony, took unfeigned pleasure in pointing out to me some of the natural beauties of his country. And the natives of the hills often show great taste in planting their temples and headmen's houses in the most picturesque positions possible.

Turning from the natural beauties of form and colour in this vast landscape, to the rocky materials out of which this landscape has been evolved, we find in these mountains an object-lesson in land-sculpture. Spread out before us, as in a map, we see how the valleys have been carved out of "the everlasting hills" by the eroding forces of rain and wind, ice and frost, and how the resulting configuration of the peaks is determined by the particular kind of rock of which the mountains are composed. Thus the straight angular outlines and crystalline form of the highest snowy peaks are due to the intensely hard crystalline rocks, quartz and granite and massive gneiss which form the axis of the Himalayas, and which have resisted so well the disintegrating forces. The irregularly jagged and bold contour of the lower peaks is owing to the unequal hardness of their constituent gneiss and granite rocks, which have weathered unequally. And the rounded broadly sweeping outlines of the lower hills are due to the thick coating of silt and debris and the relative absence there of denuded rocks, and the crumbling character of the soft shales and schists. The whole surface, too, of these outer mountains of our foreground and middle distance, so deeply carved and furrowed by the water-channels, exhibits, in the most impressive way possible, the powerful influence of denudation in the formation of the valleys.

Here, too, we see how the running water of the countless upland rills scoop out from their parent hills their threadlike tracks, and gathering strength and volume by the accession of numerous tributaries issuing from dark ravines, grow into impetuous torrents that cut deeper and deeper down into the mountain sides, and at length collect into a great river which strews the plains with the ruins of the hills. Thus we see the drainage-lines take the form of a mighty many-branched tree. This tree-like ramification of the water-channels, as seen from here, has impressed itself on the aboriginal name for the spur of Darjeeling, in our foreground. The Lepcha name for this spur is "The Fallen-Tree Hill" (*Kung-gol-l'o*). The tortuous spurs, running down from the steep foreshortened ridge of Jalapahar, represent the torn-up roots of the prostrate tree; the trunk is the ridge extending to Darjeeling; and the two main branches are the spurs of Birch Hill and Lebong, from which extend the innumerable ramifications of smaller spurs that form the branchlets.

And turning from the natural aspects of the landscape to the artificial, we find how Man himself has helped to transform this scenery, and how sudden has been this change! It is not easy to believe that all these cultivated clearings on the hill sides in the outer ranges, with their thriving settlements, busy marts and villages through which we have passed, their hundreds of square miles of tea-gardens, the white villas with their comfortable-looking curling smoke, the net-work of roads all over the mountains, and the din and stir of life, have all sprung up within the past sixty years.

Yet so it is. In 1835 when the Darjeeling hills were ceded by the Sikhimese King to the English, as a sanitarium for our troops, the whole stretch of these mountains was covered by dense virgin forest, and the scattered population, all told, numbered not more than about 200 souls; while now this settlement contains a population of over a quarter of a million, of whom some thousands are Europeans, and the tea-gardening industry alone represents over five millions sterling of invested British capital, which is steadily increasing. Such rapid progress in material development and commercial prosperity would be hard to beat even in the mushroom growth of American towns. The rapid advance of the new settlement by leaps and bounds was owing to the exertions of Dr. A. Campbell of the Indian Medical Service. He had been our political Resident at the Court of Nepal, and when he was appointed Superintendent of Darjeeling he attracted hither the Nepalese to settle in their thousands, and he also introduced the tea-plant, the cultivation of which has now become so enormous an industry.

But our reveries are cut short by the rising clouds, which gather over us into a drenching mist that drives us down the hill. Our way passes near the moss-grown chimneys of the ruined barracks on the ridge, built long ago as a sanitarium for our European troops; but as the mists and rains injured the health and spirits of the men, causing several to commit suicide, the buildings had to be abandoned. Now it is curious in this regard to find that the native name of this exposed peak (Senchal), which receives the full force of the rainy monsoon from the Bay of Bengal, and which is cloud-capped most of the year, means "The Damp Misty Hill"; so that it is possible had the Government known the etymology of the word they would have been spared much needless expense, as well as the loss of several lives of our soldiers.

On the way down to Darjeeling we saw some natives,

as well as British soldiers, armed with butterfly-nets, wildly chasing the gorgeous insects that abound here. One local species that is confined to this particular mountain, is so rare that one specimen of it fetches about a pound sterling. The pursuit, however, of these winged gems, though exciting, is not always very successful; for often, like Mark Twain's flea, "when you have got it, it is not there." We passed a picnic party, the ladies of which were dressed in silks, for Darjeeling is terribly respectable. They were travelling in "dandies", a common mode of conveyance here for those who do not ride. The *dandy* is a sort of reclining chair, fixed to a pole (which is called a *dândi* in India, and hence the name); and by this pole it is carried on the broad shoulders of three or four sturdy hillmen. Tibetan ponies are, however, the favourite "mount"; and very comfortable and sure-footed they are, though slow. But they have the awkward habit of keeping to the extreme outside edge of the path, which is rather alarming when you are skirting a precipice and the path is not fenced. This practice is said to be acquired when they are young pack-ponies in Tibet, where the bulky loads which they carry force them to keep out from the inner rocky borders of the narrow mountain tracks.

Back again at Darjeeling, as the ways of society in the Himalayas are as the ways of any fashionable European health-resort, it will be readily understood by those acquainted with the late hours and feverish energy by which the Western nations pursue health and pleasure, that active participation in the social life of Darjeeling was not compatible with the objects which had brought me to the place.

The town itself can scarcely be considered very picturesque, owing to the fewness of trees from the reckless destruction of the magnificent forest which once was its greatest glory. Of these moss-covered monarchs there remain now only a group of oaks, forming an oasis in the grounds of Beechwood, and a few stragglers dotting the hillside here and there, like solitary giants, accentuating the general bareness. At Beechwood are also a few fine pines and rhododendrons planted by Sir Joseph Hooker over forty years ago. The Cryptomerias which have been introduced from Japan, as the climate is too moist for the graceful deodars and other Himalayan pines, are so trim and solid-looking as to suggest the conventional trees in a child's box of toys. Conspicuous, too, in the long lines of the bazaar, are the inevitable corrugated iron roofs, announcing in more homely than picturesque fashion the invasion of yet another of nature's solitudes by modern enterprise and invention.

Many of the walks are very pleasant and resemble English lanes, not only those which zig-zag up and down, but also the numerous paths which stretch like ribbons over the hillsides for those who love the level. On these, however, you seldom can go far without being pestered by pedlars to buy all sorts of things that you do not want; yet these hawkers despite your protests will insist on spreading out their whole stocks before you, jewellery, plaids, daggers and swords, carvings, and the crudest of curios, including prayer-wheels, amulets, skull-drums and trumpets of human bones, and "genuine" antiquities from Tibet and China, most of which are of local manufacture, and made specially for sale to visitors.

The bazaar or market, though not beautiful in its

CURIO SELLERS.

buildings, is on Sunday morning a scene of eager bustle and bright colour, a paletteful of tints. Its varied groups of humanity, too, are most interesting in themselves to those Europeans who are not hopelessly prejudiced against everything "native". For it is too much the fashion of the Anglo-Indians at Darjeeling to put all these hillfolk, from the mere fact of their being "natives", on the same low platform as the Indian plains-people. A little more discrimination might show them that the much despised "niggers" are not really "so black as they are painted". They are not Indian at all, but despite their want of civilization, some are found to show more manly and generous instincts than many of those who despise them.

A TIBETAN.

On Sunday morning, the villagers from the hillsides, for many miles around, troop here in their thousands to do their week's marketing, decked in all their finery. The women and children are especially picturesque, dressed in all the colours of the rainbow, and laden with massive gold and silver jewellery, and necklets of rupees; they wear their fortunes on their necks.

Here you may see representatives of most of the varied native population. First there are the timid, plaided Lepchas, the aborigines of these mountains. They live in the jungles and have brought some forest-produce, such as yams, cardamoms, orchids, wild honey, and gorgeous butterflies, to

A LEPCHA.

the market to barter for salt and other articles. They are now numerically very few as they are being swamped by swarms of the sprightly little chattering Nepalese, who have immigrated in enormous numbers to settle in the Darjeeling district, as peasantry or as the well-paid workers on the tea-gardens here. The bright-eyed Nepalese women, gaily parading their holiday attire, are neatly dressed in bright colours, many of them in English broad-cloths, and they complete their toilet with a gaudy handkerchief of European manufacture thrown gracefully over their heads, in Italian style. Some of the piquant faces of the youngest would be almost pretty were their owners not addicted to the

NEPALESE WOMAN.
Moormi or Tamang-Bhotiya tribe.

unsightly practice of chewing betel-nut. Then there are many of the stalwart turbulent *Bhotiyas*, as all the Tibetan-speaking races are here called. These include the natives of Tibet proper, as well as the mixed race of Lepchas and Tibetans who form the Sikhimese Bhotiyas, the Bhotiyas from Bhotan on the east, forming the "*Doog-pa*" Bhotiyas, and the more numerous Bhotiyas from Nepal on the west, the "*Sher-pa*" Bhotiyas. Most picturesque of all are the mounted Tibetans, dashing along on sturdy ponies with jingling harness-bells, and their scarves red and blue, streaming in the wind. The Bhotiya women, especially those of Tibet, are great awkward figures, most of them, neither

BHOTIYA WOMEN SELLING EGGS.

very clean nor comely, nor over-burdened with false modesty; but all are beaming with good temper, and they wear massive amulets and charms like breastplates, of gold and silver filigree work set with turquoises; and their prayer-wheels and rosaries are also be-jewelled. The richer women wear chaplets of large coral beads, costing as much as ten to twenty pounds a set, and many wear, hanging from their girdles, various silver ornaments and Chinese chopsticks. Lounging among these groups you see several sleek priests, the so-called Lamas, in cherry-coloured robes, and usually capped with sugar-loaf-shaped scarlet hats, like mitred abbots, counting their rosary in the left

SIKHIMESE MATRON.

hand and twirling a praying-wheel in the right, and solemnly mumbling their spells; but who are always ready to interrupt their devotions to take part in ordinary gossip or a sip of beer, with as little suspicion of impropriety as the Burmese Buddhists do theirs to take a puff at their huge cheroots. Above the general hum in one corner of the bazaar, rose the wail, in a minor key, of a poor old blind beggar woman calling piteously for alms:

But quite the noisiest of all are the strident Indians—servants of the Europeans, and the followers and traders who have come in their wake, and among whom are many sly pink-turbaned usurers, the "Marwari Baniyas" and "Kaniyas," the Indian Shylocks who scheme to get the easy-going Lepchas and other simple hillmen into their clutches.

The wares are exposed in open booths and stalls in the bazaar itself as well as along the paths and road-sides leading to it; and the sellers sit behind their great piles of grain, sweetmeats, betel, tobacco, starchy yams and other food-stuffs, that are spread on green leaves, with a variety of utensils, trinkets and nicknacks. These include matches of Japanese manufacture, Manchester silks, cotton and broad-cloths; soap, tobacco, kerosine oil, and Huntley & Palmer's biscuits. But far more interesting than the wares are the figures of the sellers and buyers. The struggling, surging crowd amidst all the turmoil of the fair supplies endless subjects to the artist, if he does not mind the ancient and fish-like smells which here abound. The eager, expectant, or happy faces, and the complexions ranging from ruddy to olive and bronzy brown; the graceful drapery of the women and children, the long full flowing robes of the Lepcha and Bhotiya women, the short-kilted skirt and neat bodice of the Nepalese, with girdles of brilliant colour, and the delicate tints of many of the silk kerchiefs thrown coquettishly over the head, tints faded by the sun to tender

NEPALESE CHILDREN.

tones of green, old gold, pale pink and rose, make quite a study of colour.

Beyond the bazaar, in the picturesque little cemetery, is

the tomb of Csoma, the Hungarian, a romantic adventurer who fell a martyr here to his self-imposed task of finding out the origin of his race. The Hungarians or Magyars are the descendants of the Tartar nomads from Central Asia, who burst over Europe about the ninth or tenth century A.D. Csoma, when but a poor penniless young student, set out on his errand with only his stick, and begged his way across Asia Minor to the borders of Tibet, suffering endless hardships. In Tibetan, he believed that he had found a language cognate with his own; and after many years of seclusion in a Tibetan monastery he published his great Tibetan Dictionary and Grammar. Afterwards he tried to reach Lhasa, but died at Darjeeling, where the Asiatic Society of Bengal erected this tomb to his memory.

Soon after my arrival at Darjeeling I made the usual short excursions to see the sights of the neighbourhood—the cave of the mystic thunderbolt or "*Dorje*" on Observatory hill, from which cave Darjeeling, or properly "*Dorje*-ling", derives its name; down to Lebong, the Rang-eet valley and the Teesta-bridge, and up to the peaks of Tongloo and Sandook-phu; all of which points are easily reached by good riding-roads, with staging-houses on the way, thus enabling these charming trips to be made with comparatively little trouble or expense.

Travelling in Upper Sikhim, however, on which we are now starting, is a very big business indeed, and not to be carelessly undertaken, otherwise one's experiences are apt to be more varied than agreeable. The expedition has to be thought out and thoroughly organised beforehand. Not that there is much danger of being attacked by man, or, like Hooker, seized and imprisoned, if only one be armed against banditti, and be careful to keep outside the Tibetan frontier. Though, only a few weeks before we are starting, Darjeeling went panic-mad from a scaring report that the Tibetans with whom we had just had a little war, were swarming through Sikhim to attack the town; and the military to reassure the residents posted pickets all round the station and paraded the troops daily through the streets.

The reasons why travel in Sikhim demands costly and elaborate preparation, are because no food worth mentioning is to be obtained locally; because the roads are so few and bad, that everything must be carried on men's backs, and by porters taken through from British territory; and because frequently there is no shelter, except what you bring with you, against the sudden and trying changes of climate, which have to be encountered in the dipping in and out of tropical valleys in the ascent towards the snows.

For Sikhim so rich in scenery and in natural products is most inhospitable to the traveller. The few natives you chance to meet in the interior feed, clothe and house themselves almost entirely on the products of the jungle. Very little grain is ever cultivated by them, and never enough for their own yearly wants, so they have none to spare to visitors. Even milk and butter are seldom procurable until you reach the upland pastures of the Tibetan yak-herdsmen, where sheep also may be obtained. And shooting for the pot can nowhere be much depended on.

Not only must your own and your servants' food, cooking utensils, bedding, baggage and tents be brought with you, but the food and bedding of all your numerous porters as well. It is this last which is the most serious drag of all, for the badness of the tracks compels everything to be carried on men's backs—only for a few short distances can ponies and yaks be substituted,—and it thus requires almost a little army of porters or coolies to carry the mere food alone for your camp. This burden hampers you most heavily in your movements, for the coolies, though a splendid set of strong fellows and willing, eat up their rations as they go, and so make it difficult for you to penetrate to very distant points. To provide for this you have to send on in advance some bags of rice and Indian corn, so as to establish commissariat depots on the line of march. Then, you must not overload your coolies. Although many of these sturdy Bhotiyas can carry enormous loads of two or three hundredweight for considerable distances—and there is a story that a Bhotiya woman carried a cottage piano on her back for many miles up the mountain,—still no coolie can go at a decent pace, about fourteen miles a day, on a sustained tour in these mountains, with a heavier load than about sixty pounds inclusive of his bedding and wraps. And the more lightly your coolie is laden, that is to say, the greater number of coolies you have, the more quickly you get over the ground and with the less discomfort. So try as you will to reduce them you must inevitably take a large number in any case; and you cannot always get the best stamp of coolie, the tractable Lepchas and Sikhimese Bhotiyas, in sufficient numbers to go to outlandish places.

The enormous expense of all this porterage is indeed one of the chief drawbacks to travel in these mountains. Darjeeling is a notoriously expensive place even for a Himalayan sanitarium, but the most exorbitant item of all is porterage. Even the casual visitor finds this, in getting his baggage moved from and to the railway station. The recognised rate for each coolie is eight annas a day, or just double the rate in every other part of the Himalayas, and this notwithstanding that Darjeeling is the nearest of all to the chief source of food-stuffs in the plains, and in its railway it has quite as cheap or cheaper carriage than the long strings of toiling camels and bullock-carts which do this duty for the other Himalayan stations. Such fictitiously high rates may have been necessary in the earlier days to attract the Nepalese to settle in what was then an uninhabited country, so as to make it a recruiting ground for our Goorkha regiments. Now, however, as the population has become immense and settled, surely Government might do something to remove this anomaly; especially so, as the standard of comfort among the people here stands so very high, and is so much higher than in other parts of the Himalayas, that the women and children here are literally loaded with necklets of rupees, and many wear massive golden jewellery of barbaric size, and dress in expensive silks and broadcloths. Moreover, the persons who appear most of all to benefit by these easily earned gains, thus extracted mainly from the pockets of the Europeans, are the swarms of Indian usurers and shopkeepers and grain dealers from the plains, who keep up the prices, —the innumerable jewellers and the spirit-shop keepers.

Another difficulty that the mountaineer experiences here is the want of proper guides. There are as yet no professional guides in the Himalayas, as no natives of these regions are climbers themselves. The sportsman can always get the native hunters of the musk-deer or shepherds to pilot him along the beaten tracks, and they are especially useful in the zone of the almost impenetrable shrubby rhododendron, which is a much greater obstacle than the dwarf pine in the Eastern Alps; but these men are of little or no use to the climber who is bound for the higher slopes of difficult peaks. He must trust mainly to himself and his compass, if he has not brought with him a trained Swiss guide, as did Mr. W. Graham, who is practically the only one who has done any real ice-climbing in these parts. [9] The climber will also find some useful hints as to details and expense in Major Michell's paper, [10] though the cost of the hill journey is much underestimated there. As I did not propose at first to do any ice-climbing, I was fortunate to secure as guide, a native of Upper Sikhim, who is a noted explorer of Tibet, Kintoop by name, and whose acquaintance we shall presently make as the headman of our coolies.

The season also must be considered. The late autumn

PACKING UP THE BAGGAGE.

and spring are the most pleasant for travelling in these mountains. In the summer months, May to September, heavy rain falls almost daily on the high peaks, veiling the scenery in cloud, and the unbridged torrents, landslips, leeches and many insect pests make travelling in the lower levels difficult and disagreeable. May is the month of avalanches. In the winter the passes and uplands are, of course, closed by snow, which, however, drives the game down into more accessible places. In the middle of September, the atmosphere clears and gives magnificent views; and many plants and flowers still carpet the uplands. Snow begins to fall about the middle of October, but this month as well as November has fine clear settled weather. In March and April, though most of the higher passes are closed, and the cold is too intense on the higher peaks, gorgeous rhododendron trees cover the hillsides, from 9,000 up to 13,000 feet, with their brilliant bloom. To explore the higher peaks and the glaciers, therefore, you must endure the discomforts of the late summer rains and mists, and chance the weather. At that season, occasionally the clouds lift, giving glorious views; and milk and butter, as well as yaks and sheep for meat, can be obtained up to about 14,000 to 15,000 feet; and the yaks can carry your heavy baggage over the rocky tracks on the verge of snow for long distances, and do not require you to bring their food, as they are simply turned loose to find it for themselves. Settled fine weather usually begins about the middle of September.

Restricted in these many ways, you must draw out a plan

of your journey carefully before hand. Our present scheme is that we start in the beginning of October when the rainy season is nearly over (though a month earlier would have been preferable if we could have managed it), and follow the valley of the Teesta upwards to its chief head-water, the La-chen, and ascend that river northwards to the upper Zemoo Valley, which Hooker had been unable to penetrate; and thence pass southwards over the eastern glaciers of Kanchen-junga or Kinchinjinga to the valley of rocky avalanches (Tô-loong). This route will take us for a considerable distance over a line of country where no European has yet set foot. And we have settled all the knotty points as to the instruments we are to take, the commissariat question as to the kind and quantities of stores and their transport, the best form of tent, collecting apparatus, maps, books including Hooker's Journals and Blanford's notes, etc. And now, on the eve of our departure, as we survey with satisfaction the last finishing touches that we have put to our plans, the crowd of our coolies outside, and their head-man and our servants inside, busily sorting the various coolie-loads into which we have divided our baggage, stores of edibles, tents, shooting, collecting, surveying, photographic and other apparatus, we feel a thrill of pleasant half-anxious expectancy as to the success of our expedition, and the possibilities of the next few eventful weeks.

THE START.

CHAPTER II

THE START AND CROSS INTO NATIVE SIKHIM

> To breathe the air of Sikhim free,
> To wander by her purling rills,
>   And seek the beauty of her hills,
>   The blueness of her sky.
>
> C. Macaulay's *Lay of Lachen.*

IT was a bright smiling morning, on the 3rd of October,[11] and, beyond the blue hills, the snows stood forth invitingly clear, giving us high hopes for the success of our journey as we stepped out from Darjeeling, alpenstocks in hand, and followed by a small string of personal servants carrying our guns, field-glasses, maps, survey and photographic apparatus, collector's paraphernalia, and last but not least, that luxury of eastern travel—the lunch-basket, which it is never wise to let far out of sight in the hungry hills. Our party all told, including B. and myself, numbered fifty-three persons, of whom forty-one were porters, or coolies.

Our personal servants were mostly Lepchas and Sikhimese Bhotiyas, lissom, active, and pleasant-featured, with long pig-tails and Chinese hats, shoulders draped with blue and white striped plaids, and a sword like a Roman warrior's, suspended in an open scabbard from their belt. Of these,

ACHOOM, OUR CHIEF LEPCHA SERVANT.

the chief is Achoom, who is our courier, commissariat officer, *chef de cuisine*, waiter and valet, all rolled into one. He is a treasure of a servant; good-tempered, truthful, honest, faithful and hardworking as a slave in devotion to his master's interests, and full of wonderful resources in the many makeshifts of camp life. There is scarcely anything his deft fingers cannot do, from cooking some *recherché* dish, to carving a bamboo flute and decorating it by poker-work, or shooting game and dexterously preparing their skins for my collection, a work in which he delights, as he is like all true Lepchas, a born naturalist at heart. He is under the average height, but strong and wiry in build, has a sympathetic Mongolian face, an almost aquiline nose, slight moustache, well-formed mouth, usually relaxed in a pleasing smile, except when, in virtue of his high office, he is dressed in English broadcloth and an Indian turban on his head, when his face wears a dignified sense of his responsible position. His sword, hanging by his side, is ordinarily used for the peaceable purpose of chopping off branches of trees for the camp fire, or extra pegs for our tent, though it is ever ready in the defence of his master, whom he follows in dangerous places like a shadow.

We have also a few Indian servants. And one of us has, as orderly, a fine-looking stalwart Sikh from my old regiment of Bengal cavalry.

Our coolies are a motley crowd. They contain representatives of most of the Tartar tribes to be found at Darjeeling; and strong as horses, what a display they make of muscular strength and of vigorous animalism! Many of them have brought their wives, great sturdy good-natured women who carry even heavier loads than the men. The variety of their costumes and colours is very great, and so is their noisy chatter as they go. They carry their loads on their backs, either in large conical Lepcha baskets lined with broad leaves to keep out the wet, or tied on to a wooden framework which is strapped over their shoulders like a knapsack; and they support these loads by a broad band of plaited cane that is passed over their forehead and fixes the package from slipping on the shoulders.

OUR CARAVAN OF COOLIES.

And in their hand each carries a hollow stem of bamboo, the length of a walking-stick, to support their load when resting by the way, and it also serves as a water-bottle, while traversing the sultry ravines.

Quite a hero in his way is Kintoop, or "The Almighty

KINTOOP, THE TIBETAN EXPLORER "K.P.", HEAD OF OUR COOLIES.

One", our chief guide and the head of our transport and coolies. He is the explorer "K.P." of the survey reports, who did many deeds of daring in Tibet. With an iron constitution he has inherited, although a native of Sikhim, all the sturdy courage and roving propensities of his rugged Tibetan ancestors. His adventurous spirit found an outlet, while he was still a mere youth, in exploring many of the then unknown parts of Tibet, Bhotan, and Nepal, as assistant to the trained half-breed Tibetan spies sent by the Indian Survey to map out these jealously-guarded regions beyond our border. His qualifications for this rough and risky work, attracted the notice of Captain Harman, R.E., who sent Kintoop again to Tibet to solve one of the great geographical problems of the day—namely, as to whether the mighty river Tsang-po of Central Tibet, is continuous or not with the Brahmaputra or Dihong river which pierces the Eastern Himalayas at the plains of Assam. This problem had baffled all attempts at direct solution; for not even the Tibetans themselves know what becomes of their river after it turns southwards, a few marches to the S.E. of Lhasa, and enters a tract of country absolutely unexplored, a no-man's land, peopled by fierce savage tribes who have successfully resisted all entry of strangers into their country, indeed they kill the Tibetans on principle. How Kintoop, all alone and unarmed, forced his way far into this country, carrying his life in his hand, and almost perishing from hunger and cold; how he was treacherously sold as a slave, and on escaping, and while still a fugitive, he struggled painfully on down the Lower Tsang-po, faithful to his mission, till he came almost within sight of the Assam plains, and then, when his further progress was absolutely barred, he, according to arrangement, threw 500 specially-marked logs, each a foot long, into the river; and how this experiment, performed at such pains, miscarried, through no fault of his, but through no one having been sent to watch for these logs in Assam, owing to the death of Captain Harman from frost-bite caught among the snows of Kanchen-junga; yet how, notwithstanding this unfortunate failure to direct and establish the connection between these two rivers, he brought back particulars of the Lower Tsang-po for nearly a hundred miles lower than any previous explorer; all the details of these achievements have been repeatedly related to me by Kintoop himself, and they are summarized in the reports of the Indian Survey Department.

In appearance, Kintoop, as seen in the foregoing picture, is a thick-set active man of medium height and middle age, with a look of dogged determination in his rugged, weather-beaten features; though as he talks his little dark eyes sparkle beneath his oblique Mongolian eyelids, and prematurely wrinkled brows. His complexion is no darker brown than a swarthy Italian. His face is hairless save for one or two straggling bristles on his upper lip. And altogether he is a picturesque figure, clad in his dark crimson Tibetan coat, long pig-tail, Chinese hat, and parti-coloured snowshoes, and a dagger stuck in his belt. His deep-chested voice I have often heard calling clearly from a hill-top some miles away, like a ship-captain's in a storm. He has all the alertness of a mountaineer, and with the strength of a lion he is a host in himself. Indeed he is quite the sort of man you can depend on to stick by you fearlessly through thick and thin.

Our first day's march was only eight miles down the

BUDDHIST TEMPLE AT DORTSOOK.

deep valley of the great Rang-eet river, that here divides the British district of Darjeeling from Independent Sikhim, to Badamtam, where there is a staging-house that saved us the trouble of pitching our tents.

Scarcely had we begun our descent from the Mall, when

we overtook our coolies, who had been despatched an hour previously. They had been unable to tear themselves suddenly away from civilization and the attractions of the Darjeeling bazaar, and now they were descending the winding path in single file, like a long line of ants.

Lower down, past the white cupola of the Buddhist cenotaph or *Chor-ten* of Dortsook with its pairs of eyes (see sketch on page 64), and past the Lama-temple with its rows of fluttering prayer-flags, and its prayer-barrels turning out vicarious prayers for the neighbourhood, we meet crowds of gay holiday-makers and hear unwonted sounds of revelry proceeding from the village below, the so-called Bhotiya Bustee; and on arrival there we find it *en fête*, on account of the Feast of Lanterns of the Nepalese. The latter are small in stature, with features clearly betraying their Tartar descent. They now, however, pose as Hindoos, and have adopted the externals of Hindooism, and amongst others, this festival, which, though nominally held in honour of the goddess of good-luck—*Luckee* (or *Lakshmi*)—is really one of Nature's feasts, a harvest home, when the crops have been harvested and the granaries are full. And it is with the Nepalese the greatest gala day of all the year. All were dressed in their best, and the fun of the fair was raging fast and furious. Some were dancing and singing, others played pipes which sounded like the bag-pipes; swings, of the type of the great wheel at Earl's Court, were whirled round with screaming girls and children, and wine was being freely circulated.

During this festive outburst the Nepalese not only drink deeply themselves, but freely treat all their friends, irrespective of caste and creed; so that a sober man at such a time is quite a rarity among them. "And will the gentlemen be pleased to drink something." said one of them, offering us as we stood on the roadway, a seat and a not overclean-looking jug of beer.

We declined this proffered kindness, and began to feel anxious about our coolies, lest they might be tempted to join the general dissipation, especially as most of them belonged to this very village. We noticed with some alarm that several of them were already tipsy, and what was worst of all, Kintoop, the headman, himself was not above suspicion. This looked serious; for human heroes are, after all, only men and with men's weaknesses, and Kintoop's weakness was his fondness for wine; though I must say that he seldom did indulge to great excess, and almost never when he had important business in hand. And here it certainly was not easy for our men to resist the pressing invitations of their hospitable Nepalese friends. For we saw several of the latter, good-naturedly seizing and stopping some of our coolies who chanced to be their comrades, and forcing their not unwilling victims to have a drink.

Our march was now at a standstill, as most of the coolies had deposited their loads by the roadside, and were joining in the general merry-making. I had therefore to tackle Kintoop severely, and ordered him to collect his men and pilot them through this village without delay. And we

NEPALESE SWING AT A FAIR.

ourselves proceeded on with a few coolies who were carrying the most necessary things.

Continuing our descent we pass again into the zone of tree-ferns, of which there are eight species within a short distance, at about 6,000 ft. elevation, and giant stag-moss; and we wind along the hot shadeless flank of Lebong, or "the tongue-shaped spur", as this Lepcha name means. Axe and fire have shorn it of its trees for tea cultivation. Whole forests have been annihilated, leaving here and there only a solitary tree, or narrow belts of trees in the ravines, as evidence of the magnificent woods which have fallen a sacrifice to advancing civilization. One of the results of this wholesale removal of forest is the frequency of land-slips, through the heavy rain ploughing through the exposed soft soil. In several places stretches of the hill-sides had slid down, carrying with them their tea-bushes, so that the old adage for investors—"there is nothing like land, for it cannot run away"—is not strictly applicable to property in the Himalayas.

At the end of this spur is the little Lamaist monastery of Ging. Its altar is covered with idols, objects that are worshipped as fetishes, and candles and sacrificial implements. Its walls are frescoed with atrocious daubs, representing many devils, deities and saints of Chinese design. The place, however, is worth visiting by those who have not seen the finer paintings in Tashiding and the larger temples of Sikhim. The guardian spirit of this place is represented on the wall as a hideous, tigerish monster, gorgon-headed, with tusks and out-thrust tongue: a destructive demon who is worshipped with bloody sacrifices; and we saw his shrine drenched with the blood of kids, fowls, and other animals. Yet these Lama-priests profess to be Buddhists, with whom the taking of life is absolutely prohibited! The truth is that this bloody sacrifice is a vestige of the old devil-worship of the country. The people say, that God is a good spirit and harms no one; but the devils are actively malignant, and therefore their goodwill must be secured by peace-offerings. So God is neglected, and the devils are worshipped instead.

Still descending through tea-gardens for several miles, we enter a belt of semi-tropical forest, and about the eighth mile we reach the staging-house of Badamtam, at 2,500 feet above the sea. It is picturesquely perched in a clearing in the forest, and commands fine views of Darjeeling, 4,000 feet above us, and of the great Rang-eet river, 2,000 feet below us, glistening through the green foliage like a silver ribbon, and filling the valley with the soothing sound of its rushing waters.

After our three hours' walk we were not sorry to find on entering the house, that Achoom, who had preceded us with the commissariat, had ready waiting for us a hot lunch, to which we did full justice. For drink we had a large bamboo jugful of the refreshing beer, that the Lepchas brew from a millet seed called *Murwa.* [12] The fermented grain is put into a jug formed by cutting off a joint of the giant bamboo, and this jug is then filled up with hot water.

The liquor is imbibed by sipping it up through a thin

A MONK SIPPING MURWA-BEER.

reed like a straw. It tastes like weak whiskey-toddy or rum-punch with a pleasant acidity, and it is milder than the mildest English beer. It is the wine of the country and is a *food* as much as a drink. The men, women, and children delight to sip it at all times from morning till night. And they sing its praises in an apostrophe to the sipping reed, the best kind of which comes from the grassy hills of Sarrie *(Tsari)*, where the reed is also used as an arrow in the chase:—

O! sipping reed of Sarrie!
Thou 'rt born to make us merry.
Thy *stem* instils the luscious wine,
The drink of gods, nectar divine.
Thy *shaft* is shaped an arrow fine,
That's fit for bravest princes' bow.
Thy *top* bears up the banner-line
Of praying-flags that Lamas twine,
O! sipping reed of Sarrie!

Even the priests or Lamas are so addicted to this beverage that they sip it in their temples, and none can travel far without an attendant carrying a store of it. Indeed one of the commonest sights is to see a monk going his rounds sipping a jug of this beer as a solace to his pessimistic dogma that "all life is misery," for he then is able to contemplate the world with full approval. Whilst our truant coolies were dropping in, in twos and threes, we spent the afternoon in sauntering through the magnificent forest, revelling in the jungle sights and sounds—the flashing of a pheasant, and of the tiny sun-birds like winged gems, across the depths of green; the loud whirring of the Cicad insects on the fern-covered trees high over head, the fluty cooing of a kind of cuckoo in the thick undergrowth, the cheery chirping of the squirrels as they scamper up and down the frail ladders of climbers, the sharp rat-tat-tat of the crimson-crested golden woodpecker on the stump of a dead tree, the ringing echo of the woodsman's axe followed by the crash of falling timber, and the hoarse bark of the Kakar deer echoing up the valley. These last-mentioned deer are common here, and I shot one last year within twenty yards of this very house. Black bears also abound, not the Indian bear, but the Himalayan *(Ursus Tibetanus).* They come out freely into the clearings of the tea-gardens when the Indian corn is ripening in June and July, and are nasty customers to meet at close quarters. You must also be on your guard against even more dangerous though more lowly foes. For we here encountered a deadly serpent, with fatal results—fatal for the serpent. It was an enormous cobra, measuring 56 inches in length, and of the pale variety. It raised itself with expanded hood in a menacing manner, but quickly backed away, unlike the more aggressive dark variety which generally pursues you. It was the Malayan kind, with a single solitary spot on its neck, and not with the pair of spectacles of the Indian variety. It is somewhat reassuring, however, to know that poisonous snakes seldom ascend the mountains so high as this, though I found two as high as Birch Hill (6,500 ft.) at Darjeeling, of other species than the cobra, namely, the "Krait" *(Bungarus cærulus)* and *Calliophis Maclelandii*, yet both almost as deadly.

Going through these forests, you cannot possibly have a more interesting companion than the Lepcha, a true son of the forest. He is a born naturalist and keen sportsman. He knows the habits of every bird and beast and creeping thing; and the properties of every plant. He is steeped in romance, and few are braver than he is, or so full of resource and self-reliant when battling against physical dangers in the forest. His quiet, impressionable, affectionate nature wins its way into your confidence, and his unruffled temper under difficulties cheers on the traveller who is in his company.

It was interesting to watch them decoying some tiny brilliantly plumed sun-birds which here take the place of the humming-birds of America. When these were hiding in the thick shrubs and not one to be seen anywhere, a Lepcha who was with me, by blowing into his closed fists, imitated the hooting of a small owl which preys on these little birds, and almost immediately the adjoining shrubs were alive with these and other small birds, all twittering with excitement and craning their necks to see and to jeer at the helplessness of their nocturnal enemy, who, they well knew, could not see them in such broad daylight. And when this ruse failed to draw them after a few times, they immediately crowded out again when the Lepcha, with his lips applied to the back of his hand, imitated the squeaking of a small bird when it is seized by a hawk or other bird of prey. So curious were they to see which of their companions was being seized and devoured, that they exposed themselves freely for a few seconds, and then promptly hid away again.

Or when you see some lovely orchids growing on the top of an enormously high tree, your Lepcha asks you whether you would like to get them, and he nimbly climbs the tree, cutting notches here and there for foothold, and fearlessly fetches them to you from that giddy height. And he also gives you their names, and tells you all about their habits, and how they differ from other species.

Altogether the Lepcha is a very different sort of companion in the jungle from the Indian who knows and cares nothing about flowers, nor animals—except those that he eats or that eat him.

As the darkness closed in we watched the pretty effect of the illuminations of the Feast of Lamps at Darjeeling, mapping out the town above us, and the thousands of twinkling lights in the clearings all over the hillsides. We retired, after an early dinner, with many misgivings for the morrow, because neither Kintoop nor about a dozen of his remaining men had yet turned up.

At daybreak next morning we found a messenger from Kintoop to say that he was delayed in getting sober porters for the few remaining loads of luggage, but that we should start off and leave him to follow. But we decided to wait and see the baggage off in front of us, and it arrived in a few hours, not, however, on coolies, as no sober men were to be found, but on ponies; and fortunately the road was practicable for ponies for two more days' march. So off we started again, and our coolies, looking ashamed of their dissipation of yesterday, now that the effervescence of their mirth had subsided, seemed anxious to atone for their misconduct by extra zeal.

We dipped rapidly down the gorge of the great Rang-eet, which we had to cross. Below us, dense woolly white

RANG-EET RIVER.

clouds filled the [depths of the lower valleys, giving the appearance of a snowed-up lake or frozen Norwegian fiord, from whose white shores rose up the dark outlines of the mountain ridges, range upon range, up to the dazzling peak of Kanchen-junga.

As we descended by sharp zig-zags through almost five miles of the forest of Sal, (that timber tree inferior only to teak,) the clouds drifted in the morning breeze up the mountain sides and revealed the winding river with its silvery strands a thousand feet below us. Soon we reached the bottom of the gorge amongst whose rank vegetation and dark boulders "fever lurks in every brake". The passage of the small Rangnoo by a wooden bridge, brought us down to the bank of the great Rang-eet rushing noisily between steep mountains. This river is never fordable, and as the cane-bridge was broken we had to cross in a canoe; but the skipper of this craft and his solitary assistant, whose services are so seldom in demand, were nowhere to be found, although they had been apprised of our coming. So a messenger was despatched to search for them in their fields, a mile up the valley.

Meanwhile, we breakfasted among the boulders, mocked by the bare bones of the old cane-bridge. Tied to its piers as well as to the twigs of trees which bend over into the stream are numerous bundles of rags and prayer-flags, as offerings to the devils of the river. The water itself was deliciously cool, only 58° Fah., as it had come down from not far-distant glaciers, although the elevation was only 818 feet above the sea-level, and the temperature of the air at noon was 87° Fah. Some good rod-fishing is to be got here, including the great Indian carp or the Mahaseer. We came upon a Lepcha dining off a huge dragon-like lizard *(Varanus dracæna)*, generally called the

Bis-Cobra as it is erroneously believed to be poisonous. Another Lepcha was fishing with the rudest of nets, and in a hap-hazard way; for the Lepchas shun the great rivers, as few of them can swim. He was, however, quite content with his small bag; very unlike the native Indian fishers, who make clean sweeps of even the smallest fry; and when I have remonstrated with some of these on this point, they replied, "Why should we leave them for other men to catch?"

Geologically, we were now down again amongst the slates and limestones and carboniferous shales [13] which we encountered at the foot of the outer hills. As we descended, the gneiss formation got more and more micaceous until it became glistening mica, of which many of the boulders in the river bed are composed, though many are also blocks of gneiss, fallen from the rocks some thousands of feet above.

Our crossing-place is at a relatively narrow part of the gorge where the river rushes in a series of rapids, though the actual fall of the river in the course of twenty-three miles above this point, as measured by Dr. Hooker, is only 987 feet.

In crossing, we nearly came to grief. The canoe was only a floating beam which had been hollowed out by fire and axe. It had many ominous rifts, no rudder, and for an oar a bit of flat wood tied to a pole. When we had wedged ourselves into its narrow cavity, and several coolies had crammed in themselves and their bundles, lading it to its last inch, the two ferrymen dragged the laden crazy craft up stream some distance, and then poled it out with a long bamboo, broadside-on to the rapids, which seized it and hurled it swiftly down the stream. Then the ferrymen wildly plied their poles, and the canoe shot obliquely across the current, under the double impulse, to the opposite bank, where we bumped heavily on a boulder that sent us with a jerk into a swirl of relatively shallow backwater, at a point far below that from which we had started. It took some time to transport all our baggage and coolies and the ponies, which latter, poor things, were tied to a rope cable and hauled across, partly swimming, at considerable risk to their lives from the swift current and the great boulders in its bed. As luck would have it, the only package which was damaged in this rough transit, was my box of photographic glass plates, about which I had given the strictest orders to preserve it carefully from damp or falls; for paper and celluloid films do not keep well in this climate, and you are almost forced to take weighty and fragile glass plates. One of the men in the excitement of landing it, dropped it bodily into the river. It was quickly fished out, and fortunately, its well-soldered contents were little the worse for this ducking.

On the river bank at the bottom of this malarial gorge is a poor hamlet of charcoal-burners who suffer terribly from fever. They asked for medicine and I gave them some quinine, though this deadly fever usually lays hold of them with a grip that quinine cannot loosen.

We were now in Native or "Independent" Sikhim, and missed the good roads of the British territory. The rugged narrow goat-track which sufficed the Sikhimese for a road led past rank crops of cardamoms, growing in the rich silt on the river banks, and through tall gingers. It was a stiff hot climb up out of this gorge for about 2,000 feet, with the afternoon's sun beating down on us.

The stillness of these semi-tropical forests in the noontide heat strikes you as you rest to recover your breath in toiling up hill. Scarce a sound is to be heard, or any life to be seen, except a solitary bird, or squirrel; or sometimes a deer, as, startled from its siesta by our footsteps, it crashes through the rotten twigs and branches which strew your path; or a few gorgeous butterflies float lazily among the foliage. Even the hum of insects seems to cease, so that as you listen you are almost startled by the sound of a falling leaf.

Higher up, past the cedar-like timber-trees, "Toon" (*Cedrela toona*), of which tea-chests are made, we came to *Cheer* pines (*Pinus longifolia*), so common at the foot of the Northern Himalayas, but in damp Sikhim only found in a few relatively dry land-locked slopes like this. On gaining the shoulder of the gorge we emerged on to the open slopes of the hamlet of Kitam (2,840 feet), or "The Cotton Field", a picture of pastoral simplicity. Its well-cultivated fields and meadows stretch up for many miles to Namchi on the flanks of Mount Tendong, where we had intended to camp; but we decided, as it was late in the afternoon, to stay here for the night, especially as it seemed to be beyond the range of malaria; for after a height of of 3,000 feet or so, even dense forest ceases to be malarious, and the temperature here was 74° Fah., which was quite tolerable after the great heat of the day.

Whilst our tents were being pitched in an orange-grove on the outskirts of the village we were regaled with Murwa-beer by the headman of the place, in freshly-cut bamboo jugs, and new sipping reeds, before a crowd of admiring natives. We afterwards strolled through the hamlet, among the homesteads which dot the hillside, perched on stilts amidst clumps of feathery bamboos, broad-leaved bananas and orange trees, now bearing their bright golden fruit. And we watched many of the villagers at their primitive looms, weaving their homespun cotton and nettle-fibre, which they dye with the wild madder or Manjeet, from the jungle near by. Their very parasols grow by the wayside. It was comical to see children sheltering themselves from a shower of rain by a leaf of the giant calladium, which they had plucked in the adjoining jungle.

I experienced, as usual, much difficulty in photographing these intensely superstitious people. They exhibited a lively horror and hid away whenever the lens, or "the evil eye of the box" as they called it, was pointed at them; for they believed that it worked some dark magic on them and took away their souls with their pictures, and so put them in power of the owner of their photograph to cast his spells over them. And similarly a photograph of the scenery they alleged blighted the landscape. Some persuasion coupled with a small present, however, generally

THEIR PARASOLS GROW BY THE WAYSIDE.

overcame their scruples.

An old Lepcha woman here presented us with some eggs. A present of eggs, however, may be embarrassing at times in Sikhim; for it is a common way of proposing marriage, and the acceptance of the basket of eggs by the object of one's affections settles the question. [14] A circumstantial story is told of the sister of the present Rajah or king of Sikhim, as to how when she visited Darjeeling for the first time, she was so captivated by the charms of a certain European there, that she wished to marry him. So when he accepted her present of eggs, she bluntly asked him to marry her right away; and she was only made to understand with difficulty that he already had a wife, and could not according to our customs take another.

As the daylight faded, we returned to our tents, and after dinner, we sat outside watching the picturesque groups of our people at their camp fires. Some men and women were cooking, others fetching water in long bamboo pitchers; some men lolling lazily or stretched on the grass were singing snatches of Tartar songs in a quavering minor key:

My love is like the image, in a pure silver mirror
Beyond the reach of grasping hands and only won by loving heart.
Like a tree of costly coral, like a leaf gemmed with turquoise,
Like a fruit of precious pearls, you, my love, are rare.
You are the loveliest of lovely flowers, and where'er you go
I as a turquoise butterfly will follow my flower.

Others were jesting in rough fashion with each other, or playing games of chance, for all are inveterate gamblers. Some were piously counting their beads, or crooning some mystic spell in a low deep chant and pompous supernatural voice which seems to come from as low down as their boots; while others had already retired for the night into the flimsy booths which they had rigged up with branches, and the sheets of waterproof matting (*goom*) which we had issued to each coolie to protect our baggage from the rain; and in these rude arbors many were already fast asleep, pillowing their heads on their loads or empty baskets.

To our leeward, so that the smoke does not annoy us, is our indispensable cook's department. Achoom is at present being relieved of the drudgery of the actual cooking whilst we are in these lower valleys, by my Indian cook, also a tried man, and well accustomed to camp life, having been with me through the Burmese war of 1886—87, up to the Chinese frontier; and since then he has been regularly camping about with me. His rough active life has given him a haggard appearance very unlike the sleek comfortable cook of towns. Indeed his sharp and almost cadaverous features are so suggestive of the mummy of Rameses the Great, that we have dubbed him "Rameses"; and he takes quite kindly to this name, doubtless because his real name is Ram. Rameses may be trusted to serve up something savoury in a marvellously short time, whenever and wherever we call a halt by the way. But what a weird figure he cuts as he crouches over his pots and pans amid the smoke, his thin face lit up by the lurid glare of the spluttering, crackling log-fire; more like a magician concocting some mystic potion, than our worthy domestic preparing *al fresco* a simple meal for to-morrow.

Then Kintoop came up for orders for the morrow's

march. And after dismissing him we sat discussing our plans and other matters, until the bustle of the camp ceased, the cooking fires died down, and the eerie hooting of the great wood-owl, the screech of the night-jar, the flickering of the tiny lamps of the fire-flies, and the cry of the tiger-cat, suggested that it was time for us to turn into our tents.

CHAPTER III

UP THE TEESTA VALLEY TO THE KING'S CAPITAL

THEY journeyed over steep Tendong
And through the Vale of Teesta fair.
By Silling's slopes and Yeung's Mendong
And Kubbi's smiling pastures rare
And Ryott's roaring falls,
To where high perched on Mafi's breast
With banners gay and brazen crest
Shone Sikhim Raja's [18] halls.

C. Macaulay's *Lay of Lachen.*

THE rustle of the early breeze amongst the trees, the crackling of the freshly-lit camp fires, and the stir of our waking servants outside, awoke us next morning, just as the first streaks of daylight were stealing through the chinks of our tent. We were up, dressed, and outside in a few minutes: and whilst an early cup of tea was clearing away the cobwebs of sleep, our tent was struck and packed up; and both we and our coolies were again on the move, soon after the sun had risen. To get the men started off in the chill of the morning, cost Kintoop much trouble;

for these men, unlike the coolies of the plains, always eat before starting. Nor was it easy to get the strongest men to carry the heaviest loads, for these were usually shuffled on to the weaker back of some "willing horse", and the strongest coolie often contrived to make up a bulky-looking load, containing little else than the light wraps of himself and his comrades.

It was a real pleasure to step out briskly in the keen cool air to get warm; and to stop here and there by the wayside to pluck some of the tempting brambles and yellow raspberries that overhung our winding path, as we brushed aside the dew-drops which hung like pearls from the tips of the foliage. And we enjoyed again the delights of drinking delicious water from the crystal streamlets that crossed our path.

As we ascended this open valley of the Mangpoo, with the river far beneath us, past the picturesque huts of the Lepchas that dotted the clearings on the hill side, Achoom was hailed as an old friend by everyone we met. He is almost the only Lepcha in service at Darjeeling who has remained true to the traditions of his fathers, "among the faithless, faithful only he". One amiable old man, who was introduced as Achoom's uncle, pressed us to "honour his hut with a visit". We gladly accepted his invitation, especially as these Lepchas, who are the aborigines of the country, are extremely interesting, not only for their many charming traits, but also chiefly because they represent the state of primitive man when he subsisted by hunting, fishing, and gathering wild fruits and digging roots; and they now are a vanishing race, fast disappearing before the tide of emigrants from the more active and civilized tribes who have lately swept in great waves into their country.

A LEPCHA.

These "Lepchas", as they are called by Europeans, following the Nepalese name of the tribe;[16] "Rong", as they call themselves, and which is their proper name; are known to the Tibetans as *Mön-ba* or *Mön-rik*, that is "people of the *Mon* country"—a general Tibetan name for the lower Himalayas, from Kashmir down to Assam and Burma. The Lepchas were the sole inhabitants of these hills until about 250 years ago, when Tibetans entered the country and usurped the government, and appropriated to themselves all the best lands on the cool hills, driving the Lepchas down to seek new homes in these lower valleys and the still lower malarial gorges. These Tibetan settlers and their descendants are generally known to Europeans by the Indian term of "*Bhotiya*," that is "an inhabitant of *Bhot* or Tibet;" but we will call this ruling race of Sikhim, "*Sikhimese* Bhotiyas", to distinguish them from the Bhotiyas of Tibet proper, and those of Nepal and Bhotan, all of whom differ considerably.

Now that you see a pure Lepcha, side by side with these other tribes, you could never mistake him, not even for a Sikhimese Bhotiya, of whom many possess a considerable strain of Lepcha blood, so sharply is he distinguished from all these in physique, features, and dress, in speech and manners, in customs and character.

He is, indeed, with his distinctive traits, physical and moral, very much what his environments have made him. Living in a country which yields to him, without husbandry, a profusion of wild fruits and edible roots and other jungle products, the Lepcha is naturally indolent and easy-going. His close companionship with nature has made him a naturalist, a tender lover of flowers, and something of a philosopher; though his narrow gorges have narrowed his views. His solitary life in the peaceful depths of the great forests makes him timid and shy of strangers. His hard experience of the forces of nature, the storms and floods which wreck his home and scanty crops, and scatter desolation and death around him, has made him a worshipper of malignant devils, and intensely superstitious. His exposed bivouacking at night in malarial gorges, has sapped much of his vigour and enervated him. His roving life has made him love liberty and hate restraint, leading him to shun service, and preventing him ever combining with his fellow-tribesmen against a common foe. And this unwarlike spirit, crushed under generations of Tibetan oppressors, has left little of the heroic in his composition, when he is pitted against disciplined masses of other tribes. But, as we have seen, he is a keen sportsman, a born naturalist, sympathetic, frank and generous to a fault, and no one can be braver than he is in facing danger in the forest.

We follow, then, this genial old Lepcha to his hutlike home in one of the clearings. His mild Mongolian features, hair parted down the middle, scanty beard and moustache impart a somewhat effeminate appearance; but the frank happy look in his honest eyes stamps him as the simple contented child of the forest, who dearly loves a joke and laughs heartily at the comic side of things. And his soft, slow, staccato speech strikes agreeably on the ear after the loud harsh tones of the Bhotiya or the shrill hurried jargon of the Nepalese.

His lissom figure is clad in a long plaid of blue and white striped cloth of home-spun nettle-fibre or cotton, which is wound round his body and descends to the knee, the loose end being thrown gracefully over his shoulder, leaving the right arm free. His waist is girdled by a red or blue band, from which is suspended his long, formidable-looking, straight, one-edged knife *(ban)* in an open wooden scabbard, like a Roman soldier's sword. This knife is to him even more than the *kookrie* is to the Goorkha. With it he clears the jungle, builds his hut, skins the animal he shoots with his arrow, or snares in the forest; "it is his sword in battle, his table-knife, his hoe, spade and nail-parer," his gimlet, hammer and razor. His hair he wears in a pig-tail (his womenfolk plait theirs in two), and when a hat is added, on ceremonial occasions, as in the group at page 102, it is usually of cane-work and like an inverted flower-pot, resembling generally those of the wild Naga and Abor tribes of Assam, and bears a small plume of grass or peacock feathers in front. Around his neck he hangs small packets of charms against the evil eye etc. For leggings he has a broad tape tied round the leg from the ankle to the knee. His feet are bare; and when he travels he carries a wallet, slung over his shoulder, to hold his pipe, food etc., like his kinsmen, the Nagas and Kachins and other Indo-Chinese tribes further east, and in his hand his bow and arrows, as very few Lepchas possess a gun.

His flimsy hut is almost idyllic in its simplicity. It is perched on stout posts amid a few orange trees and bamboos, and surrounded by a patch of cultivation—a small plot fenced in by thorny branches, for a few gourds, turnips and chillies, and beyond this a few small crops of maize, barley, millet for beer, and a little terraced land for irrigated rice.

This scanty cultivation, if it may be dignified by such a term, is usually a mere scratching of the ground, and is done mostly by the women, while the men do the hunting.

The house, with the exception of the log framework, is built almost entirely of bamboo. The floor, the walls, the roof and the thatch are all of bamboo, as well as the vessels and cooking utensils. On the ground floor, in the angular space between the sloping hill-side and the platform or floor of the hut, are housed the pigs, fowls and other live stock; and I have rather unpleasant recollections of nights spent in such huts over the squealing pigs; for the Lepchas treat this animal quite as one of the family, and deem roasted pig the most delicious of morsels, an opinion which proves merely that human nature here is very much like the same brand elsewhere.

LEPCHA HOUSES.

We ascend the notched log of wood which does duty for a stair, to the landing, where we are received by the matron and her family. And we have to stoop humbly to enter the low door. Once inside, as I am putting down my hat on a clean-looking vacant spot, the good wife, with horror on her face, snatched up my hat and placed it elsewhere, and apologetically explained that the devil of the house is at present occupying that spot, and his Satanic Majesty's fearful wrath would be incurred were anything placed on that tabooed spot, and some incantations will be needed to undo the harm I have done. When we are seated on a low stool, and our eyes get accustomed to the subdued light and the smarting from the smoke—which, as there is no chimney, half fills the room before it finds its slow escape through the chinks in the roof and walls, tanning these with dark frescoes,—we then see that the interior reflects the simple mode of living of its inmates, and shows that their few wants are easily satisfied. There is no division into rooms, as the family sleep altogether, untroubled by the Western scruples on such matters; and they never think of undressing when they retire to rest, probably from the need of remaining ever ready to defend themselves and their cattle from wild beasts. At one end is an open fireplace formed of a few stones and baked mud. Beside it are a few bamboo vessels, and leaves for plates; above it hangs a frame for smoking meat, though, considering that the room is constantly filled more or less with smoke, this contrivance seems superfluous. There is also a primitive loom and spindle; but no table and no beds, for the inmates dine and sleep on the floor. At the other end is the granary, containing a few baskets of grain, with a large collection of Murwa millet and yeast for brewing beer; yams and miscellaneous roots, berries, tender shoots of ferns and other forest produce. For their ordinary food consists mainly of roots which they dig up in the forest, supplemented by berries, fungi, and spinach of boiled leaves, with occasional game; but even frogs are not refused. There is scarcely a plant too tough for them to chew, from which they do not abstract some nourishment. Salt is the only article they need which they do not find ready to hand; and this they get by barter—not by money. They never had money until lately, as they did not need it, and did not know the use of it, and have no word for it in their language. When money was first given to them, if they did accept it they used to wear it round their necks, as an ornament. Indeed they feed, clothe and house themselves almost entirely on the products of the jungle. They never depend on their few scanty crops, so that famine from which the Indians every now and then suffer so terribly, is to them practically unknown.

Amongst the rafters and on bamboo brackets on the wall are stored away some bright golden heads of maize as seed for next year's crop; one or two spare garments, a bamboo smoking-pipe, a bamboo flute and harp, and a few nick-nacks—including charms against devils. There are also some bows and arrows, and some aconite root to make a deadly paste for poisoning their arrows when used in war or against tigers and other big game.

The family relations of the Lepchas show traces of matriarchy, in which the children trace their descent through their mothers and not through their fathers. Now the

A LEPCHA WOMAN.

Lepcha has usually only one wife, and there is no ceremonial marriage. Some of the younger women-folk are remarkably comely, considering their Spartan upbringing; and many of the children are almost fair and chubby, but their hard exposed life is soon fatal to good looks, especially as most of them go naked. The in-door dress of the women is a close-fitting gown without sleeves, and this was probably their full dress originally. But now, for out of doors, they wear over all a long, loose, wrapper-like white cotton gown with long wide sleeves turned up in Tibetan fashion at the cuffs to show the red lining—a dress which effectually masks the figure and has little grace in its drapery. Their hair is parted in the middle and done up into two pig-tails which are usually gathered in a knot on the crown and secured with a silver pin. And over the head is thrown a gaudy silk handkerchief, drooping negligently over the neck, somewhat in the fashion of a Spanish peasant-girl's. Around the neck they wear as much jewellery as they can afford. Their stockingless feet are unshod. And many of them as they walk, busily twirl a distaff, acting up to the old Saxon ideal of a wife and maid—namely, *wif*, to weave, and *spinster*.

In domestic life these Lepchas are gentle and especially kind to their children and their elders. They offered us some native tea and *Murwa* beer. This "tea", however, is not made from the tea plant, which these poor people cannot afford to buy. It is a decoction brewed from the leaves of the maple, *vaccinium*, wild vine and other trees and herbs. But we must now push on with our journey, after giving each of the girls a cheap coral necklace, and each of the children a bright new two-anna-bit, like an English threepenny piece. We had laid in a large stock of these coins, as they come in handy for small services and for overcoming the objections of many of the people to have their photographs taken.

Up this valley, through old clearings on the hillside now overgrown with rank smelling wormwood, we passed some copper mines on our right. These copper mines are worked on very primitive and wasteful principles, and entirely by Nepalese lessees, for the superstitious Sikhimese intensely dread all mining operations. They believe that the ores and veins of metals are the stored treasure of the earth-spirits; and that the removal of this treasure enrages these malignant spirits, who visit the robbery with all sorts of ill-luck, plagues of sickness on men and cattle, and failure of their too scanty crops. The Nepalese call these mines *khani* or *panch-khani*, and use the copper chiefly for their coinage.

Thence through more stretches of wormwood, which with the American *ageratum* seizes on all the fallow fields, we reach the village or Mik (3,700 feet) on the shoulder of Silok-vok, or the "Stair of the Rhinoceros." These animals were once common here, says tradition, but now they are not to be found within about fifty miles down the valleys. It is to be noted, however, that "Silok" is also the name of a giant tree *(Terminalia pentaptera)* that is found here. We soon gained the ridge leading up to the graceful mountain, Tendong. Here the headman invited us to sit down in front of his house, and treated us to Murwa beer. Then continuing our ascent, we reached Namchi (5,608 feet) and pitched our tents in a grove of chestnuts near the so-called "fort" of the feudal chief of this part of Sikhim, the Lasso Kazi.

The Kazi is a sort of baron, the hereditary lord of half a hundred villages and many a mile of forest; and one of the twelve chiefs among whom Sikhim is parcelled out for revenue purposes.[17] He is of course not a Lepcha, but a Sikhimese Bhotiya.

Soon after our arrival he sent his steward to us with a

SIKHIMESE CHIEF AND RETINUE.

present of a few oranges, bananas, milk, butter, eggs and fowls; and a message that he himself would like to visit us in the afternoon. Before the appointed hour a large mat was spread near our tents, and on it were placed three European chairs on Tibetan rugs; and a message was sent to say that the chief was coming. He came, at tended by his daughters and a tail of retainers, kinsmen and vassals, including slaves,—for regular slavery still exists here, though of a mild type, and often as security for the payment of some debt. We exchanged greetings, he taking off his Chinese hat and giving a formal bow in Chinese style, after which he asked us to be seated and sat down himself. His picturesque retainers, most of whom wore Lepcha plaids, remained standing, whilst his daughters, bright-eyed, giggling girls, seated themselves unceremoniously on the mat behind him. Three jugs of his own special brew of Murwa beer were brought forth, of which one was set down on a stool before each of us, and as often as we sipped some up through reeds, the jug was replenished.

We now saw how much these Bhotiyas of Sikhim, the ruling race and to which Kintoop belongs, differ from the mild Lepchas. Although leavened to some extent with Lepcha blood, they retain most of the rough traits and features of their Tibetan ancestors beyond the Himalayas. They are tall, hardy mountaineers, who keep mostly to the cool uplands and seldom descend to the unhealthy gorges. The are powerfully built, their leg muscles are especially well developed. Their ordinary dress is like that of the Lepchas, as this suits the country better than Tibetan costume, but they usually wear a soft felt Tibetan hat. Most of them, however, are like Kintoop, dressed somewhat like Tibetans. Over their inner vest and trousers of cotton is worn a large loose woollen gown of a claret colour, high collared, and with very long wide sleeves, turned up at the cuff to show the white and blue lining, and girdled at the waist by a scarf. It contains no pockets, as the pocket is made by pulling up the front of the gown above the girdle; and into this capacious cavity is stored away a prodigious number of articles; the wooden drinking-cup *(p'or-pa)*, pipe and tobacco, matches, flint and steel, small knives, purse, charms, rosary, prayer-wheel, books, needles and thread, and varied personal nick-nacks in addition to food. Needless to say the bulging of these bulky articles often gives a Falstaffian roundness to the figure. In the girdle is stuck a sword or dagger.

Our host was dressed like a Tibetan grandee, in a long robe of flowered dark blue silk, gathered up at the waist by a red girdle, and showing an inside embroidered vest, with high brocaded collar; loose trousers of pale blue silk, and black velvet boots. On his head he wore a pork-pie hat, instead of the usual skull-cap; and from his right ear hung a long pendant golden earring, set with turquoises.

He was a middle-aged man of pleasant manners. Speaking in Hindustanee, he asked after our health, where we were going, and various questions about Darjeeling and that wonderful city, Calcutta. Whilst we were thus engaged, a noisy crowd of some hundred men came up the hill, preceded by one or two subordinate officials. This uproar we learned was a protest by the peasantry and serfs against a demand for forced labour, which they deemed unusually excessive and grievous. Sikhim has a sort of feudal or still more primitive government, which forces the people, other than the priests or Lamas, to work for it whenever and wherever called on, without remuneration. An order had been sent to this chief to send a large quantity of building materials and labour, as well as cash, towards the erection of new buildings at the Rajah's head-quarters; and these people were complaining bitterly that they had no money, and that their crops would be ruined were they to leave them at present. They were still louder in their complaints when told that this order must certainly be complied with at once. What the people fear most in such cases is not so much the forced labour and cash tax that is imposed, as the "squeezing" or unscrupulous blackmailing by rapacious subordinate officials; for even "the Kazi himself", says Mr. Edgar,[18] "as far as I can make out, keeps the greater portion himself, paying over to the Rajah a certain fixed contribution." It was some time ere the hubbub ceased, and the least noisy of all the people, though not the least numerous, were the Lepchas, whose rule of conduct almost seems to be "Give unto every man all he asketh."

This, indeed, is one of the most curious survivals of the primitive stage of Society and the Family, in that the Lepchas seem to have had absolutely no true conception of private property until they learned the idea from contact with Bengal traders. Previously, as with their cognates, the ruder Indo-Chinese tribes on the Assamese and Burmese frontiers, everything belonged absolutely to the chief, who as a rule allowed his subjects to retain possession of as much of what they acquired as he himself did not immediately want; but it was only by way of a loan. Thus, the individual had no motive for amassing property, as he could not expect to keep it. And this perhaps is the chief reason for the so-called "laziness" of the Lepcha; for, robbed of his incentive to exertion, why should he slave to amass property when he cannot keep it and reap the benefit of his labours? Even now, under the present form of government in this land of the Lepchas, the cultivator has no title to the soil. He may cultivate any unoccupied land without any formal permission. But the assessment, as in Burma and Manipur, is on the number of persons and cattle and *not* on the land. Even our host the Kazi has no real proprietary right in the land, says Edgar, though he has a kind of hereditary title to his office.

Now, however, that the English assumed, a few months ago, a leading hand in the government we may expect a re-arrangement of these matters upon more modern lines, and the commutation of service for money payment, that is to say rent; as in the old feudal system in England when liberties of all kinds had to be paid for by money. Such an arrangement is needed, not only to emancipate the servile class, but also to provide funds for making good roads and opening up the country.

A curious Tibetan code of laws supposed to guide the rulers of the country has lately been found by Mr. White. It is an odd mixture of Buddhist maxims with trial by ordeal and other barbarous pre-Buddhist practices. Its most interesting features have been thus summarized:[1]—

"The regulations regarding government servants are delightfully general in form. They are to 'leave off their own work and apply themselves entirely to Government work': they are never to use the name of Government for their private ends: they must give just judgment and not favour those who can reward them: inquire diligently into all cases and leave no case undecided, so that all men can say, 'your work has been well done.' The laws of evidence are practically that a patient listening must be given to both sides. The punishments for offences vary according to the gravity of the offence. The murder of father or mother or holy men may involve the death penalty, but the killing of others is punishable by fines varying from 10 oz. to 300 oz. of gold. Curiously enough 'old lamas' are classed with men of 'no rank' and personal servants; they can be killed for 80 oz. ahead. In cases where blood is shed, without life actually being taken, the penalties are comparatively light; though in the interests of order a man may be beheaded for wounding a superior. For wounding his own servant a man is not fined, but he must tend the wounded man. So in a quarrel, the man who first drew his knife is fined, and the wounded one must be nursed by his assailant. Blood feuds are obviously not encouraged in Sikhim: the Pathan would find no sympathy under the shadow of Kanchen-junga. For the false and avaricious, certain oaths are required; and they may even have to submit to the ordeal of carrying hot stones or plunging the hand into boiling oil. Lamas and monks should not be sworn, neither should 'magicians, shameless persons, women, fools, the dumb and children.' This categorical enumeration of persons on whom oaths will probably not be binding is not complimentary to the women-folk of Sikhim. The relations between man and wife are according to primitive ideas. Divorce is simplicity itself: a husband who wishes to be separated from his partner pays her a small sum of money, varying according to the length of the time they have been married. A wife gives a fixed sum and 'one suit of clothes'"!

Scarcely had we left the Kazi ere we received further insight into the summary methods of his patriarchal government. The headman of the village who had entertained us on our way up this morning, came running to us with dishevelled dress and uttering in loud tones the truly Hibernian complaint:—"The landlord came a few hours ago and demanded an exorbitant sum of money down on the spot for the king; and when I protested that I could not pay it and had not got it, he with his men raided my house, carrying off all my valuables and everything he could lay hands on, money, jewellery and even grain and beer; and," he added plaintively, "I implore you gentlemen of the just English Government to help me against this high-handed robbery." We, of course, could do nothing, so he left us vowing that he would go to Darjeeling to seek redress from the English Governor.

The house of the Kazi, or baron, is called a fort or castle *(jong)*; and as is usual, it is situated on a spot selected for defence against native attack, though unprotected against modern weapons. It is a two-storied stone building on a stone platform, with a balcony and several rooms, the chief of which contains the family altar with the image of Buddha and various gods ranged on shelves. The building is rather mean in appearance, although built of stone and logs in place of the bamboo of the vassals' huts, to mark the advance since the Lepcha rule, when, as with most wild tribes, the house of the chief differed little from the poorest of his retainers. There is a little rude carving on the doors. The floor is boarded with rough hewn planks; the roof of the usual mushroom-head shape, is thatched with strips of bamboo; but part of this roofing was being replaced by corrugated iron, a sign of advancing civilization!

A loud noise of drums and bells and blowing of horns at sundown attracted our attention to the monastery-temple near by. It is a barn-like building of the usual Sikhimese style, and of scarcely more architectural interest than a "Free" or dissenting church. The door, as usual, faces the east; and by its side is a huge prayer-barrel about six feet high, drowsily turned by an old sitting devotee, by jerking a string in the manner sketched by Hooker, and each half revolution is registered by the striking of a bell, giving the effect of a chime, as the bells are slightly different in tone. I was amused at the clumsy lying of the Lama-priests in charge. I had been unable to procure at Darjeeling a certain Tibetan book which gives a legendary history of Tibet, and of which most monasteries possess copies. In reply to my queries the Lamas denied having a copy, but on looking over the pigeon-holes of their library, where great bundles of books are stacked, I espied one. On this, the Lamas were not a whit abashed; they smiled and stoutly refused to lend it at any price. Here, however, I got from a Tibetan Lama, who chanced to be passing, that exquisitely carved necromantic sash of human bones, which is now displayed in my collection in the British Museum.

Over our camp-fire the Lepchas told us weird tales till phantoms seemed to flit in the surrounding gloom. There is a certain romantic prettiness in their peopling all the streams, woods and peaks with nymphs and dryads, kelpies and other sprites. One of them told us the legend of Tendong, the graceful mountain that towered above us, and which we were to cross on the morrow. Its tall cone stands between the two greatest rivers of Sikhim, the Teesta and the Great Rang-eet, at their junction.

THE LEGEND OF MOUNT TENDONG
or 'The Uplifted Horn'.

In the old, old days when there were none but the Rong (*i. e.* 'Lepchas') in this country, a great flood deluged the land. The waters drowned all the people in the valleys and covered all the mountains except this peak Tendong, and that of his sister Mainom, the adjoining mountain to the north. The few survivors who had fled to Tendong saw the peak of Mainom disappear under the water, and hence it is called 'Mainom', (properly *Ma-nom*) or 'The Disappearing Sister'; and the shrieks of the drowning can still be heard from Tendong, which then alone remained above the flood. The still rising waters lapped this peak also, and threatened to swallow it, whereupon the surviving people prayed to the mountain to save them, and it then miraculously elongated itself, and kept its clinging refugees above the rising flood. Hence this mountain was named Tendong, properly *Tün-rong*, or 'The Uplifted Horn'. After a time the waters fell, but ever afterwards the grateful Rong (Lepchas) have fervently worshipped this mountain, which had in this miraculous way saved their ancestors.

Now this legend of a Sikhimese Mount Ararat possibly preserves, I believe, the tradition of a local flood caused by the damming up of the Teesta river by a great landslip, below its junction with the Rang-eet. For smaller floods are occasionally occurring in this way; and on the other side of the valley, opposite Tendong, we have the local names of Rang-iroon and Rang-liot, which in the Lepcha mean "The Turning of the Great River", and "The Brimful Great River"; and which the Lepchas explain in a legend which tells how the Rang-eet river quarrelled with his spouse, the Teesta, and refusing to go with her, carried his waters high up the valley to the two sites above mentioned. This legend as told to me, runs:

THE STRIFE BETWEEN THE RANG-EET AND TEESTA RIVERS.

In the beginning of the world, when the rivers were first let down from the mountains, the King of Serpents, '*Pa-ril-byu*,' led the Teesta River, straight down to the plains, so that the course of this river is generally straight, and hence the Teesta was called 'The Straight-going Great Female River' (*Rang-nyo-ung*). On the other hand, the other chief river of Sikhim, the great Rang-eet, was led down by the quail-like bird, '*Tut-fo*' (*Pitta Nepalensis*). Now this bird, on the way, feeling hungry, ran about here and there searching for food, and thus it led the Rang-eet an extremely winding circuitous course, so that when the river approached the plains, he found that the Teesta had already arrived there and had occupied the only available outlet. Waxing wroth at being thus forestalled by a female, the Rang-eet turned himself round and retired amongst the mountains, till his waters rose to Rang-iroon and Rang-liot. Then, fearing lest his rashness might endanger the world, he repented and returned and espoused the Teesta, and they twain have flowed on together ever after.

These legends, of course, may possibly have arisen through false etymologies of the words, especially as the Lepcha names of the Rang-eet and Teesta may also be rendered respectively, "The Beloved Retiring One" and "The Great Sister or Queen" rivers. If such an enormous landslip had occurred, it must soon have been broken through; for no evidence of extensive lacustrine deposits have been found here, such as exist in the Valley of Nepal where such a cataclysm certainly did take place: and there tradition still tells us that the plains of Katmandu were covered by a great lake till a saint named "The Mellow-Voiced One" *(Manjusri)* cut the dam with his sword, and let the river escape; hence that river is now called "The Fleeing One" *(Baghmati)*. With regard to our Sikhim legends, it is remarkable that the bird therein mentioned is almost wingless, like most of the extinct birds, and thus presumably of a most ancient type.

THE MORNING'S BAG AT GAMOTANG.

The following morning (6th October), we crossed the steep shoulder of Tendong (8,675 ft.) through a fine forest of oaks, chestnuts, maple, birch and magnolias, and dipped down to Temi in the valley of the Teesta. We were told there were leopards about, and we saw the tracks of bears, wild goats *(thar)* and wild sheep ("*burhel*", the *Ovis nehur*). The latter animals had been digging up the ashes of some old camp-fires for the salt, for want of which they suffer so much. We also saw several Kaleej pheasants (*Gallophasis melanonotus*), and higher up, the fine red horned pheasants (*Ceriornis satyra*), the *Bap* of the Bhotiyas; but we had no time to go after them just then.

Game is not, after all, so scarce on these mountains, as is generally believed; though it is difficult to get at, in the evergreen forest, where from the numerous perennial streams it is widely distributed during the greater part of the year. Sportsmen, however, who care for something more than big bags and wholesale slaughter will find Sikhim not wanting in interest. It is possible in the higher ranges to get a fair amount of shooting, though even after long days' tramps the experience of the too eager Nimrod may often be that of the "Three Jolly Huntsmen" in the celebrated legend of the nursery. Still, several men, travelling in the upper ranges, amid scenery not to be surpassed, have brought back a goodly number of very fine horns and skins of stags, musk deer, wild sheep and goats, a snow-leopard or Ounce, silver fox, and even an occasional *Ovis ammon*, not to speak of the gorgeous *Monal* pheasants (Bhotiya "Cham-dong"), blood pheasants, snow-cocks (*Tetragallus Tibetanus*), ptarmigan, sand-grouse, woodcock, snow-pigeons, etc., that they get by the way. And on the Tibetan side of the range, game from all accounts is very plentiful.

As on this occasion we ourselves did not leave the path, in passing over Tendong, we bagged only green wood-pigeons and some small birds and animals for my collection, including the bright scarlet and blue fairy-chats (*Niltava grandis*) and brilliant sun-birds like lustrous gems, and a new species of Laughing Thrush (*Gar. Waddelli*). [20] Gorgeous butterflies abound here, more than four thousand species are found in Sikhim alone, and some of these are so beautiful and rare that collectors pay almost fancy prices for them. One of the swallow-tailed is said to be worth about £20 for a good female specimen. Especially numerous was a species (*Kallima inaches*) which conceals itself by imitating the dead leaves amongst which it lives. The under surface of its wings is marked and coloured exactly like a dead leaf, and it settles on a twig, with closed wings, in an attitude that completely supports this illusion, as noted by Wallace in regard to the butterflies of Sumatra. [21] So marvellously close is this imitation of the dead leaf carried out, that even the spots of fungus which grow upon these decaying leaves are faithfully reproduced, and thus enables these little creatures to escape their sharp-eyed enemies, and survive in the struggle for existence.

The change in the foliage was noticeable as we ascended from the evergreen forests below to the variegated autumn tints of the maples, etc., of the temperate zone. Further up, beyond the rude shelter of bamboo (*Ba-kyim*) in the forest, a path leads to the top of the mountain, where is said to be a lonely cell to which a Lama comes every year to offer prayers to Mount Tendong, to safeguard the country from another deluge; for the Lamas have accepted that old legend of the aboriginal Lepchas.

Where the path crossed the crest of the spurs there was usually a cairn of stones, or a rude stone altar, sacred to the spirit of the mountain. At these spots our men laid down their loads, and tearing a few strips of rag from their dress, tied them to a twig or a stone, which they planted on the cairn, as an offering to the mountain spirit, and called with a loud shrill voice: *Ki-ki so-so la-so-la! Lha-gyal-o! Düd-pam-bo!* (Pray accept our offering! The spirits are victorious! The devils are defeated!)

In passing these spots, travellers invariably keep them on their right side in token of respect. This is an old-world custom which still survives in the West, where it is considered the "lucky-way". Thus, it is practised in stirring the Christmas puddings etc., in passing wine at table, from right to left; in cattle treading the corn in this direction; and among the Scotch Highlanders, in walking thrice in this way around those to whom they wish well, "to make the *deazel*", as it is called. And the offering of the rag recalls the Western custom of offering a stone to the lonely cairn of an ill-fated traveller, who has died among the mountains.

Leaving to our left the dreary path through a wilderness

of bamboos, leading to the old monastery of Tashi-ding and Pemiong-chi and Sanga-cheling—visits to which I have already described in my "Buddhism of Tibet"—we struck down steep zigzags to Temi. And here our alpenstocks came in useful, as the clayey soil was very slippery from recent rain.

The first patches of cultivation appear in the forest at about 6,000 feet. Above this height little tillage is done on account of the cold clouds, and the destructive hailstones which demolish the crops, literally bombarding the cereals by their violent downfall. I have seen hailstones hereabouts as large as a walnut.

The primitive kind of agriculture which is practised here is the same which is common among the wilder Indo-Chinese tribes, and in the earlier clearings which I have seen in the back-wood settlements of America. A few acres of the virgin forest are burned down, and the rich black loam, enriched by the wood-ashes, between the charred stumps of the trees is scratched or scraped on the surface and yields abundant crops for about two years, after which period, being somewhat exhausted, it is abandoned and a fresh strip of forest is burned down, which after a year or two is in turn abandoned for a new one; and so on, until after ten or twenty years the first patch, which has lain so long fallow, has again become a jungle, and it is brought again under this "jhooming" process, as it is called. The great destruction of forest which this practice entails, is perhaps excusable in such a sparsely populated region where hundreds of miles of forest timber simply falls and rots through the impossibility of transporting it to a paying market.

As we descended, these patches of "jhoomed" fields fringed by forest belts, got more numerous, and we soon emerged on the bare hill-side of Temi (4,771 ft). Here the son of the chief of this district offered us his house for the night, but we preferred our tents. The zones of cultivation here on the flanks of Tendong and other parts of central Sikhim, as well as Darjeeling, have undergone great alteration since Hooker's visit. Much of the forest has disappeared owing to the increase of the population. The view up the Teesta valley was very fine with its interlacing mountain ridges leading up to snows; in the foreground were the dark frowning cliffs of Mainom, while to the right were the snows of the Chola pass.

Our next two days' march up the semi-tropical valley of the Teesta to the cane-bridge by which we had to cross that river, was very hot and rather uninteresting. The steep descent of over 3,000 feet to the gorge of the thundering river was no easy matter after the heavy rain of the night, as the track zig-zagged down over slippery clay and still more slippery mica-schist and chlorite slate; and over boiling and dashing torrents that we had to cross by slimy logs and saplings that were thrown across them. In the deep gorge, so intense was the heat, that one of us could not resist a plunge into the cool pool of the Rangpo rivulet, despite the risk from the blazing sun overhead. Across one of these bridges some fishermen had made a weir of bamboo, so designed that the fish in descending the rapids, are driven into this basket and captured. We tasted some of the fish, but found them very bony and

CROSSING TORRENTS.

rather insipid. The men cooked them by baking them for a few minutes in the camp-fire, inside a joint of the ubiquitous bamboo. Our little-used track led through such luxuriant forest that one of our men had to go in front to clear the way, like a sapper, cutting down projecting branches and rope-like vines that barred our path. The characteristic vegetation here was figs and nettles; and we were especially warned by our men against the so-called "deadly" nettle, whose great smooth glossy leaves look so innocent of the deadly venom which lurks beneath. The wild Mango was also common, and its fruit though small was pleasant to the taste. Amongst the birds, wood-peckers were especially numerous, owing to the large quantity of dead and dying timber. I got no fewer than eighteen distinct species of these; shewing the immense range and variety of the climate hereabout. The head-man of the village of "Fat Earth" (Nam-fak) where we encamped, brought us the usual poor presents of stale milk, rancid butter, a few oranges and bananas. He belongs to the tribe which the Nepalese call Limboo, and the Tibetans "Ts'ong-pa," (or merchants,) as they were and are still the chief cattle-merchants and butchers in Sikhim, where cattle used to be the chief import from the plains. But the people call themselves *Yak-tamba* (Yak-herds?) or "Ek-tambo". They have flatter faces, and are much more markedly Mongolian in feature than the Lepchas; though they have adopted the dress and externals of Hindooism, like most of the other Nepalese tribes.

They seem to have shared with the Lepchas the western half of Sikhim, before the advent of the Tibetans and other Nepalese tribes. At present they extend westwards into

Nepal as far as the Arun river, which pierces the Central Himalayas, and by which possibly they have descended from the plateau of Central Asia (see map in Chap. IX). The divisions of the tribe, are alleged by Mr. Risley, to be denoted

A LIMBOO BEAUTY.

by nicknames. This would be curious if true; but it is merely the result of an attempt to find the meaning of the Limboo names in an alien language, like attempting the etymology of Gaelic words by means of Greek, and the results are so absurd as to seem nicknames. Mr. Risley, however, has otherwise advanced Indian ethnology by the methods he has advocated, and it is to be hoped that on this subject he will continue to raise his voice.

Achoom tells me that these Limboos are proverbially stingy and inhospitable, even the Lepcha half-breeds of the tribe, such as the Yangmo, according to the Lepcha saying: "Though a Yangmo's door is open wide, there's nothing to eat, though plenty inside". In Nepal they intermarry to some extent with the semi aboriginal Kiranti tribe.

Our pioneer brought us the disconcerting news that the cane-bridge over the Teesta, by which we must cross, was unsafe without extensive repairs; so we despatched some men to repair it. A drizzling rain prevented our going up the hill to the Yangong monastery, which boasts a finely carved door. Its head Lama is one of the explorers of Tibet, Ugyen Gyatsho, the "U. G." of the Indian Survey Reports. Here are some caves said to be several miles long, and believed to connect the sacred mountains Tendong and Mainom, all infested of course by devils.

Higher up the ridge is the large stone carved with the mystic *Om mani*, which Hooker figures. The following day in the series of tiresome ascents and descents over spurs, a ridge which we crossed was pointed out to us as the scene of a pitched battle between the Nepalese invaders and the Sikhimese Bhotiyas in 1787 A.D., when the former were forced to retire. It is called Neh (about 2,500 ft.), and it occupies a fairly strong defensive position on a spur of Mainom.

We all suffered badly from the bites of the *pipsee* flies

that swarmed here, and worried us almost beyond endurance. This insect, in appearance like a diminutive house-fly, draws blood at once; and in so doing it poisons the wound, so that the blood continues to ooze from the puncture and also exudes underneath the skin, forming bluish patches which often end in ulcers. We cleared our tents of them for a time by fumigation with brown paper etc., but our coolies in the open suffered severely. The land-leeches were also troublesome; and several loathsome blood-sucking ticks (*Ixodes*) made us almost regret that we had not gone by the much longer road (*via* Kalimpong) to escape all these pests. A leopard, tiger-cat, civet, and red cat-bear or "white face" (*Dong-kar*) of the Bhotiyas, were shot by my collector here; and the flesh of all these animals was eaten by the Lepchas, and indeed esteemed a delicacy.

We could not but admire the very evident usefulness to these animals of their specific colours. How admirably their markings conceal these beasts, each in its special surroundings, so that they can approach their prey unawares, as well as escape from their own natural enemies. The spotted markings of the leopard render it practically invisible amongst the spotty shades of the tree-foliage where it lives; just as the yellow and black stripes of the tiger assimilate this animal to the withered yellow stems of grassy reeds with their dark shadows in the places that it haunts. So too, the broad markings of the cat-bear and the faggoty pattern of the civet are admirably suited to conceal their owners in the dusky trunks and branches among which they live.

Early in the morning, we descended the gloomy gorge of the roaring river, amid rank decaying vegetation which suggested deadly malaria. As we reached the bridge, our men sent up a loud shout, calling on the malignant water-spirit to let us cross in safety. And, certainly, it looked as if special prayers for our safety were really required, for the bridge, dangerous at all times, was a mere ragged skeleton of itself, and slippery with green slime.

Spanning the yawning chasm about 300 feet wide, in whose depths the mighty river thundered along, sixty or eighty feet beneath us, in leaping waves, dashing over great boulders of gneiss the size of cottages, and scattering clouds of spray, and hurling uprooted trees like matchwood, this frail rickety structure seemed by aspect and surroundings to suggest the horrors ascribed by the ancients to the knife-edge bridge over the Styx. And we had to cross it somewhat after the manner of Blondin on the slack rope. Here, however, we had the doubtful advantage of a loosely knotted rope of strips of rotten cane to clutch hold of. For the bridge is formed by two suspended ropes of cane thrown across the gorge, and their ends are lashed to rocks and trunks of trees in the neighbourhood; and between these two parallel ropes, and tied from the one rope to the other at intervals of a yard or so, are suspended bits of cane forming V-shaped slings; and in the narrow angle of these V-slings is laid a line of bamboos, end to end, on which you have to find your footing. It is thus like walking on a rope, for between the slings it is all open on either side, and as you cross you swing in mid-air, as seen in the frontispiece.

I had already crossed several of these primitive bridges in Sikhim, as well as the rope-bridges (*jhola*) in the Northern Himalayas, but none were ever so alarmingly rickety-looking as this. On climbing up on to it, it proved on examination to be not only frail but *rotten!* And we now found that the men who had been sent two days before to repair it, had declined the hazardous task and had decamped without touching it. These bridges last only about two seasons, and this one was already several years old and had not been repaired at all. But we must cross this river anyhow, as a night's detention in this gorge meant fever in a fatal form.

I sent one of my Lepchas, who was accustomed to these bridges, to examine it, and he managed to go over it, and returned to say that he thought it was crossable. Sending him across again, I prepared to follow, having first taken off my boots, as the bamboos on which I had to walk were so slippery. But I had not gone many yards ere I found that there was only a single line of bamboos for foothold, and that these single bamboos were neither lashed end to end nor tied to the V-slings, and that many of these V-slings were untied or wanting altogether. I therefore retraced my steps, and sent the Lepcha to tie it up a bit.

I then mounted the bridge again, and I almost shudder, even now, to think of that awful passage. Had I known what was in store for me I should never have attempted it. The instant that you step on to these bridges they recoil from you, and swing and shake in an alarming way, rolling from side to side and pitching with every step you take, like a ship in a storm. They swerve with a sudden jerk, every time you lift your foot; not only sideways and longways, but also downwards and forwards, as your weight depresses the bridge, until you pass the middle, when the oscillating structure kicks up after you, as you ascend. So, seizing the two suspension cables, one in either hand, for a railing, you have to work your way across this jerky swinging, shaking, writhing thing. I got along a short way without much difficulty, so long as I could look to see the bamboo rod on which I had to walk, although the open sides heightened the sense of insecurity. But on clearing the bank, the instant you look down to see where to place your feet, the rush of leaping water in the deeply sunk torrent underneath you, gives you the giddy sensation that both you and the bridge are running swiftly upstream. Yet, without looking down, how is it possible to see the single bamboo overhanging the abyss and on which you must find your shaky footing, and to miss which means certain death? Hitherto the line of bamboos had been tied end to end, but now, as I stepped on to the next one, it tilted up; and I could see that most of those in front were also lying loose and disjointed in their widely separate V-slings, and some also of these slings were loosened and others wanting; they had been loosened and broken away by the passing of the person who preceded me. But it was now too late to turn back, as I could not swing round; so, I went forward with long strides to get a foothold on this shaking, swinging line of slimy bamboos which writhed and twisted like a broken-backed serpent. I had to take darting, furtive peeps at the slippery, creaking bamboo, and after each step I had to half close my eyes for an instant to counteract the giddy feeling of the upward rush of the bridge. Ah, it was a creepy, ghastly feeling! One false step meant instant death in the raging gulf below. Still there was a fascination in it all, suspended at that giddy height over the rushing, swirling waters far beneath, the unceasing deafening roar, the bold rocky banks, and the rainbow tints of the clouds of spray rising from the boiling abyss below. At last, after what seemed an age, the other bank was reached and the danger, so far as I personally was concerned was past. But the others had to be provided for.

Once across, I shouted to Kintoop, who had arrived by this time, to tie up the loose parts along the whole length of the bridge, before the laden coolies attempted to cross, And it was marvellous to watch the operations of him and his assistants. They darted into the jungle with their knives, and cut the stringy bark of a giant climber into convenient lengths, and taking a bundle of these strips between their teeth, they scrambled pluckily along the ropes, clinging with their toes, like monkeys; and they deftly tied up several of the loosest parts, using only their prehensile toes in this operation, in places where they needed to hold on with both hands. Such flexibility in their toes have they acquired in climbing trees and otherwise, that they use them dextrously for gripping things; and their great toe acts almost like a thumb.

Even when these repairs were done, it was found that the great majority of the coolies, all of whom were natives of these hills, were afraid to cross it, even when relieved of their loads. Their loads, therefore, had to be broken up into small parcels, which the more steady men tied up in their Lepcha plaids and slung on to their backs, leaving both hands free; and in this way, by dint of crossing and re-crossing some scores of times, our baggage was finally got across. As for the terror-stricken coolies, it was pathetic to watch them struggling over the bridge, even after it had been repaired and they had been relieved of their loads. The thrilling horror and despair pictured in their faces as they crawled along was truly pitiful to see. At a critical moment more than one squatted down in the middle of the bridge, half-paralysed with fear, unable to go either forwards or backwards till someone stole to their aid; and two of these we thought must certainly have been lost before assistance reached them. Not a few refused to cross on any account, and bolted off. And all of us who crossed, vowed that we would rather go a month's journey round about than cross such a terrible bridge again.

We studied the mechanism of the bridge, while our baggage was crossing. [22] Its great height above the water is to provide against the rise of the flood waters. It is situated at a relatively narrow part of the river, where the latter rushes in leaping waves between the cliffs through which it has cut its way; and these cliffs of bare rock and huge boulders form the natural piers and bastions of the bridge. From these piers, two ropes or cables are thrown across the gorge and their ends lashed to these rocks, and to the trunks of trees, and pegged into the ground; and the stays and slings at either end form a network like the rigging of a ship. These two parallel cables which support the bridge, each consist of three or four plaited canes of the rattan palm (*Calamus rotang*), about 400 feet long. As these had become rotten they had been strengthened by a chain of bits of bamboo bark loosely knotted together. From these cables hang the V-shaped slings of split cane, about three feet apart, and each about two and a half feet deep. Into these hanging slings are laid the bamboos which form the platform or footway. There originally had been, we were told, three or four bamboos dovetailed side by side and securely lashed and spliced to their adjoining bundles of bamboos so as to form a continuous chain, but the bundles had got loosened and the extra bamboos had all fallen out long before our arrival. An ingenious device of outriggers prevents the bridge from closing up and choking the passenger. At intervals of every ten feet or so, a rod of bamboo is passed transversely under the platform, and from its extremities pass ropes of cane and bark that are tied to the two cables, which are thus kept apart. These bridges are called *Jalang* by the Nepalese, and by the Bhotiyas *Sampa;* and the site of the *Sam-pa* is *Sam-dong*, or the "bridge face." The Bhotiya name for this Teesta river is *Sang-choo*, or "The Pure Water", so-called because great rivers tend to purify themselves from contamination. While the temperature of the air at noon was 73° Fahrenheit, the water was only 60° Fah., owing to its having come directly from the snows. The fall of this river as measured by Hooker, not far off, was found to be 821 feet in 10 miles, and its current in places ran at the rate of 14 miles an hour.

Glad were we to get away from this fluvial horror, and emerge from the stifling gorge up on to a cool flat, where we encamped at the cairn or Mendong of Tyun-tang. amongst wild citrons. And here a refreshing cup of tea and the hot lunch that Achoom had awaiting us made us forget our troubles and fatigues of the day.

Next morning we were off early along the bold and cliffy upper valley of the Teesta, over the slopes of Silling, with fine and ever changing views of the Kanchen-junga snows, and crossing the Ryot river, reached Toomlong, "On Mafi's Breast", the mountain capital of the King of Sikhim, before nightfall. But oh, the hateful leeches and the climb!

The damp forest through which we passed swarmed with legions of voracious land-leeches. No thicker than a knitting-needle when they are fasting, they stood alert on every twig of the brushwood that overhung our track, and on every dead leaf on the path. And as we approached they lashed themselves vigorously to and fro, in the wild endeavour to seize hold of us. The instant they touch their victim, they fix themselves firmly and then mount nimbly up by a series of rapid somersaults till they reach a vulnerable point; and then they lose not an instant in commencing their surgical operations. Our poor servants and coolies who walked bare-footed were of course badly bitten. From their ankles and legs little streams of blood trickled all day, and at every few steps they had to stop and pick off these horrid little pests, and it was often difficult to dislodge them. We had dusted our stockings with tobacco-snuff, and had not felt the usual sharp nip; and our legs were well encased in *putties* or thick woollen bandages, which are wound round the leg from the ankle to the knee, over the boots and stockings, and give grateful support to the leg and more freedom to the calf muscles than leggings. We had each picked off thousands of leeches during the day, from outside our boots and *putties*, and were congratulating ourselves on having escaped, but on taking off these articles to cross the small substantial cane-bridge over the Dik-chu river, after having walked about sixteen miles through forest, we found that a large number of leeches had sucked their fill of us. They had insinuated themselves through the eyelets of our boots, and between the folds of our *putties*, and thence through the meshes of our stockings. And, after gorging themselves to repletion with our blood, some had withdrawn themselves and were lying under the *putties*, their thread-like bodies

DIK-CHU CANE-BRIDGE.

swollen with our blood, to the size of small chestnuts; while others had crept down into our boots, and had there got squashed, bathing our feet in gore; and all this had happened quite unconsciously to us. Washing our wounds only made them bleed the more profusely. B. was less bitten than I was, probably owing to his blood being so saturated with nicotine, as he smokes all day long. It was pitiful also to see the poor cattle, ponies and goats in these leech-infested forests. Their legs were always bleeding more or less, and these pests lodge in their nostrils and hang from their eyelids and various parts of their body. To dislodge them from the recesses of the nose, the herdsmen, it is said, keep the poor beasts from water for a day or so and then, when the animal drinks, the leeches show themselves, and may be removed. All the Lepchas have their legs covered with the scars of these leech-bites; and the actual loss of blood in this way must be very great. I have no doubt that these pests have something to do with the remarkable absence of four-footed game in these regions. They range in these damp forests from about 4,000 to 10,000 feet elevation. The Bhotiya name for the leech is "The Blood-drinker" (*tak-toong*). The normal food, however, of these myriad leeches, like that of those other blood-suckers, the mosquitos, is vegetable juice; and not one out of many millions of them can ever possibly taste blood.

This river, the Dik-chu or Ryot, is a snow-fed stream which descends tumultuously, about 10,000 feet in a course of about twelve miles. Its Bhotiya name means "The Staggering or Reeling Water"; whilst its Lepcha name of Ryotoong means "The Rapid Reckless Water" or "The Bristling Restless Water"—all of which names well describe the furious character of this torrent.

The leeches and the pelting rain, all day long, had so delayed us and disorganized our men, that, although it was now about 3 p.m., we had not yet had breakfast, only the morning tea and toast. We were now ravenous; but there was little chance of our getting anything till we reached the Rajah's residence on the hill, about 3,000 feet above us; for we found that Achoom and the lunch-basket had gone on ahead. So after climbing over some boulders on the river bank to wash again our bleeding leech-bites, we began the steep climb up the short cut to Toomlong. Short cuts are proverbially tedious, and this track went right up the rocky face of the gorge, rising about 3,000 feet in two miles. It would be a trying climb at any time; but coming at the end of a long fast and a fatiguing day's march, it taxed our strength severely. We had frequently to pull ourselves up over rocks by clutching hold of creepers. The ascent seemed endless. When I had climbed about 2,000 feet I sat down dead-beat, while B., puffing away at his invigorating pipe, pushed on slowly ahead. It was now getting dusk, the sun had dipped behind a peak, and the forest showed no sign of any habitation near, and not even water to quench our thirst, except the drizzling mist, as I was on a ridge; when suddenly a good angel appeared in the person of a smiling young Lama, carrying a jug of Murwa beer, which he presented to me. Refreshed by this reviving beverage, I resumed the ascent, accompanied by the young monk, who acted as my guide. He told me that the news of our approach had reached the monastery of Phodang, which was only about a mile higher up, and that the good Lamas had immediately sent him to us with the welcome Murwa. Wet and weary, we reached the monastery (5,290 ft.) just as the darkness was closing in, and here the hospitable Lamas installed us in a cloister as our tents were not up, provided us a blazing fire in the middle of the room to dry our clothes, and a lamp, and assisted Achoom in spreading our rugs on the floor round the fire, and soon Rameses brought in an ample meal which completed our material comforts.

CHAPTER IV

AT THE CAPITAL OF SIKHIM—TO THE THRESHOLD OF THE SNOWS

> AND leaving Sikhim's halls, the four
> O'er Mafi's hill, by Ringon's rill,
> 'Neath stately Narim's summit hoar,
> By Namga's shades and Chakoong's glades,
> And rapid Teesta's rocky shore
> Travelled till they the torrent crossed.
>
> C. Macaulay's *Lay of Lachen.*

I WAS rudely awakened next morning, at daybreak, by a deafening din of trumpets and drums outside our cloister; and on looking out of the unglazed window of our cell, I found the noise proceeded from a band of Lama-monks who were parading round the outside of the temple, blowing discordant horns, fifes and shell-trumpets, beating drums and clashing cymbals, and they wound up their noisy orisons with a still more ear-piercing blast at the front door of the temple. One pair of the trumpets was so immensely long—over six feet—that a young novice had to march in front to support their ends.

TEMPLE BAND AT PHODANG MONASTERY.

Our cloister in the daylight looked a severely empty room, innocent as it was of any furniture. Its walls were frescoed with the smoke of many years; and we were not the only inmates. Several bats hung solemnly in black festoons from the beams; and during the night many fleas had crept out from nooks and crannies and were much in evidence. Some Keating's insect powder, which I had provided for such emergencies, had not yet arrived, as still about a dozen of our coolies had not yet turned up. These men did not arrive till late in the forenoon.

We therefore halted here for the day, to let our men recuperate, and also to weed out the weakliest, and leave here all unnecessary baggage, such as the extra tent, and such luxuries as camp-tables and chairs. For from this point we go almost right up into rugged Alpine country where every unnecessary mouth to feed, and every extra ounce of baggage, is a drawback. We also wished to visit the King of Sikhim, whose head-quarters are here. We were told, however, that the King had just gone to the residence of our new political agent at Gantok, and had taken with him the abbot of this monastery, but the prime minister sent us an invitation to visit the palace in the afternoon.

The abbot of this monastery, which is called Phodang, or "The Chapel-Royal", is one of the most important persons in the state. He has all along been well disposed towards Europeans, and now, since the country has passed more under our control, and as he is something of a patriot, he has been made one of the chief ministers and the *de facto* primate of the Lamaist Church in Sikhim. This kindly old man is a friar rather than a monk, frequenting the busy haunts of men, and may often be seen at Darjeeling. He has imbued his subordinates with much of his own kindly spirit. The young Lama who was acting for him during his absence, and who is his nephew, and son of the prime minister, is an intelligent well-mannered youth; and as he had looked so well after us and our coolies B. gave him some bits of jewellery, and I gave him some tins of fancy biscuits, a bottle of liqueur and a Japanese teapot, all of which things he carried off in high glee.

The situation of this monastery overlooking the Dik-chu Valley is fine. It commands views up the valley to the snows of the Chola, or "The Lake Pass" (14,925 ft.), so called, it is said, from its chain of lakelets. Below these snows that rise above us only thirteen miles off, stretch the grassy and pine-clad slopes of Chomnaga (12,500 ft.), surmounting the rocky heights of Fyoom-gang, or "The Reedy Bamboo Ridge," whilst in the foreground, amongst the cottages that dot the fields of rice and maize, is the small monastery of Labrang, or "The Bishop's Palace," where resides the nominal head of the Church of Sikhim, and one of the so-called "living Buddhas" or re-incarnated Lamas, who no sooner die than they are supposed to be reborn again as the head Lama of the same monastery. The saintly reputation of this particular one, however, has worn a little threadbare through his too frequent potations of something stronger than the local *murwa* beer. And not far off is a small convent with three nuns, the chief of whom is a sister of "Tcheeboo" Lama, the friend of Hooker.

After breakfast we sauntered about the monastery, watching the routine of the monks, and the peasantry bringing their offerings to the priests, whilst our jaded coolies were preening their draggled features and dressing their leech-bites. One of the best applications to these bites, to prevent the inflammation and ulceration so apt to ensue, was, I found, the ordinary Friars' Balsam, which I had brought for that serious trouble to travellers, blistered feet, for which it is a sovereign remedy.

In the afternoon we availed ourselves of the invitation to visit the palace at Toomlong. We were escorted by some Lamas, Kintoop and several others of our henchmen. There was nothing, however, to show that this was the capital of Sikhim. There is no town, scarcely even a village, except for the huts that dot the hill-side at wide intervals; and the "palace" was most disappointing after the grand accounts of it given by Colman Macaulay and some other officials. But then we were only ordinary travellers, for whom things were not put *en rose*; and personally we prefer to see things as they really are in everyday life.

The "palace", which crowns a knoll, is a barn-like building of the usual Sikhim style, with a great thatched roof projecting in mushroom-head fashion, and tied down at the corners to prevent it being blown off. Its roof is surmounted by a small gilt turret, like a factory belfry, but of Chinese pattern, which gleams from afar in the sunlight. The whole place has a mean look; and there is nothing to suggest that it is the residence of the king, except perhaps the two or three scare-crow sentries who hang about the gate-way in the low wall that surrounds the building. They are clad in Lepcha garb and armed with antiquated match-locks.

Crossing the small garden, prolific in wormwood weeds, and passing through the squalid courtyard, we were conducted by a round-about way to the main door. For this house, as the residence of a "priest-king," is sacred, and must be approached like a holy temple, in the respectful direction; that is to say with the right hand to the wall. The chief door by which we entered was of roughly hewn timber, loopholed for musketry. It opened into a dark narrow passage, whence we were ushered up a dark ladder-like stair, and thence, groping our way, we stumbled into what has been grandiloquently called "The Audience Room", where the Sikhim Rajah held his court. It had a mean look, a low ceiling, and was floored with planks rough hewn in Robinson Crusoe fashion, and it was without any of the refinements of civilization. Here an old man with grizzled hair, shrewd features, and dressed like the ordinary Bhotiyas, in a not over-clean suit, came forward and bid us welcome with a shake of the hand. He was the Prime Minister or *Kang-sa Dewan*. Speaking in Hindustanee, as neither of us at that time were fluent with Tibetan, which is the court language of Sikhim, he invited us to be seated on chairs; and he himself sat down cross-legged on a cushion upon the slightly raised dais of the Rajah, and plied his prayer-wheel; whilst our men seated themselves demurely on the floor, behind us, with their hats in their hands. Slaves passed round Tibetan tea, a broth-like mess of boiled Chinese brick-tea, butter and flour. We, as guests, were first served with it in small Chinese bowls, but our men, as became their inferior rank, had to produce their own wooden cups, which every Bhotiya carries in his breast-pocket. This tea was followed by some *murwa* beer, which was about the worst I ever tasted. It was sour as vinegar. I conscientiously, however, sipped a little for politeness' sake, though not without alarm as to the consequences. After our host had made the customary civil enquiries about our health, and as to whether we had suffered any annoyance through the neglect of any of his people since we entered Sikhim, he questioned us closely as to why we had come and where we wished to go. But we gave him no very precise information on these points, as we did not wish him to be able to hinder our movements, as his predecessors had done Hooker's; or report our intended route to the Tibetans, with whom many of these officials are still covertly in league.

He told us that if we proposed going up the Lachen Valley, (and this we wished to do) it was not yet open, owing to several bridges having been swept away: this information proved to be true. He was anxious to know what the English Government intended to do with the

King, since our expulsion of his allies the Tibetans from the country; and he apologized for the non-appearance of the Rajah's sister, she of the story of the basket of eggs. I asked him about the etymology of some of the names of places; as to why certain mountains, rivers and places had received their particular names, for I had found that nearly all such names in this country are remarkably descriptive of their physical peculiarities. But his reply was of the usual convincing kind: "They are called so and so because that is their name;" so I had to fall back on my chief sources of information on this subject, the fountain-head itself, namely, the traditions of the aborigines of the localities in question. When we got up to go he rose and wished us a pleasant journey. We then groped our way down the creaky stair, through the dark corridor; and were glad again to get into the open air, out of this dreary building where the King of Sikhim has his home. We had no idea that he was so miserably poor. In such dismal surroundings and hedged in by his priests, it is indeed a wonder that he has not turned out more helpless than he is.

The King, or as his people call him *Gyal-po*, which is the Tibetan word for "king", is a Tibetan by descent and sympathies. The first of his dynasty, [23] which began about 250 years ago, was a pure Tibetan, and he himself, the ninth of the line, is largely of the same blood, as nearly all his predecessors married, like himself, a Tibetan wife. He was born in 1860, and bears the grand name of "The

Almighty Necromancer" (*Too'-top-nam-gyel*). His appearance is well shown in the accompanying photograph, which is, I believe, the only photograph which has ever been taken

THE KING AND QUEEN OF SIKHIM.

of him, owing to his extreme sensitiveness to the disfigurement caused by his hare-lip.

His wife, the queen, is a Tibetan, the daughter of a personal servant of the Grand Lama of Lhasa, and is named Ten-zam-drama. As seen in the picture, her headdress is a marvellous arrangement, a hillock of pearls, turquoises, coral and other precious stones. Personally, she is bright and prepossessing, and rather inquisitive. Some of the questions she asked a friend of mine at his visit, through an interpreter of course, were very personal, such as—"How old are you?" "Are you married?" "Why are you not married?" She has been credited with intriguing in political matters and causing some of our recent troubles with Tibet.

Her husband, however, like most of his predecessors in the kingship, is a mere puppet in the hands of his crafty priests, who have made a sort of priest-king of him. They encourage him by every means in their power to leave the government to them, whilst he devotes all his time to the degrading rites of devil-worship, and the ceaseless muttering of meaningless jargon, of which the Tibetan form of Buddhism chiefly consists. They declare that he is a saint by birth, that he is the direct descendant of the greatest king of Tibet, the canonized Srong-tsan Gampo, who was a contemporary of Mahomed in the seventh century A.D. and who first introduced Buddhism to Tibet. They say that a great grandson of that saintly king settled in Kham, in eastern Tibet, and was the ancestor of the kings of Sikhim, who are hence called Kham-ba, or "natives of Kham", a title which has misled Mr. Risley and other writers into stating that "Kham-ba" is the kingly section of the Lepcha tribe, whereas it is a purely Tibetan distinction and has nothing whatever to do with the Lepcha race.

This saintly lineage which secures for the king's person

popular homage amounting to worship, is probably, however, a mere invention of the priests to glorify their puppet prince for their own sordid ends. Such devices are common in the East. Not to mention the Mikado who, in the old order of things, claimed divine descent from the sun-goddess, Theebaw the ex-king of Burma was a priest-king, who claimed to be descended from the most famous king the Burmese ever heard of, to wit, a somewhat mythical king of Buddha's day and of Buddha's own Sakya tribe. And many of the modern Rajahs of India boast of even higher descent—from God himself! I have seen several examples of this process taking place at the present day among the aboriginal tribes of Central India. Certain of these non-Aryan headmen set themselves up as Hindoos, and calling themselves Rajputs, or members of the kingly caste, they pay unscrupulous Hindoo priests to invent for them an orthodox though mythical pedigree.

Without entering much into the government or mis-government of this country, there are a few points in its history that are interesting, as illustrating the principles on which the enormous British Empire has been built up.

In the building up of our Indian Empire, our policy has long been to secure along our frontiers, as buffers between these and the neighbouring empires, a fringe of thriving semi-independent states, self-governing as regards their internal affairs, and enjoying an amount of freedom that would make them a useful force in case of invasion, but under our suzerainty—as we guarantee their autonomy—

and open to our trade. For trade, after all, is the keystone of our policy, and not land-hunger or territorial expansion. "The greatest of all political interests," says Mr. Chamberlain, "is commerce, as our nation cannot exist without trade." Annexation of neighbouring states, or even direct interference in their management, is never thought of until oft-repeated aggression and aggravating injury to our commerce leaves absolutely no alternative but that the country should be brought under a civilized government. Our relations with this little Himalayan state arose in this way.

When the warlike tribe of Hindooised Mongoloids, the Goorkhas, after conquering Nepal, towards the end of the eighteenth century, encroached on India in 1814, they overran Sikhim and threatened to occupy the whole stretch of the Himalayas as far south as Assam. The British, however, drove them out of Sikhim in 1817, restored the late king, and adding to his state a considerable tract of the Terai or Morang, at the foot of the hills which had been ceded to us by Nepal, our government undertook the defence of his country, and interposed it as an effectual barrier against the expansion southwards of the aggressive Nepalese, whose growing power at that time endangered India. Then after fourteen years of peace a frontier dispute again broke out between Sikhim and the Nepalese, and to settle it the British agent, Mr. Grant, was sent. He was so impressed with the advantages that Darjeeling offered as a sanitarium for our troops, that he induced our Government to negotiate for its cession. The Rajah yielded in 1835 the wished-for territory, namely Darjeeling, and the strip of hilly land connecting it with the plains, in exchange for an annual pension of £300, soon raised to £600, which sum much exceeded the revenue that he had ever derived from it.

Whilst the young settlement of Darjeeling was growing by leaps and bounds, things went smoothly for several years between it and our feudatory king, or rather the priests who acted for him. A change came with the accession to power of a crafty Tibetan minister who ruled the country with a sole eye to his own profit. He was an inveterate slave-dealer, and made money by sending slaves from Sikhim, where slavery was prevalent, to Tibet, and he, as well as the local chiefs, with this object, raided into our territory, and kidnapped British subjects and refused to release them; while, on the other hand, he demanded the return of all his runaway slaves who had fled to Darjeeling. In the hope apparently of extorting his demands he seized the Governor of Darjeeling, Dr. Campbell, in 1849, when the latter went to try to get matters on a friendly footing, and imprisoned him for six weeks at this very place, where we now are; and along with him Dr. Hooker, who was then travelling in the country; and both nearly lost their lives here, as is related by Hooker in his Journals. These outrages were avenged by the annexation of a further strip of Lower Sikhim including all the Terai, the suspension of the cash allowance for a few years, and by the banishment of the hostile minister.

The latter, however, continued his intrigues and his evil influence over the king from the adjoining Tibetan district of Choombi, across the Chola Pass, where in order to escape from the heavy rains of Sikhim, the kings usually spent their summers. Further kidnapping and plundering led to the English occupation of "the palace" here in 1861,[24] when a treaty was exacted to secure free trade, the protection of travellers, road-making and to facilitate our trade with Tibet; and in return for this concession the king's annual allowance was raised to £1,200.

After this, though no actual conflict occurred, the King kept aloof from the friendly overtures made to him by our Government, and allowed the treaty in regard to trade and roads to remain a dead letter. In 1884 Mr. Colman Macaulay, one of the few who have realised the considerable commercial possibilities of Tibet, finding that the little trade there had been between India and that country was languishing, prevailed on the government of Bengal, of which he was secretary, to send him to open communications with that jealously isolated land. On this errand he passed through Sikhim and met the Tibetan governor of the frontier district, secured his good will and obtained a friendly letter from the minister of the Grand Lama of Western Tibet. Following up this opening, Mr. Macaulay arranged in 1885 for a commercial mission to Lhasa, and he procured from the Chinese a passport to visit that sacred city of their vassal, in terms of the Treaty of Tientsin extracted by the European powers at the occupation of Pekin. But this passport proved to be simply a paper concession, like so much of the Chinese concessions, and was never intended to be used. For it is an open secret that the Chinese, who hold most of the Tibetan trade in their own hands, sent immediately secret orders to Tibet to obstruct the mission, with the result that an armed force of Tibetans opposed it and prevented it from crossing the frontier. So jealously did the Chinese view this mission that they actually conceded us some of their territory on the Burmese side to secure its withdrawal, whilst they decorated the King of Sikhim with a grand title and a high-class button of rank from Pekin.

Our abandonment of this mission was regarded by the Tibetan Lamas as cowardice. They intrigued more actively than ever in Sikhim. They stopped all trade over the passes and they induced the King to desert his country and settle in Tibet.

For over two years there was the strange spectacle of the King absenting himself from his country, and he deliberately refused to return notwithstanding the representations made to him by our government that his country was going to ruin; that his impoverished people were being sorely harassed by orders issued in his name, extorting extravagant sums of money from them; that they were almost in open revolt; and that if he did not return soon to right their wrongs, his allowance might be stopped. He, however, refused to return and defied our Government; and his Tibetan friends, emboldened by our apparent inaction, threw an armed rabble of Tibetan troops into Sikhim in

1887 and blocked our trade-route by building a fortified barrier at Lingtoo, below the Jelep pass, well within the Sikhim territory.

This move ended disastrously for the Tibetans. In March 1888 they were driven out of Sikhim with great loss to them, and little to ourselves. Since then, the King, who had meanwhile returned, has had a British Resident imposed upon him, and the policy of desertion and misrule under which his country has so long languished is now over. The King has been made to understand that henceforward he must discharge his duties to his state and must have no more dealings with the Tibetans. A joint Commission representing England and China has been appointed to define the frontier and facilitate trade with Tibet. Good roads are being made, and torrents bridged; and already, swarms of Nepalese are being imported into the country, to reclaim its forests and give to it a large settled population of industrious peasantry. To guarantee the performance of his engagements, and counteract the intrigues of the banished minister, his own Tibetan wife, and their Chinese supporters, a detachment of our troops has been placed near his residence; and as we take our departure we can see on more than one hill across the valley the white tents of our pickets, the outposts of our little army, under whose watch and ward the country has been for several months.

Under an enlightened and efficient administration, there is not only no reason why Sikhim, so rich in fertile valleys and with some mineral wealth as well, should not become prosperous and pay its way; but, on the contrary, there is every prospect of the country becoming as rich and prosperous as the Darjeeling district. The chief obstacle to advance, now that the political power of the priests is broken, is the administrative corruption, which in the East eats deeply into every department; and the present Rajah certainly does not seem to have displayed much aptitude for his trust.

Much more hopeful is his younger son, who is his presumptive heir, as the elder son has been made a monk in Tibet. This boy, who is still a mere child, might, if suitably educated, become a creditable ruler; and those who have the best interests of the country and its people at heart, expect that our Government will see the advisability, nay, the necessity, of putting this boy, without delay, under proper European instruction, so as to train him up to an enlightened sense of his princely duties and responsibilities towards his people and country.

Such training, however, to be effectual, must be done entirely by a competent European, for it is in the last degree undesirable that the boy be made a Bengalee Baboo; and there is much risk of this happening, for even the Lama Ugyen Gyatsho has been so influenced by his few years' association with Bengalees, that our Sikh orderly stoutly maintains that he must be really one of these, and not a Sikhimite at all. It is to be hoped that our Government will see to this important matter, and so, while contributing to the welfare of his people and the development of his country, at the same time secure to ourselves a useful ally.

On returning to the monastery with its flags fluttering lazily in the wind, in lazy keeping with everything else, we found a few presents of fruit, stale milk and butter etc. awaiting us from the minister. We acknowledged these gifts in the usual way, by sending him in return much more than their equivalent in value, and also paid toll to the servants who brought the things. The remainder of the evening, after dinner, we spent in watching the curious ritual of the priests in the temple.

The monks or priests sat cross-legged in rows, according to their rank, the head-priest sitting next to the high altar, on which were ranged the idols of Buddha and the monstrous Indian and Tibetan divinities of the Lamas. On it also were set brazen candlesticks, and bowls containing holy water, flowers stuck in English beer-bottles still bearing their original labels, cake-offerings and sacrificial implements. Clouds of incense filled the building, and in the smoky gloom of the temple, dimly lit by flickering candles, the monks half veiled and half visible chanted their spells to appease the divine wrath and to banish the devils. This service, at times, was most solemn and impressive. When the sound of voices rising from a low intoned drone swelled up into a loud joyous chant, and sank again into a whisper, and the only sound was the slow deep sepulchral tones of the chief priest, the influence of the mysticism seemed to steal into your very soul. Then suddenly the thunder of drums and the shout of the priests and people and the clash of cymbals crashes on your startled ear, and the service becomes for a time noisy and discordant.

We were surprised to find that part of this service was specially for our benefit, as Kintoop had offered many candles and had arranged for special prayers for the success of our expedition and our safe return.

What immensely tickled our Indian servants was the frequency with which refreshments of soup, tea and occasional rounds of beer were served out to the monks in the temple, during the intervals of worship. They declared that they would much like to belong to a religion which provided its votaries with creature comforts so abundantly. Before we turned in for the night we noticed an extraordinary procession of some of our coolies, who had evidently been paying visits and been too hospitably treated to *murwa* to drown the memory of their fatigues of yesterday. They were stumbling along, the most unsteady bringing up the rear, but all were in good humour and not at all boisterous; and Kintoop assured us that they would be all right in the morning, and so they proved to be.

Early next morning (12th October) we were off again to Upper Sikhim, along the Teesta Valley, by the lower road, as the short cut over the Mafi pass was blocked by a landslip. Over undulating spurs we passed the small monastery of De-thang, or "The Meadow of the Scented Laurel". This is a species of Daphne from whose tough bark the natives make paper. At the hamlet of Tingcham, where we encamped, goitre was common. One of the afflicted peasants, a rosy-cheeked, buxom girl, was brought by her parents to see if I could do anything to remove the disfiguring swelling in her neck, which hindered her prospects of marriage. I gave her, as well as the others, some red iodide of mercury ointment and showed them how to apply it. But neither these people nor the headman, who brought us a few presents of food, gave us any useful information about the unexplored To-loong valley, up which we wished to go, and which we could now see looming dark and steep, some ten miles up the other side of the Teesta.

The people are intensely superstitious, and many are the wild legends related of this lonely gorge, whose very name, "Valley of the Rocky Avalanches", seems appalling. These stories tell not only of the dangers from the showers of rocks that are shot down by the spirits of the glaciers and precipices, but also of the supernatural horrors which await the foolhardy person who dares to penetrate its lonely glens since the Lamas have placed the mausoleum of the kings there, and have worked their spells over it.

One of the few monasteries of the aboriginal Lepchas is to be seen across the Teesta, almost opposite our tent. The Lepchas are boycotted by their disdainful Bhotiya rulers from the regular monasteries, and in self-defence they have established this one of Gyagong and two or three others of their own. But their form of Lamaism is even more depraved than that of the Bhotiyas. Thus they offer eggs and sacrifice fowls and other living things before the idol of the compassionate and sacrifice-abhorring Buddha!

Here we saw several birds of that well-nigh extinct family, the Hornbills. They roosted on the trees like great vultures, painting their beaks bright vermilion from the paint-box they carry under their tails. Our Lepchas told us of the curious habits of these birds in regard to their nesting, how the male bird builds a thick mud wall all over his mate whilst she is hatching her eggs, leaving only a small orifice through which he feeds her until the young are fully fledged.

Next day we crossed a valley lined with many landslips, of which one was still fresh and slightly moving as we scrambled over it. Beyond Ringon, or "The Monastery of the Hill", and its *mendong* or cairn of Sim, on a point which commands a fine view up the mysterious To-loong valley to the Kanchen-junga glaciers, we descended to the village of Singtam, where we encamped on the bank of a stream, beside two huge prayer-barrels or rather prayer-mills. They were turned like a water-mill at home, by the rushing waters of the brook. When the headman, or *Pi-pön*, came to pay his respects, bringing the usual small presents, we tried to induce him to get us some grain, as our coolies' food had already run alarmingly low, and we had been told that some maize was stored in this village. We therefore tried to tempt him to bring us some by offering four times the Darjeeling market rate, and the further reward of a fine coral necklace for his womenfolk, should he bring not less than two hundredweight of the grain before sunset. Although protesting that such a quantity could not be found, he afterwards turned up with it, and measured it out with his own hands, giving very skimp quantity. On receiving the money and the promised necklace, he put out his tongue and bowed his thanks in true Tibetan fashion (see illustration p. 172). The *Kazi* or baron who resided here in Hooker's time has transferred himself higher up to Ringon. I got some information about the lower To-loong Valley and its lonely monastery from a monk who had been there. He advised our going, as we had intended, by way of the Lachen valley. We enjoyed magnificent sunset views up the wild To-loong Valley, where the huge rock of Pon-nay stood up like a tall beetling tower or giant campanile.

Our track next day led down to the bed of the rapidly rising Teesta; here in a cliffy cañon we walked through shady groves of overhanging chestnuts, oaks, and maples, and past lovely fern and moss-grown grottoes, making many detours to circumvent precipitous rocks, over which cascades tumble down the cliffs and leap into mid-air to become lost in rainbow mist long before they reach the bottom of the cool gorge, where the thundering Teesta churns its waters into milk-white foam. At the Lepcha village of Namgor, where we were to encamp, we met a party of Tibetan shepherds, who had come with a large flock of sheep, that they were bringing to Darjeeling. They had come from the Tsang province by way of the Lachoong valley. After I had bought two sheep for ourselves and servants, they gave us the disquieting news that the Lachen route, up which we wished to go, would certainly not be open for several weeks at least. We thereupon despatched Kintoop with a letter and present to the abbot of the Choong-tang monastery at the foot of the Lachen valley, asking him to get the necessary bridges constructed at our expense without delay, and next day we pushed on ourselves to Choong-tang.

Fording a stream of foaming cataracts, we struck down again to the cañon of the Teesta, whose cool bed is now over 4,000 ft. above the sea. And after fording many tributary torrents we reached, beyond Chakoong, the open gravelly delta of the many-armed Ryot river, that rushes clear and sparkling over pebbly strands to join the Teesta close at hand. As we passed a copse of alders, on a terrace that looked like an old moraine, we heard pheasants calling in the tempting cover, and my man afterwards brought in some silver pheasants that he had shot for us here. Thence we threaded the broad ancient bed of the Teesta, now a wilderness of stones, through which the track is marked out for the traveller by small pyramids of stones, crowning the top of the most conspicuous boulders. On we went until our course was suddenly barred by a great bend of the Teesta, which sweeps round under a huge cliff. This we had to scale by ladders of notched bamboos, the "high road" to Upper Sikhim in a very literal sense! Descending again to the river-bed beyond, we threaded our way amongst the great boulders to where, at an elevation of

5,200 ft. above the sea, the Lachen and Lachoong unite their waters to form the commencement of the Teesta.

CROSSING CLIFFS ON BAMBOO LADDERS.

Here the road to Tibet branches into two, one of which leads up the Lachen, or the "Long Pass", and the other up the "Short Pass", or Lachoong, and from these two valley-passes the rivers respectively take their names. Upon the promontory formed by their junction, above a small meadow, stands the monastery of Choong-tang, or "The Meadow of Marriage (of the two rivers)."

On crossing the Lachoong torrent by a good cane-bridge, we found Kintoop and the head Lama awaiting us with jugs of *murwa*, on the marshy meadow below the monastery. The Lama, though quite a youth, was strikingly handsome and dignified, and had short curly hair like the conventional images of Buddha. He presented a ceremonial scarf, in the Tibetan style, and said that immediately on receiving our message he had collected all the available men from surrounding hamlets to make the necessary bridges; and that all these men, some dozen or more, were then present. We thereupon held a council, at which it appeared that the construction of the three bridges over the Lachen would take nearly a week, as the largest would require to be built entirely from our side without any aid from the opposite bank, as no Tibetans had yet come down that valley. There was no doubt as to the chief bridge being really broken, for Kintoop had himself gone up to the place, to ascertain the facts. This intelligence, I confess, was most disappointing, especially as such delay at this time of the year, even were we to consent to wait so long in such a hole, meant almost certainly more snow on the upper passes to which we were bound. So we decided, reluctantly, to alter our programme and go up the Lachoong Valley instead, and thence try to work round into the Lachen Valley by Kangralamo, as Hooker did, in the reverse direction, or by the unexplored pass of Sherboo. And we were reconciled to this change when we looked up the Lachoong Valley. Our hearts were gladdened by the sight of its bold pine-clad slopes and peaks tipped with snow, only a few miles off; for it rises so rapidly that it is almost Alpine at this its lower end. Whilst our tents were being pitched on the meadow and breakfast was getting ready, we responded to the Lama's invitation to visit the monastery.

We were received as honoured guests, and we must have formed quite a picturesque procession as we climbed the winding path to the convent, to the inspiriting strains of the temple band! First, there marched the band in single file, blowing horns and trombones, clashing cymbals, and beating drums that were held aloft by a handle, like huge uplifted frying-pans, such as we had seen at Phodang. After the band, and immediately preceding us, walked the stately mitred Lama, carrying burning joss-sticks or tapers of sweet incense. We were escorted by several red-robed priests, while Kintoop with a straggling tail of our followers brought up the rear.

The monastery is perched on a commanding knoll, overlooking the rivers. It is a small two-storied building of rude stone, with an upper wooden balcony reached by a notched log as a ladder. One of the chief idols in this temple is the tutelary goddess called "The Diamond Lady Sow".[25] This lady is not exactly the kind one would care to introduce to one's friends. She has the form of a woman with three heads, one of them a sow's, and her character is that of a blood-thirsty and vindictive she-devil. To account for her high position here, the Lamas say that the name of this place is not really, as the villagers call it, "Choong-tang"; but that it should be "Tsoon-tang" which means "The Meadow of our Lady (-Sow)".

This now solitary place was once a Tibetan outpost, of which the ruins are still visible; and it was the scene of much excitement about ten years ago. The people of the valleys of Lachen and Lachoong which meet here, are Tibetan herdsmen, over whom the abbot or Lama of this monastery claimed spiritual jurisdiction and extorted so many tithes that they rebelled against him. It is related, that the infuriated mob of herdsmen gathered here, and slaughtering two bull-yaks, one from each valley, at the spot where we are encamped, they dipped their hands in the reeking blood, and swore a great oath never again to owe allegiance to this Lama, or send their sons to be monks of this monastery, or do any of its drudgery or cultivate any of its lands. Then they marched up to the monastery, brandishing their swords, beating drums, and shouting vengeance on the Lama; but he, on hearing the outcry, had fled precipitately down the valley to Ringon monastery, where he still lives. The deserted monastery fell into decay, and remained in a ruinous state till 1883, when a more popular Lama was sent from Pemiongchi to re-establish it. This new Lama, however, went to the opposite extreme, it is said; and so intimately identified himself with the Tibetans, that he joined them and fled to Tibet during our recent war with that country; and at present our handsome young host is in charge.

He acts up to his Buddhist ideal in some ways, for when I was going out, gun in hand, to look for game, he lamented over my sin of shooting, and appealed to me not to take any animal life, at least within some miles of the sacred temple of Buddha. So I had to go botanizing instead. And looking up out of this deep dark gorge to the inspiriting snowy peaks rising only a few miles up the valley, we were cheered to feel that we were really on the threshold of the Himalayan Alps, at last.

CHAPTER V

THE ALPINE LACHOONG VALLEY TO THE TIBETAN FRONTIER—THE TANG-KAR, DONG-KIA, SEEBOO, PATA AND GORA PASSES

> Dong-kia's beetling bastions frowned
> A silent warning far around
> No foot may venture here.
>
> C. Macaulay's *Lay of Lachen.*

SUCH a delightful day's walk we had up the lovely Alpine valley of Lachoong. It well repaid us for all our many days' discomfort in the hot gorges below. Our path ran along the bank of the rushing river. At first it led over gravelly strands in the cool river-bed, where clumps of familiar European shrubs and flowers showed the proximity of the snowy peaks, which now almost overhung us, although the forest on the banks was still semi-tropical. But every step carried us quickly up into an Alpine climate.

After about a mile, we crossed to the opposite bank by a cane bridge near the place where Hooker lost his Tibetan dog "Kinchin"; and beyond this, over an old moraine, the valley opened out a little, and the snow fingered down the peaks on either side of us. The upper reaches of the hillsides got more and more bare and rugged, and the contrast between their southern and northern sides was most striking. The warm southern slopes were still covered by dense forest, where straggling *rattan*-cane, or climbing palms, rose to the tops of trees 70 or 80 feet high, and trailing over 100 yards through the jungle, penetrated almost to the pines

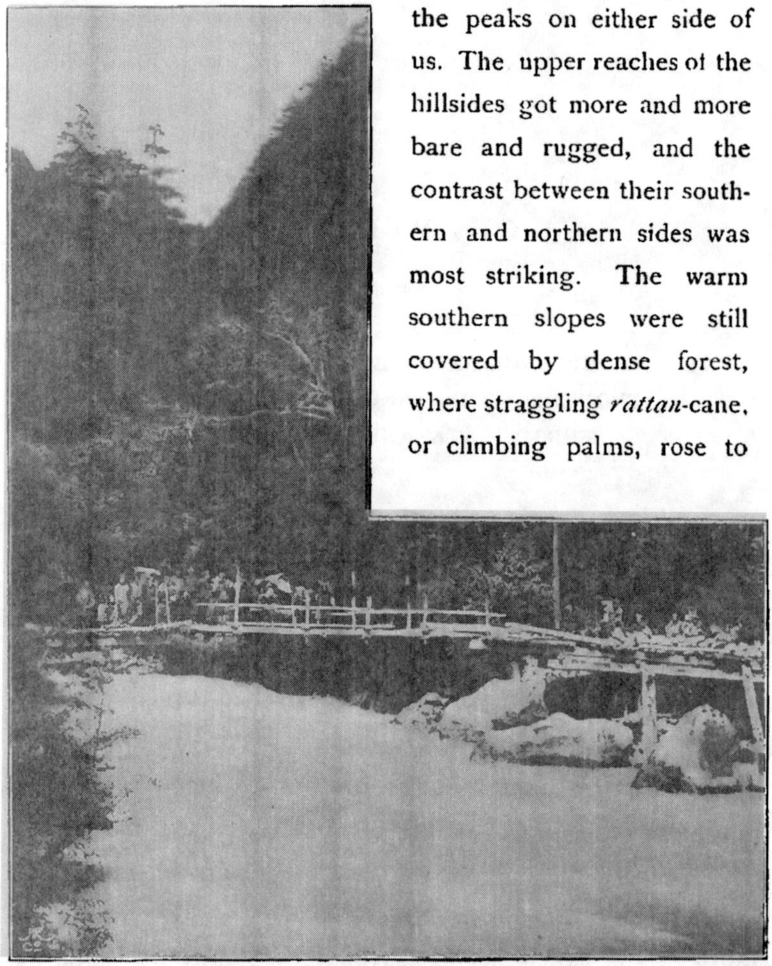

LOG-BRIDGE ON CANTILEVER PRINCIPLE.

that crowned the summits. The pines, as we moved upwards into cooler altitudes, were reaching farther and farther down the mountain sides; while in the cold northern shade, snow lay low down below the peaks, which on this side were mostly bare of trees.

At the hamlet of Kedoom (6,400 feet) we halted at a hut in an orchard of peach and apricot trees, and found the fruit refreshing, though not yet ripe. Here there is a very marked change in the flora and fauna. Indeed this place, as Mr. Blanford observes, may be considered the boundary between the Malay and Palæarctic faunas, a boundary which on the eastern Chola range is 3,000 to 4,000 feet higher. Wild goats (*Gooral*) are to be found here.

We recrossed the river by a picturesque bridge on the cantilever principle, the same which is so common in China, and figured on the willow-pattern plates; and I have seen the same style of bridge, only more elaborate, in Upper Burma. They resemble somewhat the ancient Gallic bridges described by Cæsar, and much the same are still to be seen in the mountains of Savoy. Great logs of pine, oak, or other sturdy trees, are laid down on either bank and "canted" up, so that one end projects a long way over the bank, and the beams are fixed in this position by loading down their landward ends by heavy rocks. Then across the abutting ends of these piers, stretching from the one to the other, is placed a platform of three or four logs, lashed together; and on this, for footway, some planks and brushwood are laid crosswise. It is thus a fairly strong suspension-bridge, and if made broad enough, as this one was, even cattle can cross it.

Beyond this bridge, the valley broadened out, and the undergrowth got less dense. We passed up through a fine open glade in the forest, amongst walnut trees, where the squirrels were busy at work. We knocked down a few of the nuts and found them excellent. Onwards through hazel, holly, maple, crab-apple, poplar and pines, we entered an open grassy meadow, dotted by the peculiarly Tibetan cattle, the yaks, browsing on its rich pasture.

This was the first time I had seen these Tibetan oxen, out of the "Zoo" in Regent's Park. They are shaggy beasts, in appearance something between the American bison, and the cattle of the Scotch highlands: and their curious grunting call is aptly denoted in their scientific name of "The Grunting Ox" (*Bos grunniens*). They are noble-looking massive animals, especially the bull-yaks, in spite of their oddly round and squat appearance, their broad straight backs, short legs, and long silky hair. This thick coat of hair which protects them from perishing in the arctic cold of the snows, is longest on their sides and undersurfaces, and in some of the older animals it almost sweeps the ground. The tail ends in a great bushy tuft, which serves the same purpose as the bushy tail of the hybernating squirrel, curling over its owner's feet and nose when asleep, like a rug, and thus affording protection against the intense cold of the Himalayan nights. These bushy yak-tails are much in demand in India, as fly-whisks (*chowries*) for Indian princes, and as royal emblems for the idols in Indian temples. The colour of the wild yak is a dark brown, almost black; but most of the domestic yaks acquire a good deal of white with the black predominating; and those most valued have their muzzles tipped with white, some white on their neck, and their tails entirely white. The female yaks are called *Di-mo*; and the *A-yu* are a kind of polled yak. Here also were

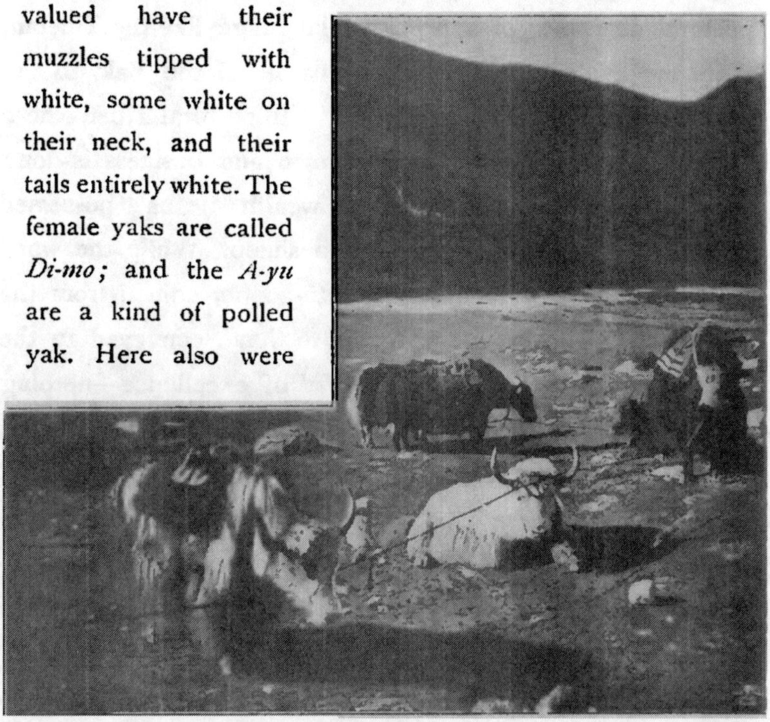

YAKS.

some hybrids between these domestic yaks and the common Indian cow; for the yak interbreeds freely with most other species of the ox tribe.[26] These hybrids are called *Zo*, and are said to stand these warmer valleys better than pure yaks, though even they cannot survive the heat of much lower elevations in this latitude. Most of these cattle are rather fierce, and we found it politic to give them a wide berth in passing.

Perhaps nothing gives a better notion of the essentially pastoral character of a primitive language like the Tibetan, than the evident relation of the name of the Yak, to the ideas of "wealth" and "excellence". In pastoral Tibet, where the use of money is almost unknown and business is done mainly by barter, the word for wealth means "possessed of cattle"—the herds of yaks and sheep. While the word "Yak" itself is evidently onomato-poetic, coined from the call of the beast: and it seems to have conveyed to the rude Tibetan mind the *beau idéal* of excellence—nothing seemed better than a good fat yak—and hence it came to form the common word for that which is "good and excellent."

The sight of these Tibetan cattle with their Tibetan herdsmen, the so-called "Dok-pa", and their fierce visaged deep-voiced mastiffs, who are marked like bears, with a white patch on the breast, and hence their usual name is "Bear" (*Tom-mo*), made us feel that we were nearing the borders of Tibet itself. And this was still more evident when the musical jingle of harness bells heralded the approach of a party of Tibetan merchants, who came riding on ponies and yaks, and driving a string of laden yaks. For baggage-animals pass regularly along this track from Kedoom to and from Tibet. Here, too, a Lammergeyer eagle came to greet us, hovering on widespread wings, high overhead, the unfailing escort of the traveller in these high regions.

The valley now had grown truly Alpine. On either side of us rose snow-capped mountains, almost bare of trees, except in the ravines where rhododendrons and dark pines clustered thickly. These elegant pines (*Abies Smithiana*), the "Spruce" of Hooker, and another (*Tsuga Brunnonia*), had been advancing slowly down the hillsides and first reached the river bank on the cold northern aspect of a head-land, about 8,000 feet above the sea-level, and about ten miles above Choong-tang, whence we had started that morning.

Suddenly, on rounding a grassy spur, we came on the village of Lachoong (8,600 ft.), lying like a truly Alpine town in the bottom of the open valley, at the junction of the Lete river with the Lachoong, and amidst the grass-covered moraines noticed by Hooker. We were met outside the village by a party of the inhabitants led by the head-man, who presented a scarf and saluted us in Tibetan style, pressing forward his right ear and putting out his tongue in his most polite way.

This extraordinary form of salutation is, I think, one of the best illustrations possible of that kind of salutation which Herbert Spencer[27] classes as expressing the self-surrender of the person saluting to the person he salutes. And it has never been properly described before. There is no "scratching" of the ear as stated by Huc and the writers following him. What is done in addition to the uncovering and low bow or prostration, and the abject putting out of the tongue, is that the Tibetan presses forward his left ear. This, it seems to me, is in accordance with the ancient Chinese custom of cutting off the left ears of all prisoners taken in war, and presenting them to the victorious chief.

The presentation of the scarf of white Chinese silk is an essential part of Tibetan courtesy. Not only is this

THE POLITE TIBETAN SALUTATION.

necessary in paying formal visits, but no favour can be asked of a superior without it, and it forms the envelope for all important letters. So extensively indeed are these articles used in Tibet, that their importation forms a considerable trade with China.

We pitched our tent on the velvety bank of grass bordering the river, and nestling under a great craggy mountain that rose abruptly many thousand feet above us. How high it rose, indeed, we could not see, as its head was hid in mist; but a glacier peeped over its cliffy shoulder and patches of snow lay low on its sides, and the chill blast blew down its slopes and made us quickly don our warmest overcoats.

Our tent was soon the centre of an admiring crowd of villagers who watched all our proceedings, open mouthed and open eyed, as most of them had never seen Europeans before. Some of the girls looked picturesque in tartan skirts and small round hats, and dressed generally like the Bhotiya women at Darjeeling. Those wearing conch-shell bracelets on their wrist are usually married. The greatest attraction of all for the people was to see us dine, which we did *al fresco* to enjoy the view. It was interesting to watch the yaks browsing high up the crags above us. How they got there and found a footing was a marvel. It made one almost dizzy to look up at these great beasts scrambling like chamois along the slippery face of the cliffs, which by fore-shortening seemed almost perpendicular. They clambered over loose masses of rock where at every moment we expected either to see them dashed down before our eyes, or send some of the rocks thundering down to overwhelm us below. At sunset, which occurred at 4 o'clock, when the sun suddenly dipped behind Kanchen-junga and threw the valley into cold shade, the herdsmen called their cattle home; and then these big beasts lumbered down the precipitous hills at a run, and gathered on the meadow near our tent, where their playful antics, so clumsy and uncouth, were ludicrous to see. Instead of lowing, they literally grunted with joy, and most of them have tinkling bells, like Alpine cattle. Here I got my first glass of yak's milk. It surpasses in richness the richest Devonshire cream, and is too rich in fact to drink, but with oatmeal porridge next morning was excellent. A young yak was bought as meat for the camp. Amongst some presents that were brought us, were some sweet little turnips, grown locally from Tibetan seed; such would be most welcome at Darjeeling, which is badly off for vegetables. They have no Murwa beer here as millet is too bulky to import so far. Instead of this they drink a coarse stuft brewed from maize, and even this is a luxury. Buckwheat and barley are the only grains grown locally.

I had some interesting conversation with several of the people, and with the Lama of the place.

The inhabitants of this valley are called Ha-pa or Har-pa Tibetans, as they came originally from the Ha province of south-western Tibet, bordering Bhotan. They are nomads in habit. Though they have fixed their head-quarters at this village, few of them stay here for more than a few months. In the early spring, as the snows melt on the upland pastures, they move up the valley with their herds, by stages, to their summer grazing-stations, which lie at intervals of four or five miles all along the upper valley.

And at each of these stations are erected rude huts as shelters, which are evacuated as the herdsmen move on. In this way, they ascend gradually higher and higher as the weather warms, till they reach the summit of the Dongkia pass (18,000 ft.) about June, when it is usually unsnowed and open. Thence, they cross the frontier into Tibet and move slowly along with their black yak-hair tents, a few of their cattle, and their produce, to Kamba-jong, the head-quarters of the adjoining district in Tibet. A few go even as far as the capital of Western Tibet (Shiga-tse or Tashil-humpo). At those marts they barter their goods for salt, tea, cloth, rugs, jewellery etc., and then they slowly return so as to recross the frontier into Sikhim about the end of August, and retreat down this Lachoong valley before the advancing snow. In mid-winter they leave Lachoong and drive their yaks and other cattle still further down, almost to Kedoom. The valley has thus practically only one village, and in this respect the neighbouring valley of Lachen is said to resemble it. These people pride themselves immensely on their pure Tibetan blood, and do not conceal their contempt for the Sikhimese, though they have to pay revenue to the Rajah of Sikhim. This is paid in kind, at the rate of two pounds of butter for each milk-yak, and a blanket and two pounds of salt for each house.

Kintoop announced that the fugitive ex-Lama of Choong-tang monastery, of whom we have heard, and of whose capabilities Mr. Macaulay had formed a high opinion, had returned secretly from Tibet and desired to see me. He came carrying a presentation scarf, which I accepted, although at that time I was unaware that my acceptance of it meant, according to the custom of these people, that I would favourably consider his request. He was a jolly-looking, typical monk of middle age, with an intelligent and shrewd expression, and he rejoiced in the title of "The Holder of the Religious Mysteries", [28] which he was careful to write on his card in the vernacular. He said that he had all along been loyal to the English, and had rendered much assistance to Mr. Macaulay, who had taken him to see the sights of Calcutta; and that as he had there seen with his own eyes evidence of the great power of the English, it was absurd to think that he had been intriguing against us, with the poor Tibetans, as his detractors alleged. "No," said he, "I have been consistently loyal to the English, and that is why the Tibetans carried me off by force."—"What other punishment," I asked in an incredulous tone, "have the Tibetans inflicted upon you?"—"None," he replied, "that was enough to compromise me; and now as they have released me, I wish to be re-instated in my monastery here in Sikhim. For," said he, "although this monastery belongs to my sect (Pemiongchi), yet the new English political officer has confiscated it, and given it to the rival sect," whose head, our old friend the Lama of Phodang, is now politically supreme. I advised him to represent his case to our political officer.

The view up the Lete Valley towards Tang-kar Pass, the "Tungra" of Hooker, was so attractive that we decided to go there next day. The only information we possess of

CASCADES OF THE LETE.

this pass is the brief notice by Hooker, of his visit to it more than forty years ago, and since that time no European appears to have visited it.

Our coolies now got quite excited at the prospect of getting into the snow, and busied themselves in preparing for this arctic weather. Several began mending their snow-boots and their blanket-coats; and the women, as if their faces were not dirty enough already, smeared more brown paint around their eyes and noses, as a protection against possible snow-blindness. The Tibetans suffer a good deal from this affection, and always use goggles when they can get them—coloured glasses stitched into a band of cloth, as metal is so painfully cold. The commonest eye-preservers consist of a gauze netting of closely plaited, black yak-hair; but the poorer people when crossing the snow merely blacken their faces around the eyes and nose with dark pigment. This latter practice is followed by the women of the lower classes of Tibet at all times of the year, even at Darjeeling where there is no snow. This hideous custom is said to have been forced on them by the Lamas, to lessen their attractions for possible admirers amongst the wavering members of the celibate monkhood.

It was almost freezing as the darkness settled in, and a few drops of sleety rain fell from the threatening sky. During the night I was awakened by a rumbling and shaking like an earthquake, but on looking out, I found that the cause of the disturbance was a yak that had strayed amongst the tent ropes, and it was more alarmed than myself.

Next morning we were off for the Tang-kar pass, leaving here at Lachoong our heavy stores and the weakliest of our coolies, as we must return this way. We crossed the river on some logs and saplings thrown over the boulders, the regular bridge having lately been swept away by a flood, which had cut a fresh section through the end of the moraine on which the village is built, and a streamlet poured over this in small cascades. The bulk of the village stands on this terraced left bank, and as we passed upwards, the score or so of houses presented a suggestively Swiss appearance with their wooden balconies, projecting eaves and truly Alpine setting, amidst dark pines and snowpeaks. Ascending this lateral moraine which belts the Lete valley, we rose rapidly, passing on the way the small monastery, where the Lama came forward and pompously presented a scarf, and received in return a couple of rupees, or eight times the cost of the scarf.

Continuing our ascent over a bare ridge, dotted here and there with the graceful Himalayan larch (*Larix Griffithii*) which grows at about from 8,000 to 12,000 feet, we struck the gorge of the tumultuous Lete, and followed up its steep bank amidst pines and rhododendrons. Here a species of wild red currant, pleasant to the taste, grows abundantly. After a time, the track got lost in the rocky bed of the stream, along which we picked our way amongst the great boulders, through most beautiful scenery: avenues of magnificent pines, graced by cascades, and overhung by snowpeaks. After a mile or so, we gained the track on the opposite side and passed up through the pine forest of *Abies Dumosa* and the silver-fir (*A Webbiana*,—in Tibetan "Dum Shing"), and here and there great black juniper trees (*J. excelsa*), the "Shook-pa" of the Tibetans, the aromatic wood of which is burnt as

HIMALAYAN LARCH.

incense in the temples, and is the "pencil-cedar" of commerce. I shot here, near an overhanging rock, a speckled wood pigeon, and higher up a snow pigeon (*Columba leuconota*), and very good eating they were—Hooker tells how these last formed his chief animal food for some months, when the Sikhim officials cut off his meat supply in the hope of starving him out of the country. Presently we reached the upper limit of trees, and here we encamped amongst the rhododendrons and red and blue barberry, at about 12,000 feet elevation. The cessation of trees was not due to any change in the geological formation, but merely to cold and height. So spongy with damp was the boggy soil, that we had to cut down a quantity of the pine branches as a platform on which to pitch our tents. Hanging from the few straggling storm-tossed pines were masses of a stringy white lichen (*Usnea barbata*), which fluttered from their branches like grizzly beards.

Our men always preferred the forest to the open as a place of encampment; not only for shelter from the cold and wind, but also for the sake of fuel for their cooking fire, and the convenient fire-place which a tree-trunk offers, especially that of a dead tree. They kindle their fire at the foot of such a tree, and the rotten touch-wood at the centre ignites, and the trunk thus getting hollowed out by the fire, acts as a reflector in throwing the heat forward. Some of the half-rotten logs were luminous, and glowed in the dark—this was due probably not to "phosphorescence", but rather to the presence of luminous micro-organisms, for this wood was stained dark green by some kind of fungus.

The morning dawned intensely cold, the thermometer registered two degrees Fah. below the freezing-point. The grass and foliage were white with frost, and the ice spangles of the frozen forest glittered in the sun. We started off in the crisp keen air, crackling the ice over the shallow puddles of yesterday. The many streamlets that we crossed were fringed with icicles, hanging from the dripping banks and stones. Ascending the bleak open valley—like a highland moor, with rhododendron instead of heather—for about two miles, the rocks closed in around us, and we entered a great rocky *cul-de-sac,* whose walls rose up like giant towers and battlements, that shut the snows from our view. Through a deep cleft in this wall, the stream tumbled down in a string of cascades, and here, at an elevation of about 14,000 feet, we decided to encamp, as the pass could be easily reached from this point the following day; and also because the dwarf rhododendron-brushwood ended here, and it was now our only fuel. After selecting a picturesque and sheltered spot for our tent, and while B. went botanizing below, I climbed the precipice to the cleft in the rocky wall, through which the rivulet precipitated itself headlong. The cliff was not so sheer as it looked from below. A steep track zig-zagged up its face, but no bridle-path could easily be made here for mountain artillery.

The view from the top was superb. At ten o'clock not a cloud obscured the summits. Westwards the view extended away down the rocky valley up which we had come, to the black tree-line, and down the deep trough to the silvery Lachoong river, over 8,000 feet below, beyond which rose range upon range of snowy mountain and blue glaciers up to Kanchen-junga and Kabroo. The contour of this latter mountain as seen from here, is a long undulating ridge, not the elegant tent-like form of its foreshortened southern view, as seen from Darjeeling. And looking upwards through the cleft where the rushing stream wrestled with the rocks that barred its progress, was a peak of everlasting snow,

DOWNWARD VIEW FROM THE CLEFT (14,500 feet).

only a few hundred yards off, dazzling white against the dark blue of the Tibetan sky.

On passing further up this narrow gorge, the stream was seen to turn sharply up to a snowfield on the right, towards the pass; so I sent on a man to report on the snow-track to the pass, and I climbed a few hundred feet higher to the crest of the cliff called La-che-pia, overlooking our camp, and found it to be a miniature tableland. This ascent was over a slope of patches of snow overlying loose shingly splinters of rock, chipped off by the frost, and which slid down under foot as you went.

GIANT WILD RHUBARB.

In this ascent, I felt for the first time the effects of the rarefied air of this great elevation, for I was now about the height of Mont Blanc, although no ice-climbing had yet been done. The slightest exertion now caused shortness of breath, and a faint headache and giddiness; but these disagreeable sensations ceased immediately I remained at rest. The natives believe that these symptoms are caused by a poison in the air, which they call "the poison of the pass" (*La-dook*).

In this treeless region there was very little grass and turf, but many flowers. Indeed the number of "living flowers that skirt the eternal frost" was here remarkable. Although so late in the season, there were still a few gentians blooming amongst the withered primroses, and a great variety of flowers of the "everlasting" kind, enveloped by Dame Nature in such warm woolly coats of hair as to resemble fleecy tufts or balls of wool. Of these the most striking were the Alpine lover's favorite flower, the Edelweiss (*Leontopodium alpinus*) or "Lion's foot", and the large woolly aromatic *Saussurea gossypiphora*, which the Lamas use as decoration for their altars. The weirdest of objects in this treeless region is the giant wild rhubarb (*Rheum nobile*),[29] the "*Chuka*" of the Tibetans. Its tall pale pyramids of about four feet high and an equal diameter at the base, standing on all the topmost cliffs ranging up to 15,500 feet, looked like sentries guarding these gigantic battlements; and more than once they misled me into stalking them for a possible snow-bear or eagle. As few Europeans have ever seen this magnificent plant growing in its home, I here reproduce its photograph, the first I believe that has ever been taken. The graceful incurving of the pale pink leaves of its tall stem to protect its bunches of seeds is remarkable. Its stem contains a large quantity of water, a grateful beverage to the thirsty traveller, and the stalks of its leaves are as pleasantly acid to the taste as our cultivated rhubarb.

No trace whatever could I find of the glacier which Hooker places here. The line of perpetual snow is uneven, and strange to say, it here descends much further on the sunny southern side than on the cool northern shade, though on the more outlying spurs the reverse holds. This is evidently owing to the greater portion of the rain-clouds which come from India on the south precipitating themselves at once, as snow, and leaving little of their moisture for the drier northern sides and Tibet. Here, the line of perpetual snow, although in places over 18,000 ft., averages a height of about 16,000 ft. above the sea-level, and comes as low as 15,000 ft., compared with about 9,000 ft. in the latitude of the Swiss Alps. In winter the snow falls in this part of the Himalayas as low down as 6,000 ft., but it seldom lies for more than a few days even at 10,000 ft.

Though it was not yet noon the clouds which had been creeping up the valley now began to drift over me, and by the time I got down to camp all the snows were hidden in clouds.

The tent was tied to rocks and boulders, as tent-pegs could not be used in such a stony place. We spent the day rambling over the hillsides. I sighted some partridges and a *monal* pheasant feeding on the rhododendron berries, but I did not get a shot at them. Achoom's trouble with this high altitude in his cooking operations was amusing. He came to me with a long face, and said, "O, sir, the water of this place is very bad! It will not boil properly. I have boiled the potatoes and the rice and vegetables for more than three hours and still they are hard." The real reason of course was that the water, under the reduced atmospheric pressure, boiled at so low a temperature that it did not burst the starch grains fully. So I told Achoom to roast his potatoes and not to try to boil them. We were now quite out of bread, which grew mouldy in less than a week, and even that also which we had toasted to preserve it for softening down in stews, tasted now like old Stilton.

We started for the pass next morning (October 19th) before day-break, so as to secure an unclouded view, and to get over the frozen snow before it began to thaw in the sun. Proceeding upwards through the rocky throat of the gorge, we entered the stony valley to the right, between bold snowy peaks, and crossing the frozen streamlet, we soon reached the snow-field, which stretches up in an unbroken sheet for about three miles to the top of the pass. From this expanse of perpetual snow the name is derived—*Tang-kar*, or "The White (Snow-) Field". On the way we had frequently to stop to recover our breath in the rarefied air.

On reaching the top, our men shouted a prayer to the spirit of this pass, and tearing shreds from their dresses, tied them to the tops of some prayer-flags which projected from a rude cairn on the fine sweep of snow on the summit.

The view into Tibet from here is striking. The snow ceases a few yards below the summit, and beyond this rises a panorama of dark, bare peaks streaked with a fiery welter of tints like the burned up hills of Aden, but set in a framework of dazzling snow, and capped by snowy peaks soaring up into a clear Italian sky. The cold was bitter, but the piercing wind that swept the top was much more trying than the cold itself. This icy blast, sharp as a razor, cut and skinned our faces, froze our breath into flakes of snow, hung icicles from moustaches, and striking our temples, through our closely-fitting woollen arctic caps, caused severe headache. Yet thousands of tiny birds, like wag-tails, annually migrate over such exposed passes to and from Tibet; though when the temperature of such winds is much below the freezing-point, we were told, even eagles

VIEW INTO TIBET FROM TANG-KAR PASS (16,500 feet).

and other large birds often drop stone dead in their flight.

We descended a short way down the Tibetan side, as there was no guard to oppose us; and Kintoop pointed out the position of a distant hot spring that he had formerly visited. Returning to the summit, we tried to boil a thermometer to control the reading of our aneroid which gave the height at about 16,500 ft., as on the survey map, but after half-an-hour's assiduous trial and the expenditure of all our fuel (spirit as well as a large bundle of firewood) and all our patience, the thing would not boil. This instrument, a "hypsometer" of the latest pattern and by the best London makers, is quite unsuited for its purpose in such altitudes. It is made of brass, which parts so quickly with its heat in these intensely cold regions, that the water cannot be heated to the boiling-point. What is needed is a less conductive metal, and a jacket of felt or other non-conducting material, also a mica-screen to prevent the flame being extinguished by the wind. It would be interesting to know how the native survey-spies boiled their thermometers in Tibet, as they were supplied with these badly designed instruments, and the heights of most of the passes in Central and S. W. Tibet, as found in the maps, are given on their authority.

Leaving the pass about 10 a. m., we found some difficulty in retracing our steps, as the snow had begun to thaw and we sank deeply in places, and the dazzling glare was very trying in spite of our dark spectacles. For the fierce sun in this latitude so heated up the air as to raise its temperature to 115° Fah. three feet above the snow, when out of the wind; so that, paradoxical as it may seem, it sometimes happens that people get sunstroke even amidst the snow.

We looked again for the glacier mentioned by Hooker, but could find no trace whatever of it. There probably has been some mistake in placing it here, for it would indeed be remarkable that a glacier should have entirely disappeared within forty years and yet have left behind no trace of any very recent glacial action. The stream from

TRYING TO BOIL AN ALTITUDE THERMOMETER ON THE SUMMIT OF TANG-KAR PASS (16,500 feet).

the snow-field had already in these few hours become swollen to twice its size by the melting snows.

At night the temperature in our tent fell four degrees (Fah.) below the freezing-point, and we needed all our warmest woollen and sheepskin wraps; and our poor men who could not be accommodated in the servants' tent, sought the shelter of some overhanging rocks to our leeward, where they huddled together; for rocks get heated up by the sun during the day, and retain much of this heat long after the ground has radiated it off. The stars in this high altitude sparkled with unwonted brilliancy.

I was roused next morning about sunrise, by a strange European voice outside, cheerily calling to my servants in Hindoostani, "Is your master here?" Wondering who this could be at such a place where no European had been for so many years and at such a time, I hurried out to find a stalwart figure leaning on an alpenstock. Bidding me good morning, he pointed to the cleft, and said, "Is that the pass?"—and seemed incredulous when I replied that it lay over two miles higher up. "For," said he, "my aneroid, which I have just received from the Survey office, registers 16,000 ft., and my map gives 16,100 ft. as the height of the pass." I showed him that my watch-aneroid had beaten his, as it recorded over 22,000 ft. for this height, whilst our large one which had been standardized a few weeks before at the Survey office, gave a reading of a few feet under 14,000, which coincided with the results of our boiling-point thermometer or hypsometer. The truth is that small aneroids are only toys, and not to be trusted. After a cup of coffee, he said he must push on as he was going over the pass down into the Choombi Valley of Tibet. I suggested that this might lead to awkward political complications, seeing that our boundary commissioners had just arrived at some understanding with the Tibetans and Chinese as to this as a boundary line which Europeans must not cross, and the Chinese ambassador was himself at the present moment on the Tibetan side, not far from this pass. Our gallant friend, however, declared that he would risk such troubles; so I wished him good luck, and he and his coolies clambered up the cliff and soon disappeared through the cleft. I afterwards heard that he was seized by the Tibetans and carried to the irate Chinese Commissioner, who promptly deported him across the frontier and required considerable persuasion to hush the matter up.

Our canvas tent was a curious sight in the crisp keen air. After our men had loosened all the ropes, it still remained standing, as it had been frozen stiff as a board with the moisture of our breath. And it had to be beaten with the tent poles and sticks to fell it to the ground, and to roll it up.

The return to Lachoong was easy, as it was directly down hill. On arrival at Lachoong, an open note was put into my hand, addressed to "The Doctor travelling in Upper Sikhim". It was from an unknown correspondent, and implored me to come at once to Kedoom where a friend of his was in an alarming and apparently dying state. Anxious as I was to push on up the valley, I could not resist such an appeal; so although I had already done a fair day's march in our descent of about 6,000 feet, I at once started off down the valley on foot, as no pony could be got, accompanied by Kintoop and the man who brought the letter as a guide. Thc man led me to the small temple-cottage outside which we had halted to eat some apricots on the way up, and there in a room I met my correspondent attending a prostrate figure, whom I found unconscious and in a dying condition. As a last resource I applied a few medicines that I had brought with me, but he never rallied, and he died next morning about 4 a.m. His was a sad death. He was the Reverend S—h, who had been in weak health in Calcutta, and almost immediately after coming to the hills had started off to the Dong-kia Pass, where the rarefied air, combined with the cold and glare of the white rocks and snow, had caused fatal inflammation of both lungs, and some sun-stroke as well. We decided to bury him here, as his remains could not well be carried back to Darjeeling, which was more than a week's journey along the hot intervening valleys. So we fixed on a romantic spot for his grave: and on a terrace above the house where he died, and overlooked by snowy peaks, the rushing waters of the Lachoong murmur unceasingly their lament over the last resting-place of our unfortunate fellow-traveller.

Returning to our camp at Lachoong, I found B. suffering from a slight cold caught on the pass. As he felt disinclined to proceed for a few days, and we had just entered the most interesting portion of the mountains, and the cloudy sky presaged snow on the higher passes, I therefore pushed on next day up the valley, leaving Achoom and Rameses the cook, and most of the other servants with B., and arranged for letters to be forwarded on to me by runners. Kintoop, of course, I took with me, and also in addition to two yaks for baggage, ten strong Sikhimese and Tibetan coolies. I was rather loth to have to take as

GRAVE AND CAIRN OF OUR FELLOW-TRAVELLER.

cook Rameses' assistant, who rejoiced in the name of "The Mighty Ocean" (*Gyatsho*), a title which aptly defined his insatiable capacity for pilfering and devouring our scanty stores; nor was his cooking very tempting, but I could not afford to be fastidious.

I was glad to be able to ride up the greater part of

the fifteen miles to Yoomtang, after the fatigues of the previous day and night. My mount was a shaggy little Tibetan pony, not much to look at, but very sure-footed. The tinkling collar bells which rang out a chime as I passed along, I could have dispensed with, nor was the high-peaked Tibetan saddle at all comfortable. Progress was slow, as I could only go at a walk owing to the uncertainty of the track. The owner of the pony acted as guide. He was a native of this valley, and told me as we went the quaint legends of the places we passed. One of these was

THE LEGEND OF THE LOST TALISMAN.

In the heart of the Tibetan mountains, to the north of the neighbouring pass, the Dong-kia, lie the vast ruins of a deserted city, near the village of Gé. In the olden times when this city was flourishing it was the size of 2,000 villages and had 4 great monasteries. One day an inhabitant setting out for the city of Tashilunpo with firewood for sale, finding that the load on one side of one of his asses was heavier than the other, he picked up a stone the size of a ram's head, and tied it to the lighter side to equalize the loads. On arrival at Tashilunpo, the Grand Lama saw the stone, and divining that it was a lucky talisman, he asked the man about it, and on receiving it as a present, he carried it off and deposited it in his monastery. Ever since that time the monastery of Tashilunpo has prospered enormously and come to rival Lhasa, but Gé has decayed. And the prophecy has come true, that when Gé loses its talisman, it will become empty both inside and out. Even so it is. Now there are only ten huts left.

My guide, like most of the Tibetans hereabout, is a polyandrist. This peculiar institution, Polyandry,—the opposite of polygamy,—whereby two or three or more men are married to one wife in common, seems to have been widely prevalent in ancient times. It even existed in Great Britain according to Cæsar. Its origin cannot, from what we know of the lack of chivalry amongst Tibetans, be explained on the principle that "the single possession of one wife is a blessing too great for one individual to aspire to"! It is rather regarded in this pastoral country as an arrangement to protect the joint-family when its head is away for weeks, herding the cattle; and it is also viewed as a device to keep the common property within the family, in a country which cannot support a large population. Here, in Sikhim, however, it is usually a *fraternal* polyandry, that is to say the conjoint husbands are usually brothers. And the practice is that if the eldest brother marries, his wife is the joint wife of all the brothers; while if the second brother marries, then his wife is common only to the second and younger brothers, and not to the elder. An exception to this rule, however, is the present Queen of Sikhim, who was originally married to the younger half-brother of the present king, and she now is the joint wife of both. The children call the eldest of the conjoint brothers their "father". The family relationships are therefore somewhat complicated, especially when, as sometimes happens, some of these ladies are the happy possessors of half a dozen husbands.

Ascending the right bank of the river, we picked our way amongst the boulders, and soon reached the junction with the Si-boo, which rushes down a fine rugged valley from the steep Gora pass, far up which we could see a glacier. Then we zigzagged up a steepish rocky track called the "Tired Yak Pass" (*Yak-che La*), the foot of which is the usual stage for tired laden yaks coming up from Lachoong; and here are some huts of a grazing-station. Beyond this we passed through a magnificent pine forest whose darkness was relieved by the golden autumn tints of the larch, and fording many crystal streamlets we reached the Po-nying rivulet (10,850 ft.), where there is said to be a detached mass of rock that rises sheer, like a pulpit, about 2,000 feet high.

Further on we came to the wreckage of a tremendous avalanche. The whole side of a great mountain, that towered above us about three miles to our left, had broken away, and come thundering down some six years ago; and the rocky avalanche had covered the valley for many miles with its *débris* and buried several miles of forest quite out of sight, leaving only a fringe of splintered pines projecting from its borders. The enormous mass of these fallen rocks had thrust the river to the opposite side of the valley, over a mile out of its course, and had dammed up its waters there, forming a lake.

This is a common way in which lakes are formed in the

AN AVALANCHE OF ROCKS.

Himalayas. Instances of it are to be found in the case of the lacustrine valley of Nepal, and probably in the Lepcha legend of the lower Teesta already referred to, and in the lake of Naini Tal, and the *Tals* or lakes in its vicinity. And such lakes thus suddenly formed and having at their outfall no rocky barriers *in situ*, are subject to quite as sudden disappearance. I myself witnessed how this occurred when travelling in the North Western Himalayas in 1882. On the night of the 23rd August of that year, the sudden pressure of water from the flood of an excessive rainfall burst through the outfall dam of Bhim Tal, whose waters rushed down the valley, sweeping away stretches of the forest, and when I saw the lake early next morning, its level had fallen over twenty feet, leaving the greater part of its bed a muddy plain.

High above this great landship we could see (*vide* illustration) the scars on the cliffs that had been rent asunder, still standing out clear and sharp. Luckily this catastrophe happened during the night, and no human lives are believed to have been lost, and only a few cattle. My guide said that all this havoc was wrought by the malignant spirit of the mountain, for some offence that had been given him; though as to what this offence was opinions differed much. The rock seems to be a weathered granite, and its fall happened during a sudden frost, which by expanding the water in the crevices of the rock, splits the latter asunder like dynamite; but probably an earthquake also had to do with it, as there are some hot springs near, which indicate volcanic action not far off.

Clambering over this great field of rock like a vast quarry, the aspect of the valley changed. It grew darker and wilder. Beetling crags and bleak stony slopes carried the blackness of the pines up almost to the snows. But our track wound along the pleasanter wooded bottom of the valley, through rhododendrons, larches and willows that fringed the river bank. Here and there we crossed the shingly bed of an armlet of the river, which split up into many branches, rushing swiftly between green turfy islets.

In this maze of tracks my guide pointed out the device of marking the trail by a handful of freshly cut twigs. Laid lengthwise on one of the diverging tracks, these twigs signify that that one so marked is the one the traveller should choose. If laid crosswise they read "no passage this way."

A hot spring (in Tibetan *Sa-choo*) marked its position far up the valley by a cloud of steam that hung over it. And my men became loud in their praises of the marvellous healing virtues of its waters as a panacea for every ailment under the sun. It lay on the opposite bank, and we had to cross over to it by a slippery log-bridge. The hot water, smelling of rotten eggs, oozed from numerous crevices in the granite rocks at an elevation of 11,730 ft. At the largest spring a well or pool of about three feet has been excavated, and this was roofed over as a protection against snow and rain. As at the pool of Siloam, the first comer was considered to get the best of it. Here he certainly got the cleanest of it. For all my men, notwithstanding the cold, quickly stripped and bathed in it, and drank deeply of its malodorous waters, and they invited me also to do likewise. But I contented myself with climbing up the hill a short distance to taste a smaller spring which there welled out, and which though not deemed sacred was uncontaminated and quite as hot. The water tasted of the usual sulphureous kind, and I collected some for chemical analysis. [30] The sides of the pool and the beds of the several issuing streams were encrusted with stringy white sulphury clots, and in this hot water, masses of a green confervoid growth waved from the stones. The temperature of the hottest spring was 114.5° Fah., which is only about 2° higher than at Hooker's visit over forty years before. [31] The contrast between the great heat of this water and the icy air (33.5° Fah.), and the cold glacier water of the river, flowing amidst streaks of snow, with a temperature of 44° Fah., only a few feet distant, was most striking.

This apparently supernatural character of the spring has, of course, overawed the Tibetans, who allege that the rock at this spring is the abode of a devil (*Chab-dü*) who causes disease if she be not conciliated. They also believe that the spring is hotter in the morning and colder during the day; whereas it is only their subjective sensations that lead them to think so, as the difference between the temperature of the spring and the air at mid-day is less marked than in the colder morning air. I had considerable difficulty in getting my men away from this attractive spot.

Above this, the valley presented a remarkably weird appearance, as most of the granite boulders, blackened by dark lichens, were covered by large patches of a bright scarlet fungus, the fiery aspect of which in such a snowy setting reminded one somewhat of the banks of that Hades-like lake at the top of the Geirangerfiord in Norway. And the splintered trees were transformed into fantastic ghostly shapes by masses of the long hoary lichen that streamed in the wind.

A sudden bend of the river revealed the grazing-station of Yoomtang (11,650 ft.) with its herds of yaks and sheep. It is beautifully situated in an open meadow, through which the river winds with many a curve; on every side are dark pine-clad slopes, leading up to magnificent snowy peaks, of which the chief is Phaloong. Several glaciers also were visible. I selected for my quarters one of the best of the empty log-huts, as most of the yak-herds had gone further down the valley; and my men occupied the others. In one of the huts, in addition to the horns and skins of several deer and boars, said to have been killed in the neighbourhood, I saw a fine pair of horns of the great "Sikhim" stag, so called, though it is not found within Sikhim at all, but only in Tibet, whence these horns had been brought. I shot here a few snow pigeons, and I sighted in the pine woods a few wary partridges and pheasants, but did not go after them. My Tibetan coolies were delighted to see a flock of the red-billed and red-legged crow (or properly, "chough"), which they said was the common crow of Tibet. The cold at night was intense, although there was no wind; and at sunrise the thermometer registered

3° Fah. of frost, while at 8 a.m. it was 36° Fah. and the water of the river 40° Fah.

Next day I crossed the "Lachoong" river (here called Yoomtang after this village) by a rude log-bridge. Thence I ascended the eastern side of the valley for about a

YOOMTANG AND ITS YAKS.

thousand feet, and over a terraced moraine, to the foot of the great glacier. This elevation, about 13,000 ft., is perhaps the lowest limit to which glaciers descend in this part of the Himalayas. On the northern slopes their position is much higher, and the glaciers themselves are larger even, although the rainfall on which glacialization depends is much less. The southern slopes seem too steep to allow of the ice forming a stream of great length. The ice falls into the lower valleys as avalanches from the fan-shaped slopes, and soons gets melted by the excessive rainfall. Here I shot a snow partridge (*Lerva vivicola*), a piping hare (*Lagomys Roylei*), and the curious wingless water-thrush, the Dipper. Continuing up the valley for four miles, we re-crossed the river, and soon reached the upper limit of trees, about 13,000 ft. Many logs were lying cut and trimmed into planks of a size that a yak could carry, ready for transport to Tibet, where timber is extremely scarce. Here we halted for a little, to carry up some smaller pieces for our own firewood. The river, now called the Riv-la, leaping over the rocks, here became a chain of foaming cataracts.

The snowy mass of Phaloong towered above the other peaks; and several glaciers came down its sides, as well as between the sharp-pointed black crags to its south. They were streaked with blue and green crevasses, and extended to within a few hundred feet of us. And it was noticeable that the valley had broadened out from the narrow V-shape of water-eroded valleys into the open U-shape, with rounded rocky surfaces, characteristic of glacier action. This configuration, however, may be in part owing to the very low dip of the rocks here; for the dip of the gneiss in the low Teesta valley is very high, and, as Blanford notes, it is still considerable as far as Yoomtang; but hereabouts, where the gneiss is granitoid, with veins of pure granite, its dip is very low and almost horizontal; and to the westward it dips at an angle rarely exceeding 10° to 20°.

Toiling slowly up the bare stony valley and over old moraines, with the snows and glaciers coming down nearer and nearer, the rarefied air began to tell sorely on us. Even the yaks and pony suffered severely from the *mal de montagne*. I suffered less than most of the party as I had been able to ride a great part of the way; but all the men who carried loads, and most of these were hardy Tibetans, were

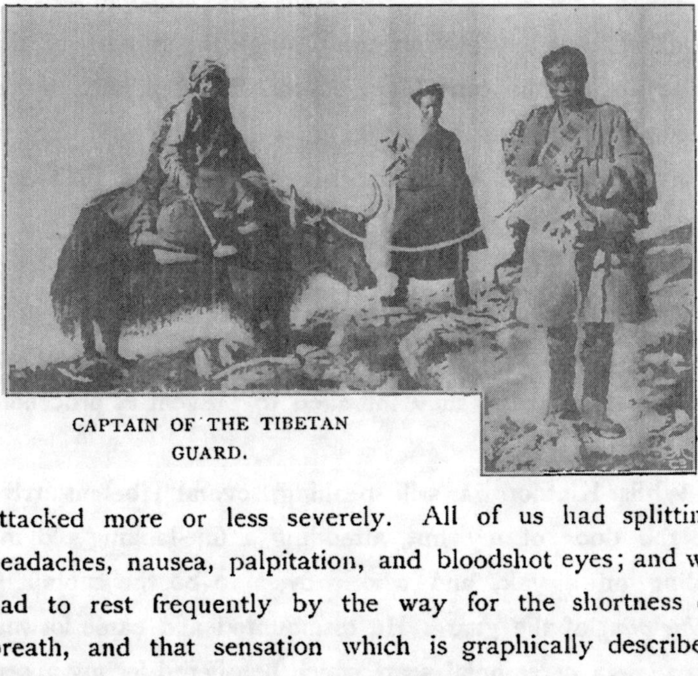

CAPTAIN OF THE TIBETAN GUARD.

attacked more or less severely. All of us had splitting headaches, nausea, palpitation, and bloodshot eyes; and we had to rest frequently by the way for the shortness of breath, and that sensation which is graphically described by Hooker as a feeling of "having a pound of lead on each knee-cap, two pounds in the pit of the stomach, and a hoop of iron around the head." I cannot explain why we were all so much more affected by the rarefied air of this place than by the much higher elevations of Tang-kar.

As we plodded painfully on, several of our men bled profusely at the nose. We were all in a sorry plight as we crossed the bridge, or *Samdong*, about the fourteenth mile, and struggled into the few bleak stone-huts of Momay (15,000 ft.). This is the highest grazing-station in Sikhim, and it is so inclement that it is only occupied for a few weeks during mid-summer by the hardy mountaineers.

These deserted, weather-beaten huts are built of rough stone without any mortar, and through the numerous chinks quite an icy hurricane blew, so that I had to pitch my tent inside the hut, and even then it was bitterly cold. The flat roof consisted of a few rough-hewn pine logs, held down by big boulders.

A few minutes after my arrival, Kintoop came to me with some alarm in his face, to say that the captain of the Tibetan guard of the pass (the Dong-kia) and his men were in this station, and they intended to prevent us proceeding any further.

Whilst Kintoop was still speaking, several Tibetans arrived at the door of my hut, attending a fine-looking old man riding on a yak, and who proved to be the captain (or *Ding-pön*) of the guard. He dismounted and came forward, carrying a ceremonial scarf which he offered for my acceptance; and on my taking it he stated who he was, and asked if it were true what he had heard from my men that I intended going up to the Dong-kia pass. On learning that such was my intention, he endeavoured to dissuade me from going, by alleging that not only was the weather up there terribly inclement, but that it was impossible to reach the pass now, as snow had fallen two days ago, and driven him and his men down; and certainly their faces with blood-shot eyes and blistered peeling skin looked as if they had been exposed to arctic weather. I found him quite reasonable and civil. He apologised for himself and his men being on the Sikhim side of the pass, and he said that of course I could go if I chose to the summit of that pass; but that it was his duty to prevent me from going beyond that point into Tibetan territory. He maintained that the summit of the pass was the boundary, although I told him that the recent agreement with China had fixed the boundary at the watershed of the Lachen, some eight miles beyond the pass, to the north. Nor would he consent on any terms to allow me to cross this way into the Lachen valley, as Hooker had done in the reverse direction. He maintained, like the guard who also stopped Blanford at this pass, that his instructions from Lhasa were positive as to the absolute closure of this pass against everyone except a few privileged Tibetans; and he added with much pantomime, the old story, that were we to force our way across, the throats of himself and his men would be cut. Under ordinary circumstances I would have felt much inclined to force my way over it into the Lachen valley, where it was so essential that I should arrive quickly, and I have no doubt that I could have done it; but unfortunately political negotiations were going on just then with the Chinese in regard to this very boundary, and the promise had been extracted from me not to cross this frontier, so as to risk any undue complications in this settlement. I therefore had to forego the attempt, and consent to go no further than the summit of the pass.

This Tibetan captain turned out to be a very interesting old man. He had attended the Tibetan governor or *Jong-pön*, who had met Mr. Macaulay's mission, and he is figured in the photograph of that group, a copy of which I shewed him. He had also been fighting against us in our little war with Tibet, the previous year, in command of a small body of Tibetans, and he had there imbibed a wholesome fear of our firearms. In referring to his experiences on that occasion, he lost all his Mongolian stolidity and grew quite excited, as he recounted to the awe-stricken bystanders how our quick-firing rifles could fire "about a dozen" shots without reloading, whilst the Tibetans took about five minutes to reload their wretched muzzle-loading flint-lock muskets, and then as often as not the flint missed fire.

My shot-gun interested him greatly. He handled it lovingly, and as he looked down the barrels, he exclaimed in astonishment, "Why, it shines clear like a mirror!"—and certainly it was even in this respect, a contrast to their own dirty barrels, deeply honeycombed as they were with rust. But it was my revolver, with its quick-repeating mechanism, that interested him most, as this was a special weapon of war. I had not brought my rifle, on account of its weight, and the few chances I expected of using it. He asked me to show its working by firing at some of his straggling sheep. I could not consent, of course, to such butchery, so fired instead a quick succession of shots into some logs of wood, and scarcely had the sharp pinging of the whistling bullets rung out, than the old man scampered off in hot haste, to see how deeply the bullets had penetrated. My hunting-knife and a few other appliances were also examined with eager curiosity. He presented me with a sheep, one of a flock he was sending to Darjeeling for sale. Tibetan mutton, though small, is not to be excelled for nutty sweetness.

At Kintoop's suggestion I offered him a little of my scanty store of whiskey, which I had brought with me in case of accident; for tea and soup were the only restoratives I ordinarily took at these altitudes, as I had found that spirit acted almost as poison, it so exaggerated the breathlessness and palpitation. He promptly produced his drinking cup from his breast pocket, and he drank the spirit with immense relish, to the dregs; though he magnanimously pretended to leave a little in the cup for his men, who passed the empty cup round from hand to hand, and each of them licked it more than clean, with so much smacking of lips and rueful countenances, that I took pity on them and poured a little more of this precious liquor into the cup for them. But the captain again took the lion's share, for, naively explained he, it was not etiquette for his men to drink until after him.

Tibetans seldom taste spirits in their own country. Their

usual alcoholic drink is the sour beer that is made from fermented barley and strained off from the seeds into vessels, and drunk cold, not hot, like the *murwa* of Sikhim. Jæsche says (in his dictionary) that spirit or *arak* is distilled in monasteries, and in the houses of the big men in Tibet; but this I am assured is not frequent in Central Tibet nor in Tsang, where spirit is very seldom drunk except by the Chinese,—and when the Tibetans specially require it, they usually buy it from the Chinese. The sour beer is served up to grandees at feasts, in the horns of the wild yak, (*Dong*) like the Urus horns which the ancient Germans used as cups for their strong drink, according to Cæsar. And these horns are mounted in silver or brass and slung over the shoulder when travelling. The Bhotanese use for this purpose the horn of the great wild ox, or *mithan* (*Bos frontalis*).

How very different are these Tibetans from the Lepchas, and even from their kinsmen the Sikhimese Bhotiyas! Yet the Tibetan too has had his character shaped largely by his environments. Though of the same Mongolian descent, he is in many respects almost the anti-type of the Lepcha. His rugged, wind-swept country has given him a rugged character and features. His cold, bracing climate and full animal diet has given him a robust body full of rude blustering animalism, that tends to make him when uncontrolled a turbulent bully, with all the fierceness of spirit which his European name of Tartar (*Tartaros,* hell) suggests. The disastrous storms and avalanches that wreck his herds and scanty crops, have caused him to worship these as destructive malignant devils, and his awestruck mind, thus dominated by the supernatural forces, has become intensely superstitious and religious. Whilst the isolation of his country by protecting and perpetuating his numerous and jealous hierarchy, has made him the most priest-ridden mortal in the world. But many of them, especially the better class of monks, I have found to be most kind and considerate, and deeply imbued with a tolerant spirit, due doubtless to education and temperament, and partly also derived from the Buddhism which permeates their religion. As a class, they cannot be said to be broad-minded, although living on broad tablelands, in the free mountain air. They are not naturalists, nor even skilful sportsmen, being forbidden to take life by their priests.

The presence of these Tibetan officials cowed my men into uncommunicativeness. The latter spoke of the diabolical tortures that would be inflicted on them as informers, by the Tibetan Government, which they said seized even people in Sikhim and carried them off to Tibet for punishment. There they do not indulge in the luxury of jails, for when they do not kill their prisoners right away, or put them to a slow death by torture, as, although professing Buddhists, they do not hesitate to do, they simply cut off their ears or chop off a hand or foot, and set the mutilated person free. Such mutilated criminals form the majority of the beggars, I am told, in Lhasa and other large Tibetan towns.

In particular, my guide, the owner of the pony, was

especially reticent, and he now tried to run away with his pony, but was caught and brought back by one of my men. And to secure his presence, or rather that of his pony, I gave the latter into the charge of one of my men, and locked away his saddle and harness.

As it was now clear that, for political reasons, I could not force my way beyond the Dong-kia pass, my only way of getting to the glaciers of Kanchen-junga was to try to get over into the Lachen valley by the knife-edge of the Seeboo La, or "Pass of Frozen Hailstones", which led into the Lachen valley. And to facilitate our journey thither, on our return from the Dong-kia on the morrow, I took Kintoop and two of my men in the afternoon to explore the entrance of the Seeboo, the passage of which seemed not hitherto to have been made by any European.

Crossing an icy torrent on boulders, under the rounded heavily snowed flanks of Kanchen-jow, or "The Great Bearded Glacier" (22,550 ft.), and below the glacier of Phaloong, we went up the wild stony valley of Seeboo for about three miles, and over the moraine and small glacier noted by Blanford, to a barren rocky plateau with a few icy lakelets, above which towered great piles of rocks leading up to the pass.

The utter desolation of this region was very impressive. The stony waste, bare of all vegetation owing to the keen winds, and buried in snow for eight or nine months of the year, stretched right up to the snow-covered slopes which, rising a few hundred feet above us, surrounded us with a circle of glittering icy spires and domes, all over 20,000 feet high. It was indeed "The Abode of Snow", the true Himalaya at last. The root of this word is the same which appears in the Greek *Imaus*, and the German *Himmel*, the Aryan "heaven"; for these snowy regions are the highest

KANCHEN-JOW AND ENTRANCE TO SEEBOO PASS.

"*heaven*-up" part of the world, and therefore nearest to the abode of the gods.

So stern, sombre, and solitary was this scene, that we seemed to have passed into a valley of distress, if not of death. The recent frost had killed even the insects, and besides ourselves there was no trace of any living thing, animal or vegetable. The solitude was unbroken, save by the sighing of the wind, and the subdued gurgle of the river, which too had lost its colour under the leaden sky, and ran swiftly dull, scarcely disturbing the universal calm which rested over all. The loneliness and fixed gloom were indescribable. Plato perhaps rightly said that "whosoever is delighted with solitude, entirely and absolutely, is either a wild beast or a god." And it is easy to see how the Tibetans, who place their gods in such regions, picture them with sullen savage features, hurling avalanches and thunderbolts, and other death-dealing weapons. Just so have the Scandinavians deified the more sublime and terrible aspects of nature. So their Odin and Thor fight with the thunderbolt, so they have their frost-giants of the Jottenheim, and their wind-giants of the Muspelheim and Nifelheim. These anthropomorphic gods are thus evidently deified natural forces, and so far support Professor Max Müller in his contention that mythology in its origin was physical, whatever it may have become in its later developments.

We did not find the hot springs of this pass, having no one to guide us. These, I was told, received more worship than those we visited the previous day, as they are the reputed abode of the powerful demon of the Phaloong glacier, who is called "His Lordship the Long-lived Devil." [32]

Returning to bleak Momay, also desolate in appearance, I saw four sleek ravens, and got specimens of that gorgeously blue-plumaged bird, *Grandula cœlicolor*. My men reported having seen some of the wild sheep, "Burhel" (*Ovis natura*). One of these was shot hereabouts by Elwes,

THE GOD OF MOUNT KANCHEN-JUNGA.

who accompanied Blanford, and in regard to which the latter writes: "We subsequently found that the '*Ovis ammon*' of which we heard so much, were all Burhel; and Hooker, I think, must have been mistaken in supposing that he saw the former in this neighbourhood, for, by the unanimous evidence of all the Tibetans, none occur to the south of the Dong-kia and Kongra-Lamo passes, although they are to be met with a little further north, in Tibet."

I also saw some tail-less rats or marmots. These small mammals called *Goomcher* by the Bhotiyas, are credited with supernatural powers, in that, if they are harmed in any way, they produce fearful and disastrous storms. This belief is evidently due, I think, to the habits of these animals burrowing into the bowels of the earth, where live, according to the Tibetans, the dragon-spirits or *Nagas* that cause thunder-storms. Owing to this superstition few natives will assist you in catching the animal, yet they do not scruple to rob it of its hoards of stored grass and grain whenever they are in need of fuel or fodder. I secured a beautiful silvery water-shrew (*Nectrogale elegans*), so unique and rare that no perfect specimen of it was hitherto known. In the icy cold river I could find no trace of life, but about 2,000 feet lower down I had seen some tadpoles and fish.

Plants, however, were not absent on the hill sides, in the crevices between the stones; but they were almost entirely the remains of flowering plants, and but very few grasses, ferns and other monocotyledons. Mr. Ball observed this peculiarity in the vegetation of high altitudes in Europe, and on this fact is based the belief that flowering plants or dicotyledons originated in the dry and rarefied atmosphere of elevated plateaus and mountains. This too would explain the absence of well-developed Exogens in the tropical coal-period, and their late and sudden appearance in the cooler times of the cretaceous period, when the flowering plants descended from their high altitudes, where the evidence of their early existence at this remote period of geological time has been destroyed by denudation of the uplands. Dwarf bamboos, which are grasses, crop up on the hot damp southern sides of peaks as high as 12,000 feet. The especial prevalence of this rich variety of flowers, especially of primroses and *pedicularis*, on the southern slopes of the Himalayas is remarkable, and cannot be simply accounted for on the hypothesis of a migration from the north during the glacial epoch. In Europe, too, "some of the most ancient fragments of the Alpine flora are now to be found only on the southern side of the Alps," as M. de Candolle has shown. [33]

The whitish colour of the flowers in these Alpine regions is also remarkable. Many of the flowers which lower down are blue are here apparently white, but they become blue on pressing. This fact, together with the excessive thickness of their petals, shews that the blue pigment is still there, and that the white colour is due to the air that inflates the interstices of their tissue.

The temperature of the air at 5 p.m. was 30.8° Fah., and

before sunset went down to 28° Fah., and snow began to fall in a disquieting way, suggesting the possibility of the valley becoming blocked, as happened during Mr. Macaulay's visit to the lower valley, when deep snow stretched down to below Yoomtang.

We all passed a wretched night, owing to the intense cold, and partly to our sudden rise in the rarefied air. My warmest woollen clothes with my sheepskin-coat over all failed to keep me from shivering in the painfully piercing cold wind; while the weight of the clothes further oppressed my breathing. I do not believe my heart is a bad one, but it now palpitated so violently as to shake my whole body, yet so slowly as not to exceed 45 beats per minute, and at times it seemed as if about to cease altogether. Yet on the slightest exertion, in walking up hill, the beats went up to 100 or 110. These alarming symptoms would no doubt have lessened, and the heart become accommodated in some measure to the altered pressure and thin air, had we remained long enough at that altitude. But even when Hooker had remained in these regions and at higher elevations for some months, he says "he never knew what it was to go a few miles outside his tent without feeling great pressure, and he always returned to camp with nausea." And he experienced the same feelings at lofty elevations in Africa and Europe, as well as in the Himalayas. Even Mr. Graham who suffered so little from the high elevations in Sikhim complained of the "very loud and perceptible beating of the heart".

To find the effect of these high elevations on our circulation, I had been carefully recording not only my own pulse-beats and respirations, but also those of Kintoop and several selected coolies, at various stages on the way up from Darjeeling, but the results are not sufficiently decided to be worth detailing. They showed remarkably little difference from the normal, even in the highest altitudes, when the men were at rest. The reduced frequency of the pulse-beats in the higher altitudes was not marked in all, and seemed due in part to the excessive work thrown on the heart by the intense cold. As Freshfield and Hooker have suggested, the breathlessness and the attendant discomfort of mountain sickness is somewhat comparable to sea-sickness, and those persons who are affected more than others need not necessarily have a diseased stomach or heart.

In the morning, as the snow had ceased, and it lay only about a foot deep, we decided to push on to the pass. But as the thermometer at sunrise registered 8° of frost, or 24° Fah., it was some time ere my shrivelled-up men were ready for starting. The Tibetan soldiers fortified themselves against the cold with bits of frozen raw meat, like Laplanders, which they shredded up with their daggers. No wind, fortunately, was then blowing, or it would have been dangerously keen.

The track was marked out by mounds of stones, and led across the river to the left bank, and re-crossed about the sixth mile, at a spot called Jarwa (17,000 feet elevation), near which are two small lakes. The Tibetan captain and his men accompanied us, and as his yak clambered nimbly over the snow-laden stones, far outdistancing my pony, which slid and stumbled so badly that I could make little use of it, he kindly offered me the use of his yak. It, however, refused to let me mount, and made several plunges at me as I approached it, although held back by the rope through its nose-ring. And I was not sorry that I had failed to mount it, for some time afterwards the tackle of ropes that fastened on the rough saddle loosened, and the captain came down from his high perch with a rush, and on the top of him came all his cooking-pots and pans, which were carried in two bags slung on behind the saddle.

Some large footprints in the snow led across our track, and away up to the higher peaks. These were alleged to be the trail of the hairy wild men who are believed to live amongst the eternal snows, along with the mythical white lions, whose roar is reputed to be heard during storms. The belief in these creatures is universal among Tibetans. None, however, of the many Tibetans I have interrogated on this subject could ever give me an authentic case. On the most superficial investigation it always resolved itself into something that somebody heard tell of. These so-called hairy wild men are evidently the great yellow snow-bear *(Ursus isabellinus)*, which is highly carnivorous, and often kills yaks. Yet, although most of the Tibetans know this bear sufficiently to give it a wide berth, they live in such an atmosphere of superstition that they are always ready to find extraordinary and supernatural explanations of uncommon events. Looking at these footprints, I thought of the poor snow-bears pent up in the sweltering heat of the Calcutta "Zoo", and what they would not give to get into such arctic regions.

Snow now fell heavily, and a driving hurricane of loose powdery snow was fast obliterating our footmarks, so that, as Kintoop pointed out, there was a great danger of our losing our way and sharing the fate which hereabout befel his former master, the late Captain Harman, in 1881. This unfortunate officer was employed in the survey of Sikhim, and on ascending this pass, he saw in the distance, the great snowy range of Tibetan peaks as seen by Hooker and Blanford, and extending, as he estimated, 150 miles from east to west. To examine them more in detail he bivouacked on the spot, but, as his baggage-coolies did not turn up, he was fatally frost-bitten.[34]

We now found that the snow-storm had increased; the wind rose furiously, and a whirlwind of fine snow, blinding and choking us, drove us down, when almost within sight of the top of the pass. Then I realized more emphatically than before, that Sherwill and Blanford had advised too late a date of starting; that I had started over a month too late in the season; and that to reach these northern passes and have time for their leisurely exploration, one must endure the discomforts of travelling in the rainy season.

The scene that bursts upon the eye from the crest of

this pass (18,100 ft.), has been described and figured by Sir Joseph Hooker. Mr. Blanford says, "it is one of the most remarkable landscapes in the world, and alone worth the journey to see it.... Cholamo lake is in front, beneath the feet of the spectator, beyond is a desert with rounded hills. Further away range after range of mountains, some of them covered with snow, extend to a distance the eye cannot appreciate. The total change of colour and form from the valleys of Sikhim, the utter barrenness, the intense clearness of the atmosphere, produce such an effect as if one were gazing upon another world in which the order of this is no longer preserved, where a tropical desert is seen amongst snow-capped peaks, beneath the unnaturally clear atmosphere of the arctic regions." [35]

The game and skins which Mr. Blanford procured from the Tibetan side of this pass through the Tibetan guards, included three perfectly fresh skins, one of the Tibetan gazelle *(Gazella picticauda;* in Tibetan—*Göd* or *Ra-gao)* the others of *Ovis Ammon*, a ewe and a young ram, and some live Tibetan sand-grouse. He was told that both *Ovis Ammon* and *Ovis natura* are pretty common in the country north of Sikhim, the Goa Antelope is less so; Tibetan antelope *(Chiru'*, the *Kemas Hodgsoni)* are never heard of in that neighbourhood; and the wild yak is not found there now.

The name of this pass, I find, means "The Frozen Wild Yak", and a legend was related to me of a herd of wild yak *(Dong)* that had strayed here, and were found frozen to death in this pass, which thus obtained its name.

The old Ding-pön and his guard of the pass seemed unfeignedly glad at our being driven down by the snow-storm, and they were still more so when, on our return to Momay, as the storm showed no signs of abating, we had to give up our proposed attempt to cross the Se-boo, and to retreat further down to Yoomtang. The Ding-pön also accompanied us here, on the plea of having some business with the Lachoong villagers in regard to the transport of wood and sheep, etc.; but it was probably to see us off his frontier, and make sure that we did not give him the slip.

On the way to Lachoong next day, I followed up the fine glacier valley of the Si-bo[36] or "Cold" river for some way towards the Gora or "Top-of-the-Wall" pass, so called from its excessive steepness. No European seems to have been up this valley before: and as I had heard that this pass, which leads into Tibet between the Dong-kia and the Tang-kar passes, was seldom used and never guarded, and I was arranging to make an expedition to Lhasa in disguise, I had sent Kintoop during the summer to reconnoitre and explore this pass and the country beyond it in a north-easterly direction, keeping above the inhabited part of Choombi, until he struck the trade route from that province to Central Tibet, on the great plateau to the north of the Tang pass.

As this line of country has not been surveyed, and even the position of the Gora pass is wrongly placed on the maps, I give here some details of Kintoop's pioneer survey, and a sketch of his route (see large map), as plotted out by me from his narrative. His directions may be taken as generally approximate, as I had supplied him with a compass; the distances in miles, however, are less correct; but he and his party certainly penetrated to a distance of seven days' hard march in Tibet, and marched beyond the Sikhimese frontier for thirteen days. There is no doubt as to his having reached the Tibetan plateau, for he brought back several plants which are peculiar to the dry tablelands of Central Asia.

Crossing the Lachoong river, 1¾ miles above the village of that name, and about 300 yards above the junction of that river with the Si-bo, and following up the latter, it was found to rise rapidly after its third mile to about the seventh mile, where, at the upper limit of trees, it turned eastward to the foot of a great glacier, one of the sources of this river. The freezing torrent, which spouted from an ice-cave in this glacier, and which was 50 yards wide and waist deep at that time in June, had to be forded. A yak-herdsman here, from whom Kintoop asked the way to the Gora pass, declared that they were all forbidden by the Tibetans to give any information as to the passes into Tibet, and he bolted off. The river above this flowed between the terraces of a great lateral moraine for about five miles, above which it divided into two headwaters. The southern of these led to the Pata pass, expanding into two lakes, each about three-quarters of a mile in length; and into the bright green water of the uppermost of these, just below the summit of the pass, the snow was falling in avalanches in June. This pass, which is not marked in any map, nor its lakes, lies about 5 miles south of Tang-kar pass, according to a herd-girl whom Kintoop met. It was not then open, but it was occasionally used by the people of that valley; whereas the Gora, on account of its steepness, was very seldom if ever used. The northern branch of the river which came down from the Gora pass was found to lead up to a grazing-station, where many dead yaks were seen lying around. A murrain had carried off about 80 per cent of the cattle. This disease, called *Yor* or *Hlak-po*, seems to be rinder-pest. It had visited these parts several times before, and is also known in Tibet, where it also attacks the wild yaks.[37] It was believed to be imported from India, through lower Sikhim. Here again, the herdsmen refused to give any information as to the passes, even when Kintoop said that he wanted to go up to worship the mountain. So he followed up the stream, which widened out into a limpid lake. The ascent to the pass beyond was excessively steep, and so precipitous as to be quite impracticable for cattle. The summit, about 17,000 feet elevation, commanded an extensive view of snowy peaks. Thence proceeding north-eastwards, across Upper Choombi, Kintoop and his companions had to go a little southwards to circumvent some great cliffs that rose over 4,000 feet high, and they had to cross torrents and spurs, till they sighted the uppermost village in Western Choombi. Then they ascended that valley of the Rido river, northwards, and crossed the water-parting into the great plain of Central Tibet. Here they followed down a stream which flowed north-westwards into a considerable lake, on the northern bank of which was a compact village of about twelve houses. On sighting this they hid away amongst rocks, but were discovered by some huge Tibetan mastiffs, whose loud barking at them attracted the attention of the villagers. The headman of the village recognizing them as Sikhimese, although they wore Tibetan dress, and suspecting them to be spies, seized them; and stripping them of the best part of their clothes, imprisoned them in his house, saying that he must carry them off to Phari in a few days, for such were his orders in regard to people entering from Sikhim. The name of this village was Kala-pak-tang; and Kintoop says that this lake resembled the Kala-tso, which he had passed several times on the way to Gyantse and Lhasa. The Kala-tso of Boyle and Turner, however, would appear to be some ten miles or so to the N. E. of this lake. During the night, Kintoop and his party effected their escape and fled back again by the way they had come over the Gora pass.

The following day (28th October) I returned past Kedoom, with its sad memories, to Choong-tang at the bottom of the Lachoong valley. The great and rapid changes in the foliage which had occurred during our fortnight's sojourn in the valley, showed that the brief flash of Alpine summer was already over. The leaves had turned to russet and orange in a few days, and soon they will be swept off by the whirlwind, and winter will have come.

CHAPTER VI

THE LACHEN VALLEY, AND EASTERN GLACIERS OF KANCHEN-JUNGA

By fairy Lachen's forest green,
And boiling Zemoo's silver sheen,
Travelled till they the torrent crossed
At Tallum Samdong hard in frost
And Tungu deep in snow.
. . . .
Down Kongra-lamo's snowy waste
The Yaks with stately movement paced,
And five score swordsmen's weapons glanced
As Kamba's chieftain grave advanced
The mystic Chorten past.

C. Macaulay's *Lay of Lachen.*

BACK at Choong-tang, we were glad to accept the young Lama's invitation to put up in his monastery. It commanded a view up the Lachen valley, which was here evergreen with semi-tropical forest, though over-topped by snowy peaks. The animals in the upper valley were found by Mr. Blanford to be more thoroughly Tibetan than in the Lachoong. This is doubtless owing to the pass from Tibet being much less high and rigorous.

The broken bridges and ladders, however, still barred all

progress up this precipitous valley, as they did at the time of Macaulay's political mission in 1884. The latter's visit was even still later in the season than our own, so that after the bridges were repaired at great cost, and after some days' detention, that party just managed to push on to Giagong (15,764 ft.) at the foot of the Kongra-lamo pass to Tibet, and then had to beat a hasty retreat before the advancing snow.

This mission of the late Colman Macaulay I have already referred to. Its leader achieved the diplomatic feat of opening communication between India and the Tibetan government, for the first time since the days of Warren Hastings, over a hundred years before. He has related the circumstances of his journey up this valley, and his meeting with the Tibetan officials, in his Lay of Lachen; and how he was benighted in the snow at the foot of the icy Chomiomo (22,385 feet) and Kanchen-jow, whose eastern slopes we had just crossed.

His ballad tells how

> The moon to nearly full had grown
> Ere they the frontier cold and lone
> Did reach, where wind-swept Giagong
> Lies white and chill and drear
> 'Twixt Kanchen-jow and Chomiom.
> No man or beast may make his home
> That barren snowfield near.
>
> The day was waning, and the crest
> Of Chomiomo paler grew,
> As sank the sun into the west
> And ever lengthening shadows threw
> The giant's hoar between.

The north wind sharp and sharper blew,
The frost was piercing keen;

Night followed day, but still no sound
Was heard the silent snow drift round
Of coming footsteps, and no light
Of lantern or of torch did peer
Across the waste of gleaming white
To say that help was near.

At length that awful night was past,
No more they shuddered 'neath the blast;
The morning smiled across the wild,
And the tentsmen followed fast,
As Kamba's chieftain grave advanced
The mystic *chorten* past.

And in Macaulay's tent that day,
In high *durbar* and bright array,
With welcome glad and presents fair
Was Bengal's greeting told.

But this Tibetan official, the *Jong-pön* or Commander of the adjoining fort of Kamba, was not to be readily coerced. He stoutly refused to receive any official message whatever, on the plea that he had no orders to do so. Mr. M. achieved his object by making capital out of the fact that the Tibetan had no orders *not* to receive any communication, and by further declaring that if the Jong-pön refused to receive his message he would himself go on to the capital, Tashi-lunpo, to deliver the message in person. This last alternative was too dreadful for the Tibetan to contemplate, so he agreed to receive the communication, and it was duly delivered; for a friendly reply was received from the chief minister of Western Tibet a few months later.

Now, however, restrained as we were by the broken bridges and ladders, we could but look wistfully up the dark vistas of this Lachen valley, so graphically described by Hooker and Blanford, trusting to be able the following year to accomplish our projected journey through it to the unexplored Zemoo glaciers, thence over the eastern glaciers of Kanchen-junga, and back by rocky Tô-loong.

This journey was done two seasons later by the political agent, Mr. White, who commanded the resources of the Sikhim State for opening the roads and building the bridges. He went in the reverse direction, entering by To-loong and returning this way; and he was accompanied by Mr. T. Hoffmann, to whom I am indebted for the beautiful photographs of the glaciers and other scenery *en route*, never visited by Europeans before. Starting at the end of June 1891, they experienced intervals of fine clear weather whilst traversing the glaciers in the middle of July.

The too brief narrative of this interesting journey, written by Mr. Hoffmann,[38] tells of their passage from To-loong to the Zemoo valley (the "Thlonok" of Hooker) with its great glacier, which descends from Kanchen-junga. He writes: "After a hard climb we reached the base of the glacier at a height of 13,800 ft. Here we counted four distinct caves in the ice. The face of the ice-cliff at the end of the glacier is about 400 to 500 ft. deep, and the immense mass of ice rested between the two slopes of the valley.... It was too dangerous to remain here long on account of the huge stones that were continually falling from the glacier. We crossed over one of the snow-bridges to the opposite bank, getting some excellent photographs of these curiosities of nature's architecture." Ascending the glacier and its surmounting *débris* to an elevation of 16,000 ft., "the mist cleared away for a short time, and we saw one of the finest-shaped peaks in the Himalayas, marked on the map D^2, or Simiolchum." Continuing their ascent to 17,000 ft., they started the following day "to cross the glacier, intending to strike a rock not far from the foot of Kanchen-junga. The glacier descends from Kanchen-junga almost in a straight line, and is fed by many minor glaciers coming down from D^2 and the peak to the north of it. We counted a dozen glaciers on one occasion, joining the main glacier. We reached a height of 17,500 ft. To the south-west was a gap in the range of 19,300 ft. The rock we had hoped to reach was still a long way off at 2 p.m., and we reluctantly turned back to camp.

PEAK D^2.

The rumbling noise of the avalanches and the crashing of falling rocks never cease, and it is dangerous to camp here, near the base of a mountain. The next day dawned gloriously. For the first time we obtained a view clear from all clouds and mist." Kanchen towered high to the west. "To the south Sim-vovon-chum (D^1) looked like a burnt-

~~NORTH~~ RIDGE OF KANCHEN-JUNGA—SHOWING GAP (21,000 FT.).

out crater filled with snow. Then came a 17,450 ft. gap in the range, with a wavy snowfield and a magnificent group of splintered peaks, not named on the maps. . . . Before leaving this neighbourhood we visited a narrow valley to the north-east of Kanchen-junga. We counted here eight glaciers coming down from the different slopes, some joining the main glacier, and others ending abruptly, forming a jagged wall of ice. The rays of the sun caused the masses of ice to act like huge prisms, reflecting the most gorgeous colours." Mr. White then followed up the Lanok (" *Thlonok* ") valley northwards to the Nakoo pass (17,000 ft.), and back by the Nangna pass (17,590 ft.).

NANGNA PASS (17,590 FEET), EASTERN SIDE.

CHAPTER VII

THROUGH BRITISH BHOTAN TO DARJEELING

In returning from Choong-tang to the capital, Toom-long, I came across some Bhotiyas making elaborate preparations for a hot bath, on the bank of a stream. They had burned out a piece of the trunk of a tree into a sort of tub, and filling it with water, they heated up the latter by throwing into it some stones which they had roasted in a bonfire; and they emerged from their ablutions with marked improvement to their complexions. So who will now say that the Bhotiyas never bathe? After all, these Bhotiyas and Tibetans have perhaps no constitutional distaste for cleanliness; but with the thermometer near, or below zero, and Boreas blowing keenly, even the most constant bather is apt to desert allegiance to his tub.

The number of snakes I found on our track was surprisingly large, though this may have been partly owing to my having been specially on the outlook for them, ever since I had been bitten by one some years previously. Here no fewer than twelve different species found their last home in my spirit-bottle. Many of them were not poisonous, and the most common were slender iridescent whip-snakes, gliding gracefully through the foliage, and several species of brightly coloured, large eyed, "keel-scaled" snakes, or *Tropidonotus*. The poisonous ones were a huge blue "krait" *(Bungarus cærulus)*, that was sunning itself on a rock, and the ugly little mountain viper *(Trimesurus monticola)* which the Bhotiyas call "The Fierce Slow-going One" *("Barop-shep-pa")*, a title that aptly describes its character; for though, like most vipers, it can only move very slowly out of your path, it bites with the utmost swiftness and fierceness. Both Lepchas and Bhotiyas have a wholesome fear of snakes, and believe that all of them are poisonous, a very safe-working theory. Such gorgeous spiders too, I had never seen before. They were resplendent in brilliant scarlet and metallic blue, and of giant size, about four to six inches in spread; and their webs so large and strong as to catch small birds, on which some of them feed. Few of these spiders have ever been collected, and many looked as if they would be nasty venomous customers to tackle. The number of small locusts was noticeable, and some of them mimicked green leaves.

Our food was now at a very low ebb, and had to be eked out largely by what I could shoot for the pot, not even rejecting plump parrots. The men stayed their hunger to some extent with wild berries and others things they foraged in the jungle, such as the tender tips of juicy ferns, nettles, etc., boiled as spinach; wild yams and other roots; mushrooms and several fruits, including wild mangoes, and when near a village, oranges *ad libitum*, for this is near the home of the orange, whence it spread west to southern Europe. But I had to be on my guard against some of the jungle products which my Bhotiya cook brought during Achoom's absence. For I found him about to cook some pods of beans, which I at once recognised as poisonous, and belonging to a kind of laburnum.

At one of the poor hamlets which we passed, a Bhotiya offered me a domestic fowl for twelve times the ordinary rate, and he would not abate the price one whit; "for," said he, with the air of a political economist who had studied the laws of supply and demand, "this is positively the last fowl left in this part of Sikhim," as the troops of the recent expedition had eaten up all the fowls and put an end to the local breed. This, I ascertained afterwards, was true, and there was probably not another fowl within five or six days' journey, and very few for much longer distances.

From Toomlong we descended to our old friend the Dik-chu river, and crossing it by a good bridge, we struck the new bridle-road, where my pony was in waiting; and then I proceeded comfortably, winding through pleasant glades and glens with picturesque views over the Penlong pass (6,250 ft.), to Gangtok, or "The Crown of the Ridge"

(5,090 ft.), where our new Resident, Mr. White, was creating an oasis of civilization in the wilds of Sikhim.

Here there burst on the view a tennis-court, rows of trim huts that housed a small force of our soldiers and police, and other signs of a British settlement, including a newly opened telegraph-station that connects us again with the outer world. Its wire, however, was, as yet, only tied from tree to tree through the forest. I got a welcome budget of letters, and tasted again some bread, an article of diet that is not sufficiently appreciated until you have been deprived of it for some weeks. Another sign of civilization we met here, in the heart of Sikhim, was the Indian money-lender usurer, the scourge of the poor natives, the pink-turbaned *Marwari*, who has come under the wing of our rule.

Next day we crossed over more hills and dales to "The Bamboo Hamlet", or Pakyong, wheret here was a stockade held by some of our troops (the 13th Bengal Infantry). It was full of life and bustle, the band was playing, and English ladies graced it with their presence.

Beyond this, we passed another copper mine, on our way down the Rarhi river. This, like the others, is worked by the rich Nepalese (or more properly *Newar*) banker of Darjeeling, Lachmi Das; and here a place was pointed out to me where, in a squabble over the revenue from these mines, the Lamas of the rival monasteries of Phodang and Pemionchi had a pitched battle in 1880, and one at least of the monks of the latter monastery was killed on the spot.

Large numbers of Nepalese colonists were busily felling and burning the virgin forest, to form settlements, in accordance with our new policy of developing the resources of the country, and raising revenue for improvements, by leasing out the land on easy terms to the Hindooized Nepalese. For these latter make an excellent settled peasantry, as compared with the easy-going Lepchas and Bhotiyas, who are neither good cultivators, nor yet do they pay any revenue worth mentioning in cash. To preserve these aboriginal Lepchas, and the nominal ruling race, the Bhotiyas, from being swept away altogether by these active Nepalese emigrants, the latter are at present restricted to the lower and most fertile part of native Sikhim, adjoining the district of Darjeeling. In the unreserved portion, the racial distribution corresponds to some extent with the geological formations; for the Lepchas down in the hot valley coincide generally with the limestones and schist rocks, while the Bhotiyas occupy the massive gneiss and granite.

In a placid pool in the Rarhi some fine large fish were rising in a most tempting manner. Thence past some silvery-barked giant *Gurjun* trees *(Dipterocarpus sp.)*, we entered British Bhotan and climbed under the old Bhotanese fort of Damsang, perched on its knife-edge cliff, up to Pedong (4,780 ft.), situated on the grand trunk road to Tibet and China.

Here we found the staging-house occupied by some of the suite of the Chinese Minister of Lhasa, the *Amban*, who was returning to Pekin *via* Lhasa to get his negotiations with the Indian Government ratified. He had crossed the frontier several days previously; but many stragglers of his party, which was said to include over 1,000 baggage coolies, were still hurrying along the road, some on mules and ponies, others on foot, laden with all sorts and sizes of packages, amongst which I noticed several cases of European wines and tinned provisions, kerosine oil, pots of fuchsias and geraniums, and some packages said to contain dynamite for blasting purposes.

At Pedong I encamped near the small chapel of Father Desgodins, the Roman Catholic missionary, who for over twenty years conducted a mission within Tibetan territory on the borders of China, and then when he was driven out by irate Lamas, who razed his building to the ground, he settled here on the Indian side, under the British flag and on the high road to Tibet, with a small staff of assistants, carrying on educational work, and lithographing tracts for distribution amongst the Tibetan traders. One cannot but admire the self-sacrifice of these men who have given up their lives entirely to this humanizing work, to labour here without salary and on a bare subsistence that affords them little better food than the poorest native; for they choose to die here amongst their life's work without ever thinking of returning, like most missionaries, to home-life in Europe. It is a pity that they have not more striking results to show for all their labours. Yet it is something to accomplish the deliverance even of a few individuals from the constant terror of malignant spirits, under which these poor natives labour. And there are not a few of their flock who regard these benefactors with the same mingled feelings of reverence and love, as the Irish peasant expresses towards his pastor, the "*Soggarth aroon*", in the song:—

"Who in the winter's night
Soggarth aroon,
When the cold blast did bite,
Soggarth aroon,
Came to my cabin door,
And on my earthen floor
Knelt by me sick and poor,
Soggarth aroon?"

Kalim-pong, which we reached next day, on the same ridge, twelve miles nearer to Darjeeling, is also a missionary station, where Mr. Sutherland and other members of the Church of Scotland Mission are doing some good work amongst the mild Lepchas, of whom a considerable colony is settled here. I was surprised, however, to find that the Lepchas were being taught through the Nepalese language, and not through their own vernacular.

This village, whose name means "the Governor's hold", as it was formerly the head-quarters of a Bhotanese district, is now the head-quarters of "British Bhotan". For this tract of hills to the east of the Teesta, from Pedong to the plains, was annexed by us from Bhotan in 1865 as an indemnity against the raids of the Bhotanese into British territory and for the expenses of the war of 1864, forced on us therewith. Their country, which is generally known by the Indian term of "Bhotan" or "The End of Tibet", has physically the same general characters as Sikhim, for it is the adjoining southern slopes of the Himalayas to the east of Sikhim. Its people, who are under fanatical Lamas

BHOTANESE CHIEF AND RETINUE.

from Tibet, call their country "The Southern Thunder-Dragon" *(L'o-Dook)*, a name which I think denotes the excessive thunder experienced in this area, which, lying at the head of the Bay of Bengal, receives, even more than Sikhim, the blast of the rain clouds, and is by far the wettest portion of all the Himalayas. Our military post stands further east at Buxar or "The Mouth of the Bamboo Bridge." These Bhotanese are naturally lawless and notoriously turbulent. They are held in little control by their nominal ruler, the "*Deb Rajah*", as he is called by the plains-people; and their Chiefs or "Pen-lows" are each petty sovereigns in themselves, as independent as they can make themselves, and are constantly warring against each other, knowing no law but

> The good old rule, the simple plan
> That he should take who has the power
> And he should keep who can.

As these predatory marauders were constantly raiding into our territory, destroying villages far and wide, and carrying off men and women into slavery and plundering their cattle, etc., our government inflicted a variety of mild punishments, without, however, any good effect. And when Sir Ashley Eden was sent in 1864 to try to make satisfactory arrangements, he was so grossly assaulted and insulted, that we annexed this part of Bhotan, as well as a large strip along the foot of the hills up to Assam, subject in the event of the good behaviour of the tribes to an annual rent of about £ 5,000 as a preventive of further aggression.

This mountainous tract, however, had previously belonged to the Lepchas, according to the local traditions, and this is confirmed by the older names of the rivers and mountains, which are mostly Lepcha.

Kalimpong crowns an open, cultivated spur. It has a

much milder climate than Darjeeling, and boasts a considerable mart to which Tibetan traders come.

Several of these were encamped in a yak-hair tent and other improvised shelters. They bring for sale or barter, ponies, wool, coarse blankets, furs, yak-tails, musk, turquoise, gold-dust, Chinese silk, brick-tea, borax and salt. These last are brought across the snows fastened on the backs of sheep. And they take back English broad-cloth, piece goods and other European manufactures; tobacco, indigo, rice, sugar, madder and other tropical products, as well as coral, pearls, glass beads and precious stones.

It is curious to find that the brick-tea is brought all the way from China, eight months' journey or more across the most difficult and mountainous country in the world, from Tasienloo through Tibet to this place and Darjeeling. Yet, after this enormously long journey it is sold at the latter place at a cheaper rate than the tea locally grown at Darjeeling. And although these compressed blocks or bricks consist for the most part of coarse twigs, caked with refuse tea-dust, still the Tibetans prefer this stuff to the good Indian tea and will even pay a higher price for it.

I bought from one of these Tibetan merchants an exceptionally fine pony. It was creamy fawn-coloured, like the best Tibetan ponies, but it was so extensively covered over with zebra-like markings that to see it would have delighted the heart of Darwin and his followers, who believe that the horse was descended from a zebra-like ancestor—though it is said that the wild horses (or *Kyang*) of the Tibetan plateaus, whose flesh is esteemed a delicacy by the native hunters, are not striped or brindled at all.

Many of the fawn-coloured Tibetan ponies are brindled, but none of the many I have seen were marked so fully as this one. It had a black stripe down the spine, the tips of the ears, nose and tip of tail were black, and it had broad black stripes over the shoulders, flanks and legs, and dappled spots over the haunches. So suggestive of a tiger were its markings that it was called "Tiger" by the natives. And it proved to be a most gentle, good-tempered beast, following me about like a pet dog.

The inhabitants of this part of Bhotan are still in considerable proportion Bhotanese. These differ in appearance from the Sikhimese Bhotiyas and the Tibetans, chiefly in that both men and women wear no pigtails, but shave their heads, like Lamas; and they often wear turbans instead of the usual Chinese hats. They are generally called by their religious title of "The Southern Dook-pa" (*L'o-Dook-pa*), as they belong to the *Dook-pa* sect of Lamaism, and own as their spiritual head or Grand Lama, the King of Bhotan, the so-called "*Dharma-* (or religious) Rajah", as opposed to his temporal governor, the "*Deb* Rajah" above mentioned. The Lepchas call them "Proo", which may be the antiquated form of their present name Dook—which is spelt "Broog".

Here at Kalimpong is a small monastery of this Bhotanese or Dook-pa sect of Lamas.

Our sudden dip down from here to cross the Teesta

river, brought us to the lowest depths we had yet reached, since leaving Darjeeling. The river here was only 700 feet above the sea, and in this deep tropical gorge it was a fine river flowing swiftly, but much less tumultuously than where we crossed it by that awful cane-bridge. Here we crossed it by an elegant iron suspension bridge, and passed up its right bank, under shady foliage that overarched our path for about a mile, to its junction with the Great Rang-eet river—the so called "Marriage-place of the Rivers", of the legend of which we have heard tell. Here the crooked Rang-eet joins the straight-going Teesta almost at a right-angle, and its clear silvery waters reflecting the foliage of its banks, refuse to mingle with the turbid Teesta till far below their meeting-place. These two differently coloured streams flow side by side in the same bed, unmixed for some hundred yards. The Teesta water, too, is colder.

Along the Rang-eet, our path led us through lovely forest, till we reached that point where we had crossed it in the canoe, and thence we ascended to our first day's staging-house at Badam-tam, amongst the tea-gardens.

Many acres of tea-bushes through which we passed were shrivelled up with a rusty blight. The tea-planters suffer much in this way by having rudely disturbed the balance of Nature, in removing the great variety of rank forest growth, and substituting for it only one kind of plant, namely tea. Thus the parasitical insects, beetles and mites, as well as moulds, finding their natural food gone, have

THE "MARRIAGE" OF THE RANG-EET AND TEESTA RIVERS.

turned their attention to the tea, and cause devastating "blights". One of the most serious of these, the "Mosquito-blight", is the commonest under 4,500 feet elevation. It is due to an insect somewhat like the well-known blood-sucker, which pierces the young shoots of the tea-bush and sucks up their juice. Another is caused by a mite known as "red-spider", and all these pests require very active measures, dosing with insecticides, liquid and gaseous, to repel their ravages.

A great swarm of locusts swept over us as we rode up next day (7th November) to Darjeeling. They came in such clouds as to darken the air, and they covered the roads, trees and fields everywhere, some inches deep in places. They were about three inches in length; and the Nepalese villagers rushed about, gathering them in basketfuls for food, as they ate them like shrimps, with great relish. So it was probably these insects, after all, that formed the diet of John the Baptist, and not the bean-pods of the same name; for the locusts thus swarming up from India were the Egyptian species (*Acridium peregrinum* and a few *A. Succinctum*); and these are said, when salted, to be a favourite food of the Arabs in Northern Africa during long journeys. I afterwards learned [39] that this particular plague of locusts was first noticed in June 1889, in the desert of Sind and Western Rajputana, over a thousand miles off, where they laid eggs in the sandhills. These eggs hatched out there into young locusts which acquired wings about August, and then they swarmed; and the flights of these young locusts spread in myriads in all directions, covering the whole of India, making their way to the Punjab in the north, to Madras and the Deccan in the south, and to Bengal and Assam in the east, doing much damage to the crops. In the arid Punjab, where vegetation is so precious, the troops were turned out to destroy them, and rewards were offered for their destruction. In this way in one station alone (Kohat) twenty-two tons of these insects were killed in a single day.

They did little damage in well-wooded Sikhim, beyond stripping many of the trees and tea bushes bare. They penetrated even to Tibet. More than one trustworthy traveller told me that the dead insects lay several feet deep on the Tang pass (15,700 ft.) to the east of the Dongkia, blackening the snow for many miles. And, curiously, a plague of locusts was predicted in the Tibetan astrological horoscope of this very year, as a Lama proudly pointed out to me.

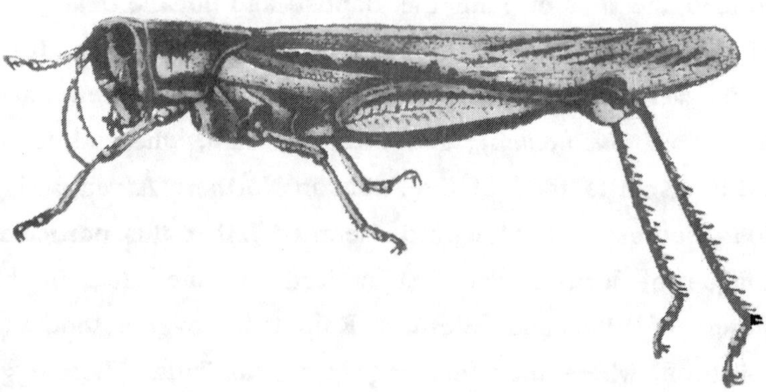

A LOCUST (*A. succintum*).
Natural size.

CHAPTER VIII

TO THE EASTERN PASS OF THE JELEP, AND THE SCENE OF THE LATE WAR

No travellers come from far Tibet,
From the mystic land no tidings yet
  For many a month are sent;
No more the tinkling bells ring clear
On Lingtoo's heights, by Bedden's mere,
On Jelep's pass no step resounds,
No smoke at even upward bounds
  From weary traders' tent.

C. Macaulay's *Lay of Lachen.*

AS soon as the snow cleared from the uplands in the spring, I set off for the Jelep pass, on the direct overland trade-route by way of Lhasa to Pekin. This, too, was the scene of our late war with Tibet, of which many traces were still visible.

An easy canter of about half an hour, one morning in the middle of April, carried us up from Darjeeling, over Jalapahar, dotted with its white barracks of the military sanatarium and artillery batteries, and gave us as we rose, magnificent views of the snows. Thence we descended to Jor-bungalow, or "The Two Cottages", the seat of a Tibetan colony, where about a month previously I had seen these people joyously celebrating their belated new year. Like the ancient Romans, they begin their new year in the spring, when the winter season of suspended life has passed away, and when the fulness of Nature's reawakening energies is delightfully exhibited in the wondrous profusion of blooming orchids and magnolias in the fine forest of Rang-iroon, that we now entered, on the dripping damp northern slopes of Senchal.

This magnificent forest, which has been preserved by government, gives us some idea of the luxuriance of the virgin forest that once covered Darjeeling and its surrounding hills; but which has been ruthlessly swept away since Hooker's visit. It stretches for several hundreds of square miles, more or less continuously, from the top of Senchal down to the upper limit of cultivation, at about 6,000 feet; and our road runs through it for about ten miles. Its giant oaks, chestnuts and magnolias are thickly draped with moss and wreaths of aerial orchids, ferns and festooning climbers and parasitic plants, which hang in great tufts and pendants, waving over the blue hydrangeas of the undergrowth. Some of the branches of these trees are perfect gardens in themselves. In the soft drapery of moist moss that thickly clothes these branches, and in the beds of fine mould from the decaying leaves that fills their crevices, are to be found not only luxuriant clusters of exquisite

ORCHID AND MOSS-COVERED OAK-FOREST.

orchids *(Pleurothalis etc.)* and many kinds of other epiphytic plants, but even large woody shrubs and evergreens *(Vaccinia etc.)* with a variety of flowers and foliage. A gorgeous feature of the forest, at this season, is the blaze of crimson blossoms of the *Magnolia Campbelli*, a tree which has just flowered for the first time in Europe. Here, in its home, it is a forest monarch over 80 feet high, and its huge flowers, like those of the cotton tree below, appear curiously on its bare branches before its leaves. White magnolias also abound, scenting the air with their fragance. Delicately pink hydrangeas 18 to 20 feet high are common, and ferns are so numerous that over sixty species may be found along this forest road within a few miles.

The glimpses of the snows, framed in this rich forest foreground, were very varied, and there vistas comprised the deep valley of the Rang-eet, and to our left Darjeeling in the middle distance, and Kanchen-junga more fascinating than ever. And we passed several mounted Tibetans and Chinese, with strings of laden pack-ponies, also several detachments of our troops going and coming, which reminded us that we were on the trade-route to Tibet, and on a line of march held by our forces.

After winding above a mineral spring, and past a few clearings of the herdsmen who supply milk to Darjeeling, and who are Bhotanese of the Moo-sepa clan, we emerged from the forest at the open slopes of Lop-chok, or "The cool stone," where Achoom promptly brought us breakfast, in the little rest-house, with its wide views of both the Teesta and Rang-eet valleys.

Thence a steep descent, by rapid zig-zags, led us through the trim tea-gardens of Pashok, or "The Giant-bamboo Jungle", for here begins the zone of this valued bamboo *(Dendrocalamus Hamiltonii)*, whose stout stem, 7 to 9 inches in diameter, supplies the Lepchas with their large jugs and cooking-pots. Further down we re-entered the forest, and at about 4,000 feet below Darjeeling, reached the staging-house (3,300 ft.) in a semi-tropical forest, which generally resembled that of Badam-tam, the first stage of our previous journey. Here we heard again the shrill chirping of the cicad insects, and the subdued roar of the great river below. Near the house amongst the undergrowth of thick stalked *arums*, spotted like serpents, were a few of that curious old-world type of tree, the cycad, which is somewhat between a fern, a palm and a pine.

The descent to the Teesta bridge, next morning, had to be done on foot as the road was too steep to ride. On the way down through the Sal woods to the tropical forest bordering the river, we got occasional glimpses of the river, and a fine bird's-eye view of its junction with the Rang-eet; and we sighted a marsh-deer or *Sambhar*, (Lepcha, *Sa-ving*,) of which the species found in these hills are decidedly smaller than those of the outer plains.

At the bottom of the gorge, the mighty Teesta, now only 710 ft. above the sea, thunders down, carrying a tropical climate and vegetation up along its banks thus far within the mountains. We soon reached the iron bridge which we had previously crossed in coming from Kalimpong. Here, in this deep hot gorge, quite a large village is springing up since the increase in the military traffic that has followed our little war with Tibet. And now we realized that we were on the line of communications of a small army in the field. The road was thronged with small detachments of troops and endless strings of transport coolies, laden mules and pack-ponies going, and empty ones returning with their drivers, and droves of cattle and sheep for slaughter for the commissariat.

The mouth of the bridge was quite blocked by the trains of transport bullock-carts that had come directly up the Teesta valley from the Indian plains of Siligoori, to avoid the needless climb up to and descent from Darjeeling. The block of carts here was especially great owing to the bridge having, through an oversight, been built only for foot-passengers, and so narrow that no cart could cross it. These vehicles therefore had to be unloaded, their wheels unshipped, and both their loads and the bits of the carts carried over piecemeal, and put together and reloaded at the other side; all of which meant a chronic block of the traffic at this narrow throat of the bridge.

The frequency and severity of the "Derbyshire neck" here is remarkable. Most of the residents suffered from this disfiguring swelling; and whilst I was at breakfast at the rest-house, I was surprised to see that several of the goats and the domestic fowls, as well as some of the ponies of the place had the same large swellings. The villagers blamed particular springs in the neighbourhood, which they said gave goitre to every one who drank that water. Probably the complaint is connected with the limestone-rocks that crop out hereabouts; but I had already found that most of the goitre-causing springs in the submontane plains, contained in addition to lime an excess of iron, which we know produces readily fulness of the blood, and thus a swelling of this large vascular and unsupported gland of the neck might be accounted for on physical principles.

At the entrance to the bridge a warning placard caught the eye. It bore the very necessary military notice to safeguard this slender vibrating structure:—"Troops crossing this bridge are *not* to keep step." And all along the bridge were tied countless parti-coloured streamers and fluttering prayer-flags, the offerings of the Tibetan passengers to the spirits of the water. I helped myself to a few of these flags for my museum, as curios are seldom to be had free, gratis and for nothing.

Once across this bridge we were again in British Bhotan. In the steep ascent to Kalimpong we followed at first the new cart road which had been made since our last visit here, but after a time we took to the short-cut, which, rising over 3,000 feet in five miles, is always hot work to climb, and tries the breath of the pedestrian. Our troops found it especially trying when they were pushing on in

1888 to fight the Tibetans. On that occasion one of the British soldiers is said to have exclaimed, after toiling, under a broiling sun, up some 2,000 feet in two miles, "I've heard that Tibet was a *table*-land, so these must be the legs we are climbing!"

Beyond Kalimpong, after several miles of hot shadeless road, we rose into some grateful forest at Rissisoom, or "The Three-spur Ridge", where three spurs diverge; and descending the northern of these, past Choo-mik, or "The Spring of Water", where there is a Lama temple, we reached again Pedong, and encamped not far from the French missionaries' chapel, near the solitary "incense-tree" *(Sal;* in Tibetan, *Po)* which gives its name to this village. The resin of this tree is largely used as incense in the Lama temples of Tibet. It is found in the ground at the foot of certain of these trees in Sikhim, in large masses, often nearly 30—40 cubic inches in size, but how it is produced is not yet known exactly.

Pedong is now a considerable military station and commissariat depot for our small army of troops in Sikhim. The mere cost for the transport of the rations for our troops, in this little war and the subsequent occupation of this mountainous country, must have been enormous. All the food was brought from the Indian plains, and for the greater part of the way, within the hills, it had to be carried by mules and ponies, and on men's backs. The carriage of only one hundredweight for the short distance from the Teesta bridge to here is one to two rupees (one shilling and threepence to half a crown), according to the number of porters available. In this way these thousands of coolies have been making a month's wages in a few days. And as I came along I saw scores of these coolies seated by the roadside gambling, with little heaps of rupees changing hands; and it was no uncommon sight to see coolies resting beside their loads, throwing up rupees and striking them against each other, and gloating over the sight and sound of their new-found treasure. Yet what solid advantage have we yet gained for all this enormous outlay!

From there, several more aggravating descents and ascents, and again further descents still awaited us ere we reached the final climb to the Pass. These ups and downs seriously obstruct the flow of trade along this route; although the map distance from Darjeeling to the Jelep is only about 40 miles, the distance by the undulating road is over 80, and the ascents must be over 20,000 feet and the descents over 15,000! A descent from here to about 2,800 feet brought us to the *Rishe*, or "Hillhead", torrent, which comes down from a high hill of that name (10,400 ft. high), and which we crossed by a strong bridge, at an elevation of 2,030 feet above the sea, and we were then once again in "Independent Sikhim". Thence we ascended through cultivated fields to Rhenok, or "The Black (-earth) Hill"; and crossing that ridge at an elevation of about 5,000 feet, we wound through copses alternating with many fallow fields strongly scented with rank wormwood, to "The Great Flat

Stone", which gives its name to a small hamlet at a traders' halting-place. The deserted barracks that we passed on the way had to be abandoned a few weeks previously by the artillery, on account of a bad epidemic of fatal fever that claimed here many victims, as was evidenced by the fresh graves with their wooden crosses. This epidemic was caused, so my Tibetan porters alleged, by the sylvan deities and water-sprites of this place, in revenge for some outrage perpetrated on them by our soldiery; but this "fact" will not, I fancy, be found in the records of our army.

Pushing on by the good bridle-path that wound through rank jungle infested by venomous *pipsee* flies, we dipped down to the fine river called "The Water of the Lepcha's Hut" *(Rongli-chu)*, so named after a Lepcha's house at the crossing. We had a refreshing bath in the river after our hot march, and halted here for the night; for although the elevation was only ,2,590 feet above the sea, the site was exceptionally cool and was reported to be free from malaria, at least at that season, and here was a staging-house prettily situated on the river's bank.

The woodwork of this building bore abundant marks of having been tenanted by the British soldier. He had spared few of the beams and posts in his eager desire to carve down his initials or name to posterity, whilst halting here with his detachments of troops that were frequently passing this way to and from the frontier fort, near the Jelep Pass. Our men caught a few fish in the stream, but they were aggravatingly bony and rather insipid to eat.

From this place the ascent was practically unbroken. The road led up a finely wooded gorge, and crossing several tributaries, carried us into open glades where permanent cultivation was possible. Here were several new settlements of the Nepalese colonists whom our government was inducing to settle in these hitherto uninhabited tracts, so as to create a fixed population, and provide a local supply of food and labour, on this solitary trade-route. Higher up we reached "The Great *Se*-tree" *(Sedong-chen)*, where, at 6,500 feet elevation, and in a temperate forest of oaks, there is a rest-house, in which we halted for the night.

Towering some 6,000 feet above us, and scarcely two miles distant, rose, like a black wall, the beetling heights of Lingtoo, the strongest of the fortified Tibetan positions which had to be taken by our troops, and which we had to cross in the morning.

It is marvellous how our forces were able to carry such a strong position in the face of a swarming foe, even though badly armed, so excessively steep is the ascent, not to mention the difficulties of making active exertions in the rarefied air of such an altitude (12,617 ft.), and the badness of the track at that time. Even with the present good bridle-path, the strings of baggage animals have to stop every few dozen yards to take breath. The first Tibetan stockade was built on a ridge at 9,060 feet high, thickly covered with dwarf bamboo, beside a small tarn, called "The Fine Sheep-pond" *(Jeluk-Tso)*. Here some of my coolies who had accompanied our troops, pointed out the spots where the Tibetans had lain in ambuscades, screened by the undergrowth and mist, and the remains of some of their dead were still to be seen not far from our path.

TIBETAN FORTIFICATIONS AT YATOONG.

The steep ascent up the cliffy Lingtoo led us beyond

the bamboos, winding through rhododendrons ablaze with blossoms, on which honey-suckers were feeding, and up through dwarf junipers *(J. recurva)* and silver-firs to the bleak summit, which was crowned by the long lines of Tibetan masonry fortifications, after the style of the Tibetan block-house at Yatoong, here figured. I roamed over these, examining their details, whilst Achoom kindled a fire in one of the deserted barracks, to prepare some tea and hot luncheon.

The storming of this Tibetan stronghold by our troops, under General Graham, was effected with marvellously little loss of life on our side, seeing that the natural strength of the position made the place practically impregnable, if it had been held by any well-armed and disciplined body of men. But the Tibetans were only armed with wretched rusty matchlocks, and some had merely slings and bows and arrows, which latter are still the native weapon of the Tibetans. Indeed, the Tibetan word for "gun" is "fire-arrow" *(Me-dah)*, and their commanders are still called "Lords of the Arrows" *(Dah-pön)*. More than to their weapons, however, did they trust to the spells of their priests, and especially to the divinations of the Ne-choong oracle. These spells they believed secured to them, not only the supernatural assistance of the gods; but also rendered them individually invulnerable against the shots of our rifles. And even when their men were being rapidly shot down, still the survivors did not lose faith in their spells; but afterwards with complacent confidence they asserted that something had gone wrong in the casting of their spells, but that in the next war they must certainly prove efficacious. Amongst several of these spells found in their camp, was one like a windmill, inscribed with the words "Break them! Destroy them!" A curious Tibetan map of Sikhim

TIBETAN SOLDIERS.

and Darjeeling was also picked up, and a lithograph of it is now displayed in the Survey Office in Calcutta.

Their code of rules to be followed in warfare, though quaintly worded, is generally admirable in theory, as seen in a manuscript copy found in Sikhim by Mr. White. They read:

"Before going to war, the strength of the enemy "should be carefully ascertained, and diplomacy is to be "exhausted before a campaign is undertaken; and care "should be taken that by going to war no loss be sustained "by your Government. Anyone coming with overtures of "peace should be well received. Should two or more "enemies combine against you, no means should be left "untried to separate them, and if possible to bring one "over to your side; but false oaths should not be resorted "to, nor the using of God's name. See that there are no "lazy, sick, or timid in the ranks; but only those who fear "not death. Experienced men only should be sent. The "army should be divided into three divisions under differ- "ent officers. Your horses, tents and arms should be kept "in good order. A doctor, diviner, astrologer and Lama "should be appointed. On moving, the tent fires should "first be put out, the wounded be cared for; and in cross- "ing rivers, order should be kept, and those behind should "not push forward. Things found should be returned with- "out asking or reward. Any disputed booty should be "drawn for by lots. The General should appoint sentries, "who must look to the water-supply, and see they become "not easily frightened. They should allow no stranger to "enter the camp armed; but should be careful not to kill "any messenger. If a sentry kills a messenger coming to "make peace, he shall be sent to his home in disgrace, "mounted on some old useless horse with broken harness.

"Again, when a fort is surrounded, those in it should

"remain quiet and show no fear. They should not fire "off their arms uselessly, and with no hope of hitting the "enemy. The well within the fort should be most carefully "preserved. If you be defeated you must give up your "arms, and those who give these up must not be killed. "Should anyone kill one who has given up his arms, he "must be derided and scoffed at as a coward. If you "capture a General or officer of rank you should bind his "hands in front with a silk scarf; he should be allowed to "ride his own horse or another good horse, and should be "treated well; so that in the event of your ever falling "into his hands he may treat you also well. Prisoners "should receive necessary subsistence, and also expenses for "religious ceremonies. Should an army be defeated and "obliged to fly, nothing should be said to them, but they "should not be rewarded or receive any presents, even "though the leader be a great man."

Our artillery proved too much for them. When it poured its withering shells into their midst they broke and ran, and though they made several stands higher up, they soon were driven from their position, swept over the pass, and pursued into the valley of Choombi beyond. This charming Tibetan valley could easily have been held, even by a small force of police; but our troops were quickly withdrawn, out of consideration for the feelings of China, the nominal suzerain of Tibet.

The Chinese immediately on hearing of this defeat of the Tibetans, despatched an envoy to Darjeeling to settle this frontier trouble, although they had hitherto professed their inability to influence the Tibetans. This envoy was Sheng Tai, the chief Chinese Resident or *Amban* at Lhasa, and he was accompanied by a large suite of Celestials and Tibetans, who astonished us during the past winter at Darjeeling, by appearing like antediluvian monsters, dressed in the most

CHINESE ENVOY FROM LHASA, AND SUITE.

The chief Mandarin of Lhasa. The Amban—Sheng Tai. Secretary to Amban. General of Troops at Lhasa.

formidable trappings to keep out the cold, such as they use in the arctic winters in Tibet, including nose-pads, ear-pads and temple-pads, and huge padded goggles.

And, only a few weeks before our visit here, a convention was signed between these Chinese and England, which recognised the English protectorate over Sikhim, defined the boundary in general terms, and appointed a commission to facilitate trade across this frontier. The ceremony of signing this convention was done with much pomp at Government House, Calcutta, before the Amban with his Chinese suite returned to Pekin over this demolished Tibetan fort, by the way we had come.

The Chinese plenipotentiary, the *Amban,* whose official designation is "Chinese Imperial Associate Resident in Tibet and Military Lieutenant Governor" accompanied by his suite, as shown in the accompanying illustration, was received at the bottom of the grand staircaise by the Under-Secretary of the Foreign Department, and conducted to the top of the stairs where Mr. Cunningham, Foreign Secretary, was waiting to lead him to the Council Chamber, along a passage lined by the body-guard. The Amban wore a dress of blue and black silk, with a richly jewelled belt from which hung a short sword. He and his secretaries and suite all wore their official caps with their buttons of rank. A couple of minutes after they entered the chamber, the Viceroy and staff, with two members of council came in, in procession, and the Imperial resident was presented to His Excellency by Mr. Cunningham. The Viceroy showed the Amban to his seat at his right hand, and all the other officers took their seats, two of the Chinese having places at the table, and four standing apart. Then the powers of the Plenipotentiaries were presented and acknowledged. The door was then closed, while the Convention was read out, and compared in the English and Chinese versions; and after about a quarter of an hour the door was opened, and four copies of the Convention were signed by their Excellencies. The Amban used a brush like a camel-hair pencil, with a plain wooden handle. He dipped this in a small metal dish of Indian ink held by one of his attendants, and stooping over the parchment, slowly inscribed two characters, one below the other, and both together not more than half an inch in length. Beside the Viceroy's "Lansdowne" written in a bold hand, they had the appearance of a mistake that had been scratched out. When the copies were signed they were sealed by attendants, and here the stamping of the red seal of China was done in a moment; whereas the great fan, or *punkah,* had to be stopped, and a number of matches struck under the table and in sheltered corners, before the wax seal of the British Government was affixed.

From this rugged crest of Lingtoo, with its ruined fort, a sweep of fine rolling downs, the upland pastures, stretch away up to the snows of the Chola range and its pass of the Jelep. At first the knolls, amongst which we find ourselves, are covered with clumps of rhododendrons, now in full bloom and clothing the hillsides with almost every shade of bright colour, from brilliant vermilion *(R. cinnabarinum)* to pale rose, blue and yellow. And the grassy depressions between the lichen-clad rocks are enamelled with purple primroses *(petiolaris)*, blue gentians *(quadrif.)*, pink and white anemones, buttercups and other bright yellow Alpine flowers, already taking advantage of the brief spell of sunshine by bursting into blossom; for even in these high altitudes many flowers are "born to bloom and blush unseen", and summer is as sweet as down below. Magnificent views of the snows, too, are to be got; that of Kanchen-junga is especially fine, from the boldness of the foreground. The numerous little pools in the marshy hollows which are found here, are considered by Blanford to be traces of former glaciers—the dams, being little moraines,—and he says, "I had been carefully watching for marks of glacial action at a lower elevation, but could find none whatever; if any ever existed they have long since been obliterated by the tremendous rainfall and consequent disintegration and denudation of the surface."

After a slight descent through a pine forest with some stunted junipers, a turn of the road reveals the frontier fort of Gnathong, or "The Black Meadow", so called by the

Tibetans, as its dark pine-encircled meadow is the first traders' camping-ground on this side of the snowy pass. In regard to this name, as in so many others, it is a pity that in spelling it, our map-makers should have gone out of their way to introduce an initial *G* that does not exist in the Tibetan, or "T*h*ibet*i*an" as they would have it, for the native word is plain Na-t'ang.

The fort here is perhaps the highest military post in the world which is held by Europeans. Its elevation is 12,030 feet above the sea-level. It lies in the bottom of a bowl-like valley, commanded all round by heights at no great distance, so that it is only tenable against a timid and badly armed foe like the Tibetans. Its fortifications are, like the barracks themselves, of wood, backed by shallow earthworks and trenches. Yet it looks picturesque, especially as the small stream that meanders down the land-locked valley has been dammed up to form a considerable sized lake, which gives the troops who are cooped up in this dreary place some recreation, bathing, boating and swimming in summer, and skating in winter, in addition to a plentiful supply of water.

Through the clouds of thick mist which were fast settling down, we saw as we crossed below the dam, some scores of European soldiers, and our ears caught the cheery brogue of the jovial Connaught Rangers, who held this post, assisted by some artillery, Goorkhas and pioneers; and soon we experienced the warm welcome from the hospitable officers, who ensconced us in one of the spare log-huts within the fort. It was amusing, if not pathetic, to notice that the streets inside the fort in this outlandish edge of the world, were named "Hyde Park Corner", "Rotten Row", etc.; showing how the Britisher in his exile here, still clings in loving fancy to the land of his birth.

The bitter cold of the winter may be imagined from the extra warm clothing that was needed for the troops *in addition to their ordinary winter clothing*. The extra clothing issued on this account to the troops (2,000 British and native and 930 followers) employed in Sikhim, is given officially for the year ending 1st April, 1889, as:—11,000 blankets, 4,100 pairs of boots and shoes, 3,600 cardigan jackets and warm coats, 2,200 sheep-skin coats or poshteens, and over 8,000 pairs of worsted socks, as well as 8,500 warm jerseys and pyjamas. About 4,000 waterproof sheets were also issued, besides mittens, putties or woollen leggings, turbans, and warm waistcoats in proportion; 650 waterproof capes were supplied for the use of men exposed to the wet during guard or picket duties. The protection of the men's eyes fom snow blindness was not forgotten, the force being supplied with 1,200 pairs of goggles.

As is usual at most military stations on the frontier, the natives were especially polite. The Tibetans, of whom there were a goodly number here, kowtowed and put out their tongues in their most respectful way; although several of them were men who were fighting us a few months before, but who were now profitably employed in building, road-making and carrying loads, for which they got good pay. This peculiar Tibetan form of polite salutation which we have already seen, was not at first understood by the British soldiers here, one of whom complained to his officer, that one of these "dirty rascals" put out his tongue at him, and "I knocked him down; and when he got up again he put out his tongue even more than before, then again I knocked him down."

Next morning we ascended to the Jelep pass, riding most of the way. A zig-zag led over the "Derby Downs", as the undulating hill to the north of the fort is called, to commemorate the charge of the Derbyshire regiment in driving the Tibetans from the Tooko ridge above. It was along this ridge, at an elevation of 13,550 feet, that the Tibetans built their famous wall during the night before the last fight. As has been remarked, it seems scarcely credible that this wall which was breast high, and extended for four or five miles, could have been erected in a single night. When our picket was withdrawn from this Tooko ridge at dark one evening, not a Tibetan was to be seen near, nor was a sound heard in the night at Gnathong, which was only a mile and a half below, and yet next morning there was this wall completed, and lined by a mob of yelling thousands. Some evidence of the havoc wrought by our bullets was still to be seen in a few pierced skulls lying about, and gruesome piles of dead Tibetans showing through the thin graves, trenched open by the heavy rains.

From the pass through this Tooko ridge, we passed over open grassy downs and moorland, and descended through scrubby rhododendrons to a little lake about half a mile long, the Bidang-Tso (12,700 ft.), fringed with ruby-coloured primroses (*P. Kingii*). This lake is, as noted by Mr. Blanford, one of the best examples of a glacier-lake. Just at the upper or north-west end there is a horse-shoe moraine, which has formerly enclosed a second lake, now converted into a marsh. At the south end is a second well-marked moraine, damming up the lake.

A sharp rise up the craggy, yet swampy Kapap valley, and a sharper rise through a snow-streaked gorge, and still steeper bit over frozen snow, on foot, brought us, at 14,390 feet above the sea, to the summit of the "Lovely Level" pass, as the name *Jelep*, I found, means. And certainly it deserves this name, for it is the easiest of all the passes between Tibet and Sikhim. It is relatively low, and can be crossed on horseback both up and down, and is seldom closed by snow for more than a few weeks during winter. We went down the other side some distance.

The view into Tibet from the top is much finer than from the Tang-kar pass; for here, one sees away down into the bold pine-clad valley of the inhabited Mo river, where lies its capital town of Choombi, and beyond it rise the heights of Phari fort, leading up to the snowy peaks, the most conspicuous of which is the sugarloaf-like cone of the sacred Chumo-lhari (23,940 ft.), or "The Hill of the Lady-goddess", the tutelary spirit of this valley, as well as of the adjoining Tibetan tableland to the north. In the foreground, a few feet below the pass, on the Tibetan side, is a small lake whose waters leap down through dark fir-woods, past the site now occupied by the Tibetan block-house of Yatoong, (figured on page 267,) into the Mo river, only about six miles distant, at the flourishing town of Rinchen-gong, and three miles below the fort of Choombi, at an elevation of not more than 9,400 ft.

This fine valley of Choombi, though at present closed to Europeans, has been visited by several Englishmen. Manning passed this way to Lhasa last century, as well as the missions sent by Warren Hastings—Bogle's in 1773, and Turner's in 1783. Some of our troops also, as above mentioned, lately pushed into this valley. And all testify to its splendid climate and scenery, and the signs of material well-being and comfort there, in such striking contrast to Sikhim. The houses are said to be well-built stone buildings, two to three storeys high, surrounded by fertile meadows and orchards; and in the river, good fishing is said to be got.

What a pity it is that this fine residential valley was not annexed by us, when we had the legitimate opportunity of doing so two years ago, as some indemnity for the enormous cost of that little war which the aggressive Tibetans forced upon us. The cost to our Government of that expedition, and the subsequent military occupation of a position in Sikhim which it entailed, can scarcely have amounted to less than a million sterling, and was probably much more. Yet all this expenditure, so far, has turned out dead loss, without the slightest prospect of advantage in any way. And even China, in view of all the circumstances, could not have seriously objected to its annexation.

Amongst other reasons for this annexation in these days of geographical boundaries, is the fact that this valley is not geographically a part of Tibet at all, but lies within the *cis*-Himalayan water-shed, like Sikhim, Nepal and Bhotan; and it is believed to have belonged to Sikhim or Bhotan, until about two hundred years ago. Several of the inhabitants have told me that they would welcome annexation by the British Government, as they are so harassed by the Chinese and Tibetan officials, who receive no wages and who "squeeze" the inhabitants accordingly. And the political as well as the physical desirability of acquiring it is immense. Its climate is far better fitted for a sanitarium than Sikhim, for it is screened from the rains which make residence in Darjeeling so unpleasant during those very months when a cool sanitarium is most needed;[40] and its bold Alpine scenery is said to be scarcely equalled by the best parts of Kashmir.

Then, this valley is the only natural trade-route from India to Central Tibet, and is therefore of commercial as well as strategical importance. The route through Sikhim by which we have come is so extremely circuitous, so bristling with endless ups and downs, dipping into tropical valleys and ultimately rising to the 14,390 feet of the Jelep, only to dip down again to the 9,000 feet of this Choombi valley, that it is indeed remarkable that any trade at all finds its way by the present route through Sikhim, or "The Crested Country," a peculiarly appropriate name. On the other hand, as a reference to the map will show, the natural and direct route from India to Central Tibet is up this Mo or Torsha river from the plains of Jalpaigoori, the British district which adjoins Darjeeling on the east. Here are no trying ridges to cross, but one simple gradient all the way, through a productive country that would carry a remunerative railway, and over which trains could easily run from India *via* an extension of the existing Bengal-Doars or Rangpur railway, into Choombi in a few hours.

The advantages of this route struck Sir Ashley Eden so forcibly, when he was crossing this river on his mission to Bhotan in 1864, that he wrote: "If the country had been in any hands but those of the Bhotanese, a road into Tibet would have been taken up this (Mo) valley, and would have opened communications with the plains, *avoiding all snow-passes*" —an important record which seems to have been forgotten.

Between this Choombi valley and the plains of British India, a corner of Bhotan intervenes, it is true. But this doubtless could be easily acquired from the impecunious Bhotanese, who have already ceded to us, for nominal sums, so much of their territory; and especially as this small tract in question is so sparsely populated, and has already been shorn of most of its marketable timber and india-rubber trees, so that it is now of little value to the Bhotanese themselves.

I advocated these views at the time of the late war; and I believe that eventually we shall have to take over

Choombi. Once we have got the railway there, there will be relatively little physical difficulty in extending it up to the Tibetan plateau, and to the great central river, the Tsang-po, if necessary. For Tibet is certain to become of considerable commercial importance—its rich gold-fields, perhaps the richest in the world, are alone sufficient to make it so. And it lies in to India much more closely than to Russia. On the disintegration of China, or other crisis, demanding the occupation of Lhasa, an Indian army could reach that city from Choombi in about a week's march; whereas between Kashgar and the Pamirs lies an almost impassable desert which would take many months, indeed the greater part of a year, to cross. The easiest route of all to Lhasa would, of course, be up the Tsang-po or Dihing river from Assam.

The cheapness of living in Choombi and in the adjoining plateau of Tibet is remarkable, and all the more so when compared with that in Sikhim. I was told by some of the natives of this valley of Choombi (which is generally known as "To-mo", after an edible tuber, for which it is famous), that an ordinary native traveller, who purchases his provisions with money (though in some places in Tibet the people do not sell goods for money, but only barter them), can live on about $1^1/_2$ to 2 annas (or pence) a day, compared to the 6 annas or so, that it costs in the neighbouring British territory of Darjeeling. And carriage is still cheaper. The ordinary means of transport is by ponies, mules or yaks, that carry about $1^1/_4$ to

2 cwts., for human porterage is deemed degrading in Tibet. The cost of the carriage of one *maund* ($^2/_3$ of a cwt.,) all the way from Choombi to Gyantse, the large mart of Central Tibet, six or seven days' march distant, is said to be only about four annas (fourpence) all the way! In this march, two days are usually taken from Choombi to Phari fort, where the customs are levied, and Phari is ordinarily five days' march from Gyantse, seven from Shigatse, and thirteen from the holy city of Lhasa, the Mecca of the Tibetans; though I met at the Jelep a man who had left Lhasa only eight days previously. The trade-duties are said to amount to four annas (pence) a head going, and three annas returning, in addition to about one-tenth of the value of the goods imported, and this is often taken in kind. The Nepalese levy heavier duty on their Tibetan frontier, as much as five rupees (over six shillings) *per* head, and about ten *per* cent of the value of the goods, except gold, which is always passed free of duty so as to encourage its import. Silver, on the other hand, whilst it is freely exported to Tibet, and usually of a base quality, is strictly forbidden to be imported from Tibet into Nepal.

Returning from this Jelep pass, we saw other tracks going off to the right and left, to the neighbouring passes, between the jagged snow-streaked peaks of this so-called Chola range—to Pemberingo, 15,000 feet on our left, and to the Nathu, Yak and Cho passes on our right. Following this last track over the moors for a short distance, we reached the wild gorge of the diamond-shaped Nemi lake, fringed with firs, beyond which, after about two miles, the track goes up to the Nathu pass, where a limited view of this Choombi valley is obtained. About three miles farther on, through a picturesque valley with a succession of little lakes, is the steep Yak pass with a fine view of the Choomolhari peak. The Cho or Cho-La pass is long, steep and tedious, and commands a restricted view. This range consists of a pale-coloured gneiss with a remarkable low dip, so that the peaks are somewhat flattened.

Through the thick mist that now set in, we heard the musical tinkle of ox-bells, and met several yak-herdsmen on our way back to Gnathong; we bought some milk and butter from them. They are nomads like the herdsmen of the Lachoong valley. They graze their cattle on both the Tibetan and Sikhim sides of the frontier. In the summer they drive their cattle across the Jelep and adjoining passes, into the Choombi valley, where they grow a few crops, and in autumn they recross the passes. As the snow falls, they descend into the lower valleys of Sikhim, where they have scanty crops of barley and buckwheat. The latter is a hardy cereal of the dock family, which is made into poor girdle cakes; it is called *phyo* by the Bhotiyas, *pru* by the Lepchas and *pha-phar* by the Nepalese.

One of the few pedestrians we met was a Sikhimese going to Choombi, carrying a heavy load of *Murwa* seed of his own growing. It was said that a load of this seed, which in Sikhim brings only Rs. $4^1/_2$, sells for Rs. 6 in Choombi; and this amount, if invested there in

Tibetan salt, buys about $2^1/_2$ cwts., which sell in Darjeeling for about Rs. 30—a good stroke of business!

Some of the legends of these passes were related to me as I descended to Gnathong: how that the wizard-saint, Lo-pon Rimboo-che, the founder of Lamaism in Tibet, passed over this way to introduce his religion into Sikhim, and the devils of these mountains conspired against him. He entered by the Cho-la, hence called "*Jo-la*", or the "Pass of the Lord", to which he thus gave his name; on the east side of that pass, a rock is pointed out as "the throne" *(zooti)* on which he sat; and close to the pass, is a spot where he surprised some she-devils cooking human beings, and two masses of columnar rock there, are alleged to be two of the stones that supported their colossal cooking-pot. He, too, created the pass through that ridge on which the Tibetans built their long wall—the Tooko La, or "Up-torn Pass", by tearing up the rock there to crush an obnoxious demon, whom he buried in the Bidang lake near by. And all these lakes are tenanted by mermaids, sirens and dragon-spirits who allure the unwary to destruction.

The names of these mountains, places and rivers hereabouts, I find, give us great insight into the way in which primitive people have coined their names for places, and given names which now convey to us little or no meaning. In England and most parts of Europe, where so many waves of different races have swept into the country in ancient times, and so little is known of the language and customs of the aboriginal natives who were thus displaced or driven out, it is not easy now to find a meaning in the names of many of the rivers, mountains and places. Here, however, the aborigines, who gave the original names, are still in possession, and as they themselves have occupied much of their country only comparatively recently, the reasons for their name-giving have not yet been lost sight of. But there is no time to lose in investigating this subject, for the language of the real aborigines, the Lepchas, is fast becoming extinct. They have not a written language, nor has any full vocabulary of their language ever been published. Thus the names that they have given to the places and rivers might, through much longer delay, prove unintelligible by their meaning becoming lost.

I had, therefore, in this research, to prepare a vocabulary for myself by taking down the words phonetically from the lips of the elder Lepchas, and to hunt for the precise shade of meaning of each word. And then I had to elicit by enquiries at each spot, the special reasons as to why that place or river had received its particular name.[41] Here I shall only mention that while all the oldest names in this part of the Himalayas are of Lepcha origin, there are also many Tibetan names which have been bestowed by the immigrant Bhotiyas who settled here; and there are also now in the lower ranges recently occupied by the Nepalese, several Nepalese names for places already bearing aboriginal names, not to mention several English ones. So that several of the hills and rivers have now come to possess three different names or synonyms, according to these three ethnic groups. Thus, the river which the Lepchas call "The Great Straight-going Water" (*Rang-nyoo-Oong*), and which the Bhotiyas call "The Pure Water" (*Tsang-Chu*), is called by the Hindooized Nepalese, "The Three Currents" (*Teestota* or "Teesta"), on account of its stream breaking up into three main branches in its course through the plains.

It will already have been noticed, how remarkably descriptive these native names are, as a rule; and they usually embody information that is useful to the roving Lepcha aborigines of the forest, or, in the case of a trade-route such as we were now traversing, to the Tibetan traders who frequent it. The names usually well express some very obvious physical feature of the site or river; *e.g.*, of rivers, an especial tortuosity, steepness, impetuosity, shallowness or otherwise of a course or channel; of mountains, their shape, appearance, etc.; of village sites, the stony, precipitous, meadow-like character, quality of soil, jungle-product, conspicuous tree, etc.

Thus, most of the names of places along this road denote halting-places, or stages presenting a rock-shelter, or a clearing in the jungle with water near, and occasionally pasture. These sites, being on lines of communication and always near a water-supply, occasionally develop into villages. The names were probably first given by Tibetan merchants or other travellers, such as priests or monks; and the process of such name-giving probably arose through a pioneer merchant or other traveller, narrating the stages of his journey, and his successors adopting his stages and nomenclature.

Such a traveller might be supposed to describe how on going from "The *Tomo*-tuber" country (*Choombi*) to the "Country of Rice" (or "*Den-jong*" as the Tibetans call Sikhim, for it is one of their chief granaries for this staple food), and on crossing "The Lovely Level Pass" (*Je-lep-la*), he passed "The Saints' Mount" (*Ku-phu*) and the "Uptorn Pass" through the ridge (*Tooko-la*), and reached "The Black Meadow" (*Gna-thong*), where he halted. Next day he proceeded down "The Steep Descent" (*Ling-tu*, or properly Loong-tu) to "The Big *Se*-tree Clearing" (*Se-dong-chen*). Next day, continuing his descent past "The Big Pigs' Wallow", (*Pha-dom-chen*) he crossed "The Water" (*Chu*) at the Lepcha's house (*Rong-li*) and ascended to "The Big Flat Stone" (*Do-lep-chen*), where he halted. The following day he crossed "The Black Hill" (*Rhenok*) and "The Mountain-Head Torrent" (*Ri-she-Chu*) and ascended to "The Incense-tree Clearing" (*Pe-dong*). Next day he lunched at "The Big Spring" (*Choo-mik chen*), and crossing the ridge at the junction of "The Three Hill-tops" (*Risisum*), reached "The Governor's Fort", or "*pong*" as the Lepchas call it (*Kalim-pong*) etc., etc.

On returning to Pedong, I proceeded eastwards along the frontier of Bhotan. A charming walk through a fine temperate forest led over the exposed crest of Labah, or "The Windy Site" (6,600 ft.), down to Ambiokh (2,920 ft.). On the way, we saw the tracks of wild elephants, and the damage they had done to the trees as they passed. Large herds of these animals roam hereabouts, and are said to ascend as high as 10,000 feet on the flanks of Lingtoo; and every year numbers are caught by the Indian Government, in the unreclaimed forest of the adjoining plains below.

Near my tent in the forest, at Ambiokh, rose the picturesque ruins of the old Bhotanese fort of Daling (3,350), that gave its name to this part of Bhotan, which was known to the Bengalees as the Daling-*Dooar*, or "pass." This fort, which occupies a very strong position, is perched, as its name "The Rocky Site" implies, on the precipitous edge of the gneiss-rocks, which rise here at a very high angle. It was stormed by our troops in our war with Bhotan 1864, already referred to. This fort overlooks the great Terai jungle at the foot of the Himalayas, and the sea of outstretching plains, seamed by the ever-shifting channels of the great rivers. We saw that the impetuous torrents which had hurried down from the cloudy mountains into the sunshine, now formed majestic rivers that creep sluggishly along their winding way over the plains, depositing as they go the debris of the hills in such enormous quantities, that the river-beds become raised above the surrounding country and force the rivers to seek new channels, oscillating for many miles on either side. One of the largest of these rivers that we saw is thus called "The Hidden Water" (*Jal-daka*), because it sinks down and disappears for several miles, flowing underneath the porous gravel and loose detritus.

I descended this Terai jungle by following a path past the "cow station" (*Gooru-bathan*) of some Nepalese herdsmen. These shallow passes or entrances from the plains into the hills are here called by the Indians, *Doo-ars*, equivalent to and having the same Aryan root as the Saxon "door". Several others of these shallow valleys or Doo-ars [42] have been ceded to us by the Bhotanese as waste-land, and now form some of the richest tea-land in India.

The jungle here, is so thick and dense that it was not practicable or wise to go very far from the path, especially as I had no elephant to ride; for on the sandy bank of one of these streams, amongst tracks of rhinoceroses and deer, I came across the fresh foot-prints of a tiger. Here I got several birds of Malayan type, including two fine grey pea-pheasants with gorgeous iridescent spots on their wings and tails, a Bhotanese partridge, and the great racket-tailed Drongo, a sort of bird-of-paradise (*Dissemurus paradiseus*). Jungle fowl were common. These ancestors of our common domestic fowl are said to have been domesticated in India and China before 1400 B.C., and introduced into Europe amongst the Greeks as early as 600 B.C. The shrill clarion call of the wild bird is much more sharp and staccato than that of the domestic. The variety of butterflies and other insect life is even greater than in Sikhim, also the rankness of the vegetation, for the rain-fall in this outer tract, to the east of the Teesta and in the basin of the Brahmapootra, is almost double that of the corresponding parts of Sikhim.

The semi-aborigines who inhabit the "Doo-ars" and the adjoining plains of the Brahma-pootra, the river beyond, are in many ways an interesting people. They do not, as is stated by Colonel Dalton, Mr. Risley and other writers, belong to the dark negro-like aborigines of India, the Dravidians; but they are a distinctly Mongoloid race, a branch of the "Kooki" that seems to have entered Bengal from the east, by way of the eastern valley of the Brahma-

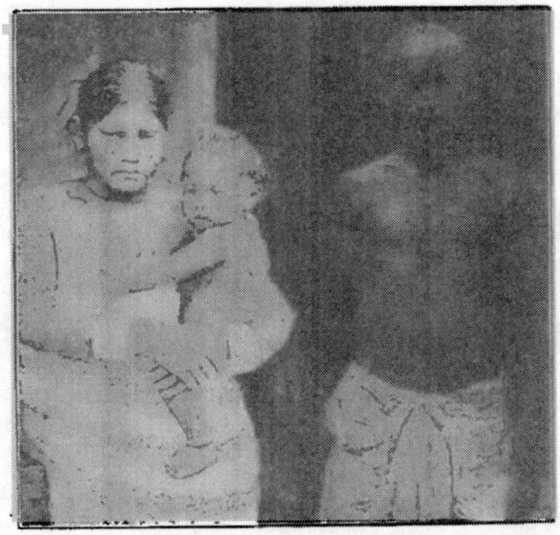

KOCH OR "COOCH" TRIBE.

pootra and not, I think, from Tibet. They have become so much Hindooized by contact with Bengalees, that they have lost not only their own language, but even their tribal name, and are now known by the Bengalee epithet of *Koch*, or "the Terai" (people), just as their kinsmen across the Brahma-pootra are called "*Kochari*" or "Cachari", an identical term. Most of them, however, prefer to call themselves by the Hindoo title of "*Raj-bansi*" or "The Royal Race", to affiliate themselves on their nobler kinsmen, the reigning chiefs of Koch or Cooch-Behar, Tipperah, Hajo, etc., in lower Assam and Bengal. A few of the still more aboriginal tribes are to be found in the deeper parts of the forest, these are the *Mech* or *Boro*, and the *Dhimal*. All of these people have a curious form of inheritance on the mother's side, instead of the father's, as is usual; and some traces of this are also, as we have seen, to be found amongst the Lepchas.

These sturdy, industrious people of the Koch tribe enjoy remarkable immunity from the deadly malaria of the Terai and adjoining plains. This is owing, in some measure, I think, to the high platforms or plinths on which they raise their huts, and to their clearing away the rank jungle from the immediate neighbourhood of their dwellings, where their trim plots of tobacco cultivation, their unveiled women in brightly striped skirts, and the straight ridged huts alongside a few areca-palms, contrast pleasingly with the squalor and rank setting of the hog-backed huts of Bengal.

In a cultivated clearing here I came upon a young leopard in broad daylight, skirting a field of sugar-cane only about a hundred yards away. It was peering so intently into the dense cane-thicket that it did not see me for some minutes, and just as it was disappearing into that tall growth, I sent a shot after it. Immediately there rose a dreadful outcry from a village which, unseen by me, lay a few dozen yards beyond where I had fired. Thinking that I must have shot some person, I rushed up to the village, and was relieved to find that no one had been hurt, but that the excitement was owing to a herd of wild pigs which the leopard had been stalking, and which on hearing my shot and seeing the leopard, had bolted pell-mell through the village, scaring the inhabitants.

I should not advise anyone to return to Kalimpong directly across the hills as I did, for the seeming short-cut turned out deceptively to be much the longer and more fatiguing route, on account of the circuit and badness of the tracks. These hill-people have even less true conception of distance than the people of the plains. They under-estimate distances, so that in their "two miles and a bittock" the latter usually turns out to be much the bigger half, and, curiously, they often tell you that a place is double the distance going up hill, to what it is coming down.

On the way, I passed through several flourishing settlements of the Lepchas. The families averaged four to five children, and several numbered seven or eight; so that the current statement that this race is dying out through sheer inanition is scarcely correct. The real reason for their disappearance in British Sikhim, is the disappearance or "conservation" of their forests, which by cutting off in great measure their sources of food, forces them into the unreserved tracts of Bhotan and Nepal. They are also losing their identity by the extensive absorption of their women into the Bhotiya and Limboo tribes, with whom they freely intermarry, as they find that their own race is so much despised by the more civilized tribes.

Two of these Lepcha girls, after a good deal of persuasion, sang us some songs to the accompaniment of a bamboo flute, and a Malayan harp like a Jew's harp,—all decorated with poker-work of a plaited basket-pattern. As none of the Lepcha songs have ever been recorded before, and they are unlikely to survive much longer, I have noted down a few of them from the lips of these people, and translated them with the aid of Mr. Dorje Tshering, and one of us has rendered their simple melody into European notation.

The words of these idyllic songs refer not only to the primitive passion of love, but even to the inscrutable mystery of the origin and destiny of man. And in this last respect it is pathetic to notice how these Lepchas or Rongs specially associate themselves with their ubiquitous bamboo, whose stout stem supplies them with huts for shelter, with fuel, bows and arrows; its larger joints afford water-jugs, cooking-pots and pans; its smaller joints bestow bottles, smoking-pipes and flutes: its branches make a springy couch; its bark supplies ropes to span their raging torrents, also baskets and umbrellas; and its tender young shoots are eaten as food. Indeed, the Lepchas believe they could not exist without their beloved bamboos, and no wonder they glory in having been "born of equal age with the bamboos."

A-CHU-LE:

A SONG OF THANKSGIVING.

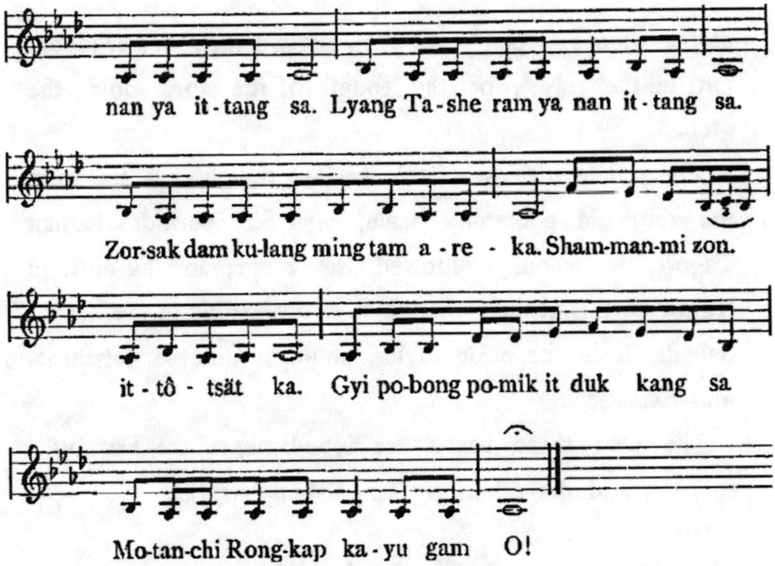

I.

O Joy! In the olden time the Head-Father-Spirit made the earth,
(He) the Sky-Existing-One made this earth,
He clothed the stony bosom of this tearful earth with fertile fields.
When the men were made and the jointed bamboos and the trees,
At that same time were we, the sons of the (one-) mother-flesh jolly Rongs.[43]

2.

O Joy! The mulberry trees were made with the rice and other vegetables,
The running rivers were made with their fleeing fishes,
The fleeing sky-birds were made with the worms and insects,
And the rainbow was made by our old first great-grandfather,
(But) our troubles were made by our old first great-grandmother!

The plaintive wail of these wild tunes reflects the stern surroundings that tinge the lives of these poor people with sadness. You seem to hear in their ancient airs the moan of the wind sweeping over their rugged rock-cave or lonely hut in the forest, or the sough of the storm down the glen.

The simple melody of this ancient tune shows traces of the very old pentatonic scale, says Sir Sourindro Mohan Tagore, to whom I showed the score; and he adds in regard to this scale, "though it is observable in the Scotch ballads, it is the scale in use amongst Chinese, Japanese, and Siamese".

The next three songs are love-laments, the first by a spinster, and the others by languishing swains.

U-LA-DUNG DÜT:

A LOVE-LAMENT.

I (am) a maiden like an unopened bud,
like a pretty supple shuttle,
like a whirling spinning staff.
I am a maiden standing like a twirling spinning thread,
like a bright golden tassel,
standing (forlorn) behind.

I am a maiden like a tender coiled bud
Shung like a sorrowing bird,
loudly lamenting like the *Tak-mok* bird,
I feel very sad, very sad!

The reference, in the above and in the following song, to the "respected sisters standing behind", relates to the custom of the girls of the family of standing behind the guests, as waitresses to replenish their drinking-cups.

THE PANGS OF LOVE.

Eh Yeh! I feel very sad, very sad.
Listen! O maidens behind,
My heart is pierced through and my breath is chill,
Alas! I feel very sad.
O great head-father, maker of Fate,
Pray tell me my luck.
I feel very sad.
I am only but a *Sham-man* youth, a mere boy!
Why have you troubled me so?
I feel very sad, very sad!

O fair one with the flowing hair!
O fair one with the straight-parted locks!
Why have you charmed me so?
O fair one with the neat parted hair!
O old great-grandmother Nyezong, the joiner of our breath!
O old great-grandfather Fadung, praised be your names!
But why have you created me
To suffer such heart-breaking sorrow?

Other songs sing the praises of their legendary chiefs, called Tekong-Tek and Fadung Ting, and their wives Nye-kong Nal and Nye-zong No, all of whom are deified and invoked in worship.

Down again in the Sal-tree forest, in the tropical gorge of

the Teesta, we saw one of the great breeding-grounds of the myriad butterflies that swarm over Sikhim. At this season, May, and on till the middle of June, the tender leaves of the great *Sal* trees were literally alive with voracious caterpillars, whose droppings fell on the dry leaves underneath, with a noise like a brisk shower of hail; and this was going on all day long, for several miles deep, in a forest that belts the Teesta and Rang-eet and other tributaries for some hundreds of miles. These caterpillars seemed mainly of two species, and both were distasteful to birds, which explains their presence in such overwhelming numbers. I collected several of these larvæ and offered them to some fowls, which, however, rejected them after a trial, with disgust, and went on wiping their bills for sometime afterwards. One of the species was a bright coral colour; and the other greenish with longitudinal stripes, and when disturbed it exuded a bead of malodorous fluid. It broke its fall from the tall trees by letting itself down by a long silky thread.

Continuing down the right bank of the Teesta, to its dark affluent "The Black Stream" (*Kali-jhora*), and then ascending towards "the height of the great bent-going river" (*Mahaldi*), we reached, at the "Foot of the Hill" (*Rishap*), the great Cinchona plantations on the eastern flank of Senchal. In this dense, damp, dripping forest the Cinchona plant finds a climate like that of its home in the Andes of Peru. The Government factory here was well worthy of a visit. The successful cultivation of this Peruvian bark, and the invention of cheap methods of extracting its quinine, by Sir George King and Mr. Gammie, have reduced the price of this drug to almost nominal rates, and so prevented this valuable aid to life in the fever-stricken tropics from getting into the hands of commercial monopolists.

A ride of about 18 miles by the new road, up through fine moss-covered forest, brought us again to Rangiroon, by which we had gone, and thence back to Darjeeling, which now justified its name as "The Place of the Thunderbolt". For, whilst the lower ranges were bathed in bright sunshine, a mass of thunder-clouds hung over the town, hiding its houses from view, and the rattling peals of thunder of the first burst of the rains, echoed up and down the valleys. And here in the drenching downpour of the 120 inches of rainfall, and the clinging dampness of the next few summer months, one has almost to live in a waterproof, to escape being soaked by the rain, through and through like a sodden sponge. Darjeeling, however, is going to make some capital out of her misfortune in this respect, for a movement is afloat to light the town by electricity generated from its excessive rain-supply.

CHAPTER IX

ALONG THE NEPAL FRONTIER TOWARDS EVEREST, ETC., TO SANDOOK-PHU AND FALOOT

TO see Mount Everest from closer quarters, and the rhododendron forests in full bloom, we set out for Sandook-phu and Faloot, going northwards along the spur which tends southwards from Kanchen-junga, for about sixty miles, towards Darjeeling and the Indian plains, and which forms the natural boundary between Sikhim and Nepal. This journey can now-a-days be done with very much more ease than in Hooker's time, for an excellent riding-road now runs along the Nepal frontier, with comfortable staging rest-houses *en route;* and Tonglu, the nearest of the higher peaks, which took Hooker three long and laborious days to reach by a bad native track from Darjeeling, is now one day's easy ride of about twenty-three miles, and all the way along the cool crest of the spur.

So, taking advantage of a spell of clear weather at the end of March, when a slight fall of snow on the nearer ranges had swept the hills from the haze that had hid their features for some weeks, we cantered along the road to Ghoom, past the large rock of gneiss, and thence on foot we threaded the fine forest to the staging-house of Jorpokri, on the frontier of Nepal.

This ferny and moss-grown forest resembled somewhat that of Rangiroon, and a walk through it was especially exhilarating in the crisp air of early spring. Here and there we passed fluttering prayer-flags, tied to twigs where water-kelpies haunt the mossy burns; and we met strings of sturdy Nepalese trudging along with huge baskets of provisions that they were carrying to or from the Darjeeling market.

These hardy Nepalese are of many different tribes; and though of Mongolian blood, they are all now adopting the externals of Hindooism, since their ruling tribe—the Goorkhas—have set them this example.

This ruling race of Nepal, or the "Goorkhas" as they call themselves, after the name of their former headquarters at Goorkha,[44] in the Central Himalayas, were little over a hundred years ago a small band of military adventurers, the descendants of a few quasi-Rajpoots, or members of the Hindoo warrior caste, who had emigrated from India and settled at the town of Goorkha, and had intermarried with the Mongoloids there. Seizing advantage of the breaking up of the old powers and petty dynasties at that time, when India and the principal states of Asia were in transition, they carved out for themselves a little kingdom there. And attracting to their ranks the more warlike members of the other tribes, by giving them the honour of their own tribal name of "Goorkha", and a share in their spoils, they carried their victorious arms for nearly a thousand miles through the length and breadth of the Himalayas, covering

A GOORKHA.

the country with blood. They invaded Tibet in 1792, and were spreading beyond Nepal, northwards towards Cashmir, and southwards into Sikhim (in September 1788) and the Indian plains, until they were hemmed in and defeated, in 1814, by the British troops under General Ochterlony, to whose memory was erected that great tower of victory, which is the most conspicuous monument at Calcutta.

Now-a-days these Goorkhas have almost disappeared from modern politics, though their name is still famous as the title of some of the bravest of our native regiments, which are recruited from their ranks. As mercenary troops, they have fought so gallantly under British officers, covering themselves with glory, that their name is almost a household word in England. And they have been induced to settle in large numbers in British territory, in the Kumaon Himalayas to the north of Nepal, and in Sikhim to the south-east, in order to supply recruits to our Indian regiments as well as to secure them as industrious colonists.

The pluck and good comradeship of the Goorkhas has been attested on many occasions, both when they fought with us and against us, and I myself have experienced it in the Burmese and Chitral wars. So long ago as 1790, when, after returning from Tibet, they were assisting our forces in the storming of Bhartpur, the chronicler of that campaign, Captain Smith, says: "It was an interesting and amusing sight to witness the extreme goodfellowship and kindly feeling with which the Europeans and the Goorkhas mutually regarded each other. A six-foot-two grenadier of the 59th would offer a cheroot to the 'little Goorkhee,' as he styled him; the latter would take it from him with a grin, and when his tall and patronising comrade stooped down with a lighted cigar in his mouth, the little mountaineer never hesitated a moment in puffing away at it with the one just received, and they were consequently patted on the back, and called 'prime chaps.'" And when they were pitted against us as our foes, Mr. Marshman, the historian, writes:—"The Goorkhas were not only the most valiant, but the most humane foes we had ever encountered in India, and they also proved to be the most faithful to their engagements." They can, however, be savagely cruel in their own country, where they often gave no quarter, and killed women and children. It is probable that in addition to the admiration which we cannot help feeling for their bravery, the Goorkhas have won our sympathy and confidence by their unswerving good faith, and they on their part seem to reciprocate our sentiments. As an instance of their desperate courage may be cited the deeds of Colonel Bahadur Gambar Singh, when assisting our troops at Lucknow, during the Indian mutiny. At that time he was only a private, but on one occasion he captured three cannon single-handed, and killed seven mutineers. This deed of daring was performed with only his knife or *kookree*, and he received twenty-three wounds.[45]

Politically, although within the British "sphere of influence", and acknowledging, like most outlying Mongoloid states, such as Burma, by its periodical embassies, the nominal suzerainty of China, the state of Nepal is absolutely independent in its government. And it has all along jealously closed the interior of its country against all Europeans, not excepting even our political residents, from the illustrious Brian Hodgson downwards. Its government is of the autocratic, oriental kind. The present Prime Minister, who is the real *de-facto* ruler, is called "*Maha-rajah*", or Emperor,

THE RULER OF NEPAL
Sir Bir Shumshere, K. C. S. I.

while the king is called *Adi-rajah*, or "Primordial King". This minister, who is also father-in-law of the present king, won his position by a *coup d'état* in 1885. He was educated at Calcutta, I have heard, and has proved himself an enlightened ruler, introducing several useful European reforms.

We are now passing, on their way to and from Darjeeling, many representatives of the various Mongoloid tribes of

KIRANTI OR JIMDAR TRIBE OF NEPALESE.
Aged 31.

Nepal. Those who have adopted the externals of Hindooism, who crop their hair and wear the Indian Rajpoot dress, are broadly classed as the Nepalese proper or "*Pahāriyas*", *i.e.*, Highlanders. These comprise, in addition to the Goorkhas proper, the *Khas* tribe, the *Mangar* or *Magar* (see portrait on page 309) of the lower ranges, and the

Gooroongs, a nomad pastoral tribe of the uplands; and also the following *non*-Goorkha tribes: First of these come the *Newārs*, who were the semi-aborigines and the ruling race of Nepal until displaced by the Goorkhas. They are more civilised than the Goorkhas, and form the chief clerks, traders and artisans, and some of them still adhere to their old religion, Buddhism, despite the ridicule of the Goorkhas. Somewhat resembling the Newars, but more purely Mongoloid and less civilised, are the *Kirānti* (or *Kirat* or *Kichak*) tribe of the wilder valleys of Eastern Nepal. The *Limboos*, still more distinctly Mongoloid and intermarrying with the Kiranti, we have already seen. And in addition to several others, there are those semi-Tibetans, the *Moormi* or "*Tamāng* Bhotiyas", who also have adopted the habits and dress of the Hindooized Nepalese.

But as yet, the Nepalese allow their caste rules to sit very lightly upon them. A Hindoo's caste, in practice, usually resolves itself into what he will eat and drink, and what he will not. The Nepalese, however, have not yet much altered their habits in these respects, but eat and drink things that are tabooed by every strict Hindoo. Thus, most of the Goorkhas, at home, eat buffalo-flesh, sheep and pork, and are very skimp with their ceremonial ablutions. The Newars and the other above-mentioned tribes eat also goats and fowls; and the highest Nepalese take water from the hands of the pork-eating Bhotiyas, a thing that would scandalize the lowest out-caste Hindoo of India.

Though small in stature, these Nepalese have big hearts;

and in many ways resemble the bright joyous temperament of the Japanese, though lacking altogether the refinement of the latter. Naturally vigorous, excitable and aggressive, they are very law-abiding, driven as they have been to obedience by the draconic punishments of their Goorkha rulers. The people are hanged or decapitated for very trifling offences, as was the case in England not so many decades ago; and this doubtless must tend to purify the race by preventing the perpetuation of imperfect types! Certainly in Nepal, these heavy punishments have made the people afraid to commit crime. But though the Nepalese are becoming plodding cultivators, they have not yet degenerated to the dead level of the present day caste-bound Indian cultivator. In appearance the various tribes vary considerably, in proportion to the extent of their admixture with Aryan blood. Scratch a Russian, it is said, and you'll find the Tartar; but the Nepalese, even with their thin veneer of Hindooism, do not require this operation to reveal their Tartar character. The features of the great majority are markedly Mongolian, with oblique eyes, and little or no moustache.

They are generally undersized, but tough and wiry as whipcord, and so full of energy that it is quite common to see old people scampering nimbly up and down hill in preference to walking. Their rough exposed life so furrows their features that the flat wrinkled faces of some of the older men, as in our illustration, almost suggest gorillas.

All dress in the same Hindooized style, and none wear pigtails. The men's dress is not by any means picturesque.

MANGAR NEPALESE.
Aged 65.

It is that of the Hindoo Rajpoots of the Northern Himalayas. It consists of cotton trousers and puny jackets, originally white, but so dirty that it is remarkable to find any at all approaching this colour. And into their bulky towel-like girdle they thrust their peculiar curved knife, the *Kookree*, of which the leather sheaths are sometimes richly encased in ornate silver-work. Their head, closely cropped—except in the wilder tribes, whose matted hair reaches to the neck—is covered by a small pork-pie cap, worn perkily on one side, after the manner of our smart cavalry soldiers. And most of the younger men beautify themselves by sticking large flowers behind their ears, and the more wealthy ones insert plugs of gold into holes drilled through their front teeth.

The Nepalese women, as we have seen, have often bright and pleasant faces, and are picturesquely dressed in a close-fitting bodice and kilted skirt, with bright coloured girdle and sash; and a gaudy silk handkerchief is thrown negligently over their head. They overload themselves with massive jewellery; enormous gold or silver ear-rings, nose-rings, bracelets, anklets, finger-rings, and necklets of huge size, made of coral or thinly beaten gold or massive silver, or strings of coins reaching down to their waist. Indeed, most of the women wear all their wealth as well as that of their husbands on their necks and faces; and whenever they get hard up they pawn or sell their jewellery.

Their position is decidedly free, quite as much as in Europe. Indeed in married life, like their Lepcha and Bhotiya sisters, they are much the better halves. Marriage is with them almost always an affair of the heart. Young men and maidens become acquainted with each other, and courtships and real love-matches are the rule. Whereas, with the Indian plains-people everything is arranged by the friends, and it is seldom that the bride and bridegroom see each other before marriage. The Nepalese are monogamous as a rule, and seldom take a second wife unless they are not blessed with a family. They are uncompromising in their punishment of infidelity, and are allowed by the laws of Nepal to cut down their aggressor with their *Kookree*. In British territory, however, where they cannot take the law into their own hands, they have to be content with a fine only.

All these tribes agree in the one respect, that personal cleanliness is rather at a discount amongst them. Like most mountaineers, they seldom use water for ablution, nor do they often change their clothes, but sleep in the same suit at night. While the Bhotiyas are certainly the most immoderately dirty of these hillmen, perhaps the Nepalese are the cleanliest on the whole, though most of these satisfy their religious scruples by performing the daily ceremonial bath that is prescribed to professing Hindoos, by merely touching their lips with water, and one or two rubs with a few invisible drops of water on the finger-tips, without undressing. You must not, however, with your European dress and known nationality, attempt to enter their houses unceremoniously, as you would a Lepcha's or Bhotiya's; for in such matters they put on all the airs of the most prejudiced of high-caste Hindoos, and would bluntly ask you to withdraw, although your pork-eating Lepchas and Bhotiyas and native Christians have the run of the house. For your intrusion, if it were noticed by outsiders, would necessitate the throwing away of all their cooked food, and even the burning and rethatching of their hut. But you lose little by not entering their houses, for these resemble, as a rule, those of the very meanest class of Hindoos, and have not the redeeming interest of those of the unpretentious Lepchas.

With their thin veneer of Hindooism, the Nepalese have adopted a Hindoo dialect, called "the hill speech" (*Parbatiya*), and it is throughout Nepal like what French used to be on the Continent, and what Hindustanee or "*Oordu*" is in India. It forms the chief medium of communication between the heterogeneous tribes peopling Nepal, each of which has its own peculiar language or dialect; but by means of this common *Parbatiya* speech all are able to converse with one another.

They are great believers in witch-craft, like the Lepchas or Bhotiyas, and regularly employ exorcists whenever they fall ill, instead of a medicine-man, as they attribute disease to an evil spirit who must be driven out. These exorcists they call "the spell-throwers" (*Bijooas*), as they cure by charms and enchantments; and, like the Lamas, with their magic they ward off dangers from the people, their cattle and crops; and on the middle of the road on the outskirts of more than one village, we passed a small heap of bits of cloth, and rice, an old shoe and reeking embers, as a peace-offering by these exorcists to the evil spirit who had possessed the sick person, after it had been driven out by their beating of drums, etc., and bidden to depart elsewhere.

Their ascetics are somewhat more decently clad, and less hideous, than those of the Indian plains. We passed a party of them coming down from their penance in the wilderness of snows, to taste the luxuries provided by their lay patrons at Darjeeling. Their faces were ghastly, smeared over as they were with ashes.

The personal titles of the Nepalese are peculiar, in that the proper personal name of the individual is scarcely ever used, even by their nearest friends. This is not done, apparently, because it is deemed unlucky. As all men are brothers, they are usually addressed simply as "elder brother" (*dāju*), and the women are called "elder sister"; or they may be called by one or other of certain titles, all of which are considered to be more polite than the proper name of the individual. These tribes do not appear to have any totems, or beasts specially sacred to the clans, like the mountaineers of Central India, as found by V. Ball and others.

In our walk, after passing the old Lepcha custom-house (*Jagat*) and "The Pen of the Pigs" (*Soongri-tār*), those animals so dear to the Nepalese, we reached "The Dried-up Tarn" that gives its name to a considerable market village (*Sookee-pokree*) of the Nepalese, where we met a marriage procession of Limboos, preceded by pipers who skirled like Scottish bagpipers. Thence, we ascended through the woods to the rest-house at "The Pair of Tarns" (*Jor-pokree*), where we tasted the good things that Achoom had provided for us.

Here we were serenaded by a wild-looking, unkempt mu-

A HILL MUSICIAN.

sician on the most primitive of one-stringed fiddles, an instrument that one of us became the proud possessor of for sixpence. And we had other serenaders. Swarms of frogs, embowered among the reeds of the adjoining tarn, kept up a nocturnal chorus of murmurs. The natives of these parts, the Newars just mentioned, worship these animals in the belief that they send rain to their crops.[46] And here also were tree-frogs with a bell-like call, who capture insects, as do the lizards, by darting out their tongue on which is a sticky secretion to which the insects adhere; the pity, however, is, that not only are vermin thus captured, but lovely species of butterflies that would gladden the hearts of entomologists.

Next day our path led us through a grand old forest of stately oaks and magnolias that stretched out high over head, their giant arms draped with a thick mantle of velvety moss and lichens, and garlanded with ferns and ropes of twining creepers. Magnificent orchids clung to their moist mossy bark, with flowers of many colours and fantastic shapes. One of them is sweet-scented like the climbing orchid of Brazil, which yields vanilla. The number and variety of the orchids hereabouts is prodigious. They are scarcely less numerous than in the adjoining Khasia Hills, where Sir Joseph Hooker discovered fully 250 kinds.

For some of the rare kinds of the "aristocratic orchid" fancy prizes have been offered by devotees of the cult. The *Englishman* announced recently and authoritatively, that "£1,000 is the reward attached to the re-discovery of the long lost *Cypripedium Fairieanum*. A popular description of its leading 'points' may encourage some enthusiastic planter to the search, may induce him to follow out its romance of botany, unless, indeed, the plant is extinct in its native habitat, wherever that may be. The flowers are produced singly and are exceptionally attractive; the dorsal sepal is large and white, yellowish green at the base, beautifully streaked with brownish purple; the two necktie-like petals are similar in colour, fringed with black hairs, deflexed and curiously curved at the ends; the pouch of the "lady's slipper" is a dull purple, suffused with dull brown and veined with green—one of the prettiest of the *Cypripediums*. Big sums have been spent in the search for it, and the offer of Messrs. Sander is surely sufficient earnest of their confidence, and they ought to know best, that it will yet be found, probably at the foot of the hills in Assam, probably in Bhotan (probably in Sikhim). The 'long-felt want' among orchid growers is a blue orchid. Curious it is that while the flowers are arrayed in all the tints of the rainbow, every conceivable gradation of colour, tones and shades innumerable, blue is almost unrepresented. There is a legend that a blue *Habenaria* is to be found in Sikhim, somewhere beyond the frontier; that it has been found, and that it has a place in the great orchid herbarium bequeathed in trust to Professor Reichenbach to be kept sealed for twenty years, the contents of which will, however, be ultimately given to botanical science in the stately *Reichenbachia*, an illustrated work in folio. A work which is understood to be in course of preparation on the Orchids of Sikhim, by the learned Director of the Royal Botanical Gardens, Calcutta, Sir George King, may give some clue as to the whereabouts of this rarity. Queen of its class is the *Cœlogyne cristata*, in great vogue in cultivation. It is plentiful above Darjeeling, at 8—9,000 feet, whence it was introduced about fifty years ago. The flowers are pure white, two to three, sometimes as much as four inches across, with a batch of yellow on the lip. One seldom fails to meet with good specimens of it in those baskets of miscellaneous orchids that are offered for sale in Darjeeling, products of a vandalism that is as wanton as it is wholesale. It is a great delusion, only too commonly experienced, to attempt to cultivate these plants in the plains. They may flourish quite fashionably one cold season, but they can seldom muster sufficient courage to endure a second. They will expend all their strength in producing new leaves and have none left for the supreme effort of flowering, unless they are sent to the hills to recuperate. One hesitates to compute the number of thousands of plants that are thus aimlessly destroyed in each year, lost not only to cultivation, but to science, for not a few species are being rapidly and surely exterminated." It is to be hoped that the authorities of Darjeeling and Sikhim may discourage and prevent this wholesale and woeful waste of these "glories of floral creation."

Some of the giant acorns (*Quercus lamellosa et annulata*) strewing our path, exceeded two inches in diameter.

Winding down this forest, over veins of brittle white quartz rock amongst the dark grey gneiss, we reached the saddle (*bhanjan*, as the Nepalese call it) in the ridge at a crumbling cairn or *Mani* (6,500 ft.), where we halted for lunch; and then zig-zagged up through a burned forest,

THROUGH A GLADE OF FEATHERY BAMBOOS.

where the array of tall charred stems stood weird and uncanny-looking. Thence we ascended through a glade of feathery bamboos, through more gnarled oaks, and, more steeply, through dense thickets of dwarf bamboos, relieved by the peach-like blossom of the still leafless paper laurel (*Daphne papyrifera*), from whose tough bark the natives

RHODODENDRON TREES.

make their Japanese-like paper,—to a ridge, at about 9,000 ft. elevation, where there burst upon our view the gorgeous rhododendron forest in full bloom.

This glorious sight is to be equalled nowhere else in the world, for this is the home of the rhododendrons. The whole hill-side for miles was aglow with the brilliant colours of the rhododendron flowers. These ranged through almost every hue, from the bright vermilion of *cinnabarinum*, the blushing scarlet of *fulgens*, to the crimson of *arboreum* and *barbatum;* the rose-red of *nivale* and *Hodgsoni*, the purple of *virgatum*, the yellow of *Wightii*, the bluish of *campanulatum*, to the cream of *Falconerii* and the white of *Dalhousii*, *anthopogon* and *argentum*. The variety in form and size of the plants was equally great, many of them were huge *trees* like great oaks (as seen in the illustration on previous page), and the profusion of their fallen petals carpeted the ground deep with fiery flakes like rosy snow, recalling somewhat the aspect of Japan during the gay festival of the Cherry-blossoms. Ascending through this gorgeous mass of colour and along a path lined with pink primroses (*P. denticulata*), we reached the rest-house of Toom-ling, or "Tonglu" as it is called on the maps, at 10,074 ft.

We spent the afternoon in the rhododendron woods. Hooker has described and figured about 24 species found hereabouts. The first that we met on the way up is a parasitic species (*R. Dalhousii*). It grows upon and covers with its beautiful large bell-shaped white blossoms, often seven inches in length, the highest branches of the highest oaks and chestnuts. After it, appears the large tree-rhododendron (*R. arboreum*) and then the more brightly coloured forms. A strikingly beautiful specimen is the creamy flowered *R. Falconeri*, which grows about thirty feet high. Its large leaves are covered with a rusty down underneath, and its pale pink bark peels off in flakes,

SEA OF CLOUD RISING FROM THE PLAINS.

giving the smooth silky stem a strikingly fleshy and naked appearance, as no moss or orchids can cling to it. *R. argentum* differs from this last in its having a silvery under-surface and its flowers pure white; whilst *R. Campbellia*, with its bright orange downy leaves, is only found above 10,000 ft. Several have sweet-scented flowers, for example, *R. Dalhousii, Edgworthii* and *Wightii;* and the leaves of some of the dwarf species are aromatic and are burnt as incense by the Lamas. We did not, however, relish the rhododendron-tree as fire-wood for our log-fire, as its smoke was most irritating and malodorous. Its dark heart wood is used for making the handles of *kookrees* and other knives. Our Lepchas cooked and ate the petals of this and some other species; the *cinnabarinum*, however, they said was poisonous, and often killed sheep, as Hooker has noted.

The sunrise over the snows as seen from the summit of this mountain was very fine. Especially graceful as viewed from here is the outline of Kanchen-junga, or Kanchen' as we shall now call it for brevity; but Everest is not visible, as the dark hill of Sandook-phu shuts it out, nor is the range of view so wide as that to be seen from our next stage, Sandook-phu, to which accordingly we now set out.

The road descended gradually to 8,250 feet, passing on the way a yak-grazing station—Ghairi-bāns, as the Nepalese call it, where some half-breed yaks or Zo were kept; and here we met a whole village of Nepalese emigrants who had left their native hills and were *en route* to settle permanently in some tea-gardens near Darjeeling. The party numbered about a hundred individuals, men, women and children; many of the latter were scarcely able to walk, toddling at their mothers' heels; and the dust of travel was thick upon them all, as they had been about a week on the march.

Beyond a deep saddle on the ridge, where on a previous visit I had seen a pack of wild red dogs hunting a deer, we emerged all of a sudden from the denser forest on to the open grassy slopes of Sandook-phu. Here at a tarn of dark peaty water (*Kala-pokree*), at 10,130 ft. above the sea, we halted for lunch.

Here the grassy slopes, which, sprinkled with pines, stretch up to the summit for about 2,000 ft., are thickly covered with the deadly nightshade or aconite plant; and it is from this feature, I believe, that this mountain derives its name—to wit, Sandook-phu, which means in the Bhotiya or Tibetan language "The Hill of the Poison-plant or Aconite." So abundant is this plant here, and so deadly to the cattle of these pastoral people, that all the sheep and cattle passing over this mountain are muzzled by their drivers. And at the foot of the mountain are great heaps of these discarded bamboo muzzles.

The curious circumstance is also noted here regarding this poison, which Marco Polo records of this or a similar plant in Mongolia—namely, that it only affects fatally those cattle that are newly imported from the plains or lower levels; whilst those that are bred in the locality do not appear to suffer. [47] This is believed to be owing to the native sheep learning to avoid the poisonous leaves or to shun the youngest leaves, which are the most virulent; but it is difficult to see how they can entirely succeed in doing this where the poison grows so abundantly. It is, I think, more probable that they get habituated to it, by eating the drug in small quantities, as opium-eaters do opium, and as snake-charmers are believed to render themselves and their performing animals immune to serpents' venom, by the repeated injection of small doses of the venom, a method which I had many years ago ascertained by experiment to be somewhat prophylactic against snake-bite. [48]

Much of the aconite of commerce, that finds its way to Europe, and which is so largely used now-a-days by homœopaths, is gathered on this mountain; and I have found the Bhotiyas in the autumn, digging up the roots wholesale for transport to Calcutta. They pay a small fee to the Rajah of Sikhim for this privilege, and they get from the native dealers at Darjeeling about fourteen shillings for three-quarters of a hundredweight of the dried roots. There are several species of the plant growing here, including the greenish *A. palmatum* and the deeper blue, the virulent *A. ferox* that is exported for its poison, and which Hooker says is merely a variety of "the monkshood" (*A. napellus*) of our gardens at home. [49] The men dig up its roots in late autumn after the plant has withered and when its juices, on which its activity mainly depends, have mostly returned to the roots.

This root is also extensively employed throughout the

Eastern Himalayas to poison the arrows that are used

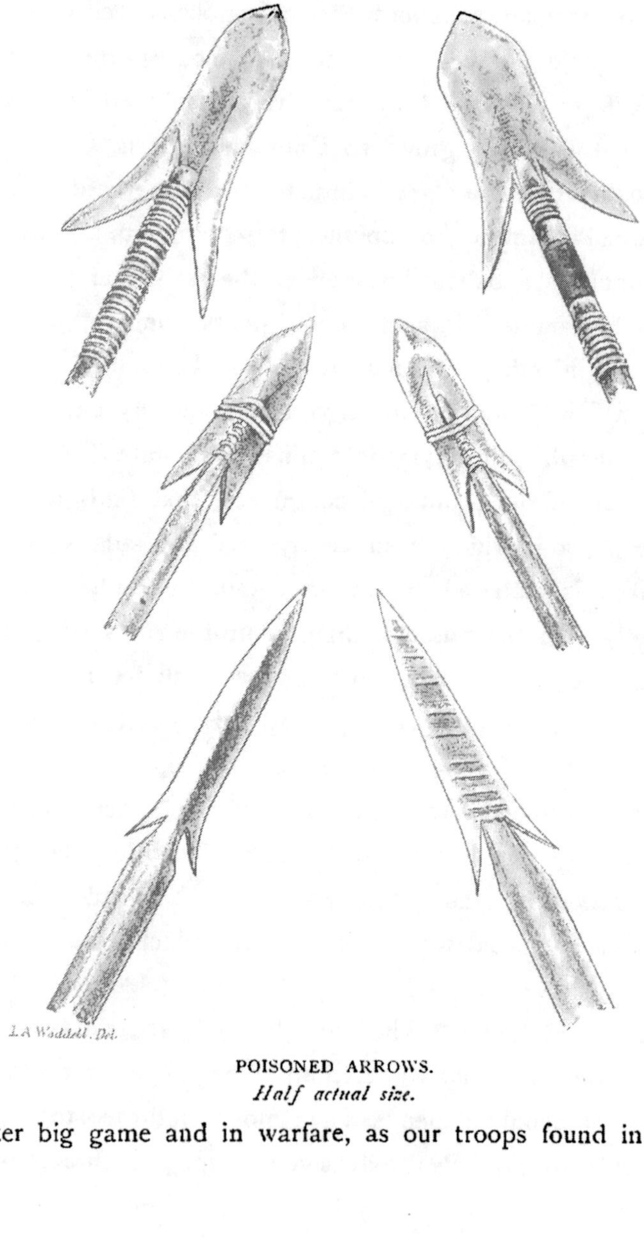

POISONED ARROWS.
Half actual size.

after big game and in warfare, as our troops found in the

SNOWS FROM SANDOOK-PHU.

expeditions against the Sikhimese, and also the Abor and Aka tribes of Assam. These arrowheads are sliced with valvular crevices to hold the poisonous paste, or made of barbed pieces so cleverly pieced together, that any attempt to drag them out of the wound, causes the splinters to penetrate more deeply. It is noteworthy that the Lepchas eat the cooked flesh of the game that they have killed by these poisoned arrows, without any bad effects to themselves.

Snow lay in patches on the path as we zig-zagged up the northern slopes of the mountain, through clumps of silver pines, and it covered the summit with an almost continuous sheet, over which, in the bitter wind, we made our way to the rest-house. Here we found the front room invaded by a pile of driven snow over a yard deep, that had been blown in through a chink in the door. Fires were soon lit, but it took us some time to thaw our frozen limbs, while Achoom was busy in the kitchen, and we needed our warmest wraps.

Outside, the baffled tempest still howled and whistled furiously. The storm-tossed pines threw their splintered arms about and sighed, poor things, in the piercing wintry blast. But at night the wind died down, and the view of the snows in the moonlight was sublime. After the storm

> "the mute still air
> Was Music slumbering on her instrument."

From a background of almost inky blackness, the graceful white-robed peaks and icy horns of the Kanchen-junga range gleamed out clear and colossal in the dry frosty air.

The ice-spangles on the dark pines and rhododendrons sparkled like diamonds in the pale moonbeams; whilst in the fore-ground, fringing the ice-covered lakelet, the frozen "everlastings" projected from the snow, bright and pure—a picture in frosted silver.

The sunrise over the snows was magnificent, and the stretch of these latter much wider than that seen from Senchal, extending perhaps for nearly 200 miles. We were up early to the topmost of the three nipple-like peaks of the craggy summit, to see this famous view. As the eye wanders over the vast amphitheatre of dazzling peaks it is at once arrested by the great towering mass of Kan-chen-junga; and the first thing that strikes you is the altered outline of both it and its group of peaks, as compared with that seen from Darjeeling. The long straggling lines of its outlying snowy peaks and ridges, the tent-like Kabru, etc., as seen from the south-eastern aspect from Darjeeling, are now foreshortened, and the peaks cluster closely together under Kanchen', which towers up majestically over all. This dazzling mountain, almost the highest in the world, is magnificent, even as seen from here, in its dark setting of pines, and without the deep intervening valley of the Rang-eet. It is, after all, only 852 feet less in height than Everest itself.

The Everest group, no longer shut out by the dark ridge that hid its peaks from view at Senchal, soars up through banks of clouds far to our left, and beyond a deep gulf of valleys. This group, however, lies much lower on the

EVEREST GROUP RISING ABOVE THE CLOUDS FROM SANDOOK-PHU (12,000 FEET).

horizon than Kanchen', being so much further away—about, 90 miles—whilst the latter is about 43 miles. Only the peak of Everest is visible. Its base is hid behind the shoulder of a great armchair-like snowy mountain, the "Peak No. XIII." of the Survey (see p. 342).

Scarcely less magnificent than this view up towards the snows was the view looking downwards to the plains. Some ten thousand feet below us, the rising mist and clouds formed a vast woolly white sea, whose tide of rolling billows surged in amongst the mountains, of which the dark rugged ridges stood out against the fleecy foam, as bold capes and headlands and dark islets in this sea of curling clouds. And as we gazed, some of these fleecy clouds surged over us and crept slowly, like "sheep of the sky" as the Lepchas call them, upwards to the snowy pinnacles, on which they settle down in flocky masses, veiling the peaks against the staring mid-day sun. Towards evening, however, these clouds disappear, probably condensed into snow in the colder atmosphere, and then we get again clear views at sunset.

The track to the next peak led along the undulating crest of the pine forest, through patches of rhododendrons blooming brightly amid the snow, past some juniper trees after a few miles; and the ranges of the hills got more and more rugged and rocky, as we approached the everlasting snows. Amongst the patches of rhododendrons by the way I got two *Monal* pheasants and one blood pheasant; and I saw a wild pig, also tracks in the snow of deer, goat-antelope, and a bear.

The pine forests, however, seemed to harbour little life, and their stillness at times seemed uncanny as I walked through them a long way ahead of my men, and especially so near the ridges, where there were many gaunt splintered pines struck dead by lightning, and gnarled trunks and writhing roots tortured into weird shapes by the icy blast. As I was climbing up the ridge called *Sabar-goom*, or "The Cliff of the Musk-deer", so called after those animals (*Sa-bar* in Lepcha and *Lao* in Tibetan) which used to frequent this ridge, I saw a ghastly sight. Athwart the path, stretched on the snow, lay a Nepalese frozen to death. Several jackals and an animal like a hyena surrounded the dead body, beside which were the embers of a small fire, and not far off lay the deceased's basket filled with his food and belongings. It was evident that he had perished through the cold; that he had arrived here benighted after the snowfall had ceased, and, unable to proceed further, had lit a small fire, and had been betrayed into a sleep which proved his last. There was no evidence of a struggle. His foot-prints in the snow led up to here, and the jackals had evidently come only a few minutes before I appeared on the scene, for they had gnawed only one arm, and were searching in his basket when I disturbed them at their unholy feast.

Hurrying onwards out of the cutting blast that swept over this exposed crest (11,640 ft.), we emerged from the pine forest on to the treeless slopes of Faloot, properly *Fok-loot*, or "The Peeled Summit" as the Lepchas call it,

A NEPALESE FROZEN TO DEATH IN THE SNOW.

for it looks from the forest-clad ranges below, as if its summit were "peeled" of trees; and my Tibetan porters on seeing its bare grassy snow-streaked slopes, sent up a shout of joy, and exclaimed, "Now we are again in a treeless country like our own Tibet!"

It was a long and cold zig-zag up its sides to reach the rest-house nestling on the leeward side of its windy top (11,810 ft.), and I arrived about an hour before my porters, with a perfectly ravenous appetite, but with nothing to satisfy it except some Indian corn and capsicums, which was the only food that the caretaker of the house possessed. He made up for me some of the Indian corn into a sort of porridge-like mess, but the capsicums proved excruciatingly hot. I was foolhardy enough, on his recommendation, to eat two when I was almost paralysed with the cold. Their effect was instanteous, and for hours my blistered tongue reminded me of this fiery food.

The sunset on the snows was almost as splendid as the sunrise had been. As the crimson ball of the sun dipped to the western horizon, the snowy pinnacles, gleaming fiery red, soared out of the purple sea of pearly haze that filled the dividing valleys, up into a sky of deepest turquoise, laced here and there with shafts of burnished gold. Then followed a swift kaleidoscopic play of colours, in which the glittering fiery peaks faded to crimson, pale rose, and a cold steely grey that seemed to carry them far away, spectral-like, into another world.

A bear had mauled badly a brother of the care-taker of

this desolate hut, tearing out his eye and the side of his face. Such shocking mutilations are not very infrequent, and explain why these people dread a bear even more than a tiger or leopard. Not long ago in these same hills an excited Nepalese came breathless to my tent, with the news that a large bear and its two cubs had mangled two men of his village, and had for several days been chasing others, so that they were afraid to go about; and hearing that a European traveller had arrived, he had come to beseech me to go to their aid, promising that if I would go, all the villagers would turn out and assist me in slaying these animals. As it was then too late to go that evening I started early next morning, with my shot-gun and shells and a few of my best coolies armed with their knives. It was a long and hot way to the village, down many miles of ravines. On reaching it, a powerfully-built man was led slowly out to me. His head was swollen to twice its size, and both eyes and his two cheeks were torn out, and their tattered shreds were hanging down his neck, and he was groaning in agony. I had no narcotics with me to relieve his pain, but I had him laid down and bathed his poisoned and inflamed wounds with tepid water. I was then told that he was the village blacksmith, and that his children had for some days been complaining to him that they had been chased by these bears while herding his cattle, and yesterday one of his children had been overtaken and clawed in the back by one of the young bears. Whereupon the indignant blacksmith, relying on his great physical strength, and he was indeed a Vulcan in physique, went unarmed to the bears' den and there he shouted to the bears to come out. The old bear rushed out, and in an instant inflicted on him the terrible wounds that we had seen, and so terror-struck were the villagers at the sight of these proofs of the power of the bears, that although I had come at their special invitation, they refused to go with me to attack the bears. The wives pushed their husbands inside their huts and barred the doors. And it was some time ere my men could force open the doors of several of the huts and drag out some of the men. With these and my informant of yesterday and a few others who showed less cowardice I went off to seek the bears. The cave lay about a mile from the village, at the junction of two streams, amongst cliffy rocks overgrown with a good deal of brushwood. I took up a position about a hundred yards off and sent the beaters to throw in stones, but the bears seemed to be not at home. At least they gave no sign, and did not appear even when I approached to the mouth of the cave and fired into it; and we scoured the hillsides for some distance without finding them, though the trees bore fresh marks of their claws. I sent the poor wounded man some opium from my camp to relieve his pain, and advised his friends to carry him into the nearest hospital, about four days' journey distant, but from subsequent enquiries there, I learnt that he had never come; he must certainly have died.

The view from this peak of Faloot, or "Fa-le-loong" as

the Tibetans mispronounce the Lepcha name, gives much nearer views of the Kanchen' group, of which the culminating peak is now only about thirty miles distant. And the horn of "Jannu" in Nepal stands grandly up on the left.

Everest, however, is scarcely visible from here, as it is hid by that great arm-chair-like snowy crater, the "Peak No. XIII" of the Survey Department. To see Everest we must go further north along this ridge, or return to Sandook-phu, from which latter place the top of its peak comes into view over the shoulder of this much more imposing arm-chair peak, as is shown in the previous illustration and in the annexed sketch by Colonel Tanner. And this view, small as it is, is one of the very best that is to be got of it, outside Tibet and Eastern Nepal, which unfortunately are at present closed to Europeans. Indeed, so inconspicuous is Everest from any point of view to which Europeans have had access (in Sikhim or the Indian plains, or in Central Nepal), that it is extremely doubtful whether any of the older travellers in these regions were ever able to distinguish Everest at all, or as a pre-eminently high mountain. For even from Sandook-phu and its other available points of view (it is not visible from Tonglu or the Kakani ridge above Khatmandu), owing to its great distance in the interior, behind the outer snowy peaks that tower in front of it, its enormous height is not apparent, and this was only revealed by the scientific measurements of the Indian Survey Department.

When the great trigonometrical survey of India had,

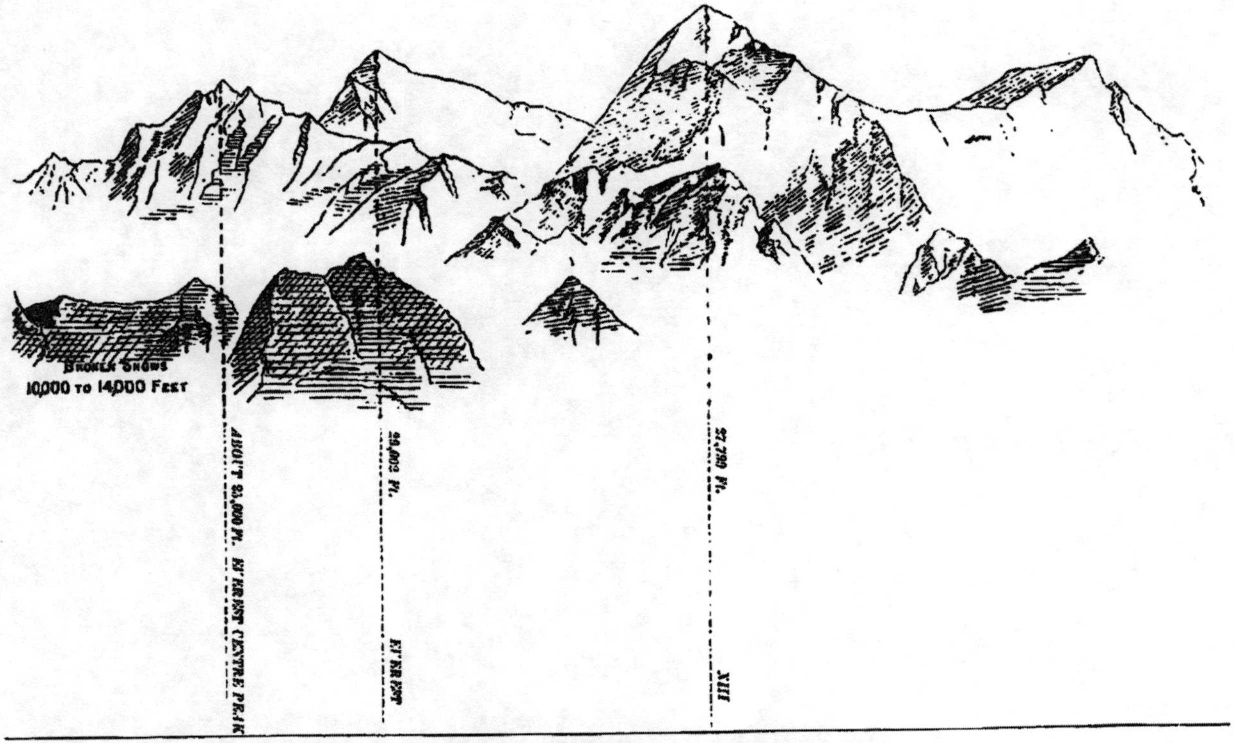

KEY TO THE EVEREST GROUP FROM SANDOOK-PHU.

EVEREST FROM SANDOOK-PHU.

about the year 1850, extended their triangulation to the foot of the Himalayas, from this newly gained base, measurements were made to the snowy peaks beyond the frontiers, and it was discovered, between November 1849 and January 1850, that in Tibet at 27° 59.3′ north latitude and 86° 54.7′ east longitude from Greenwich, a peak rose to the enormous height of 29,002 feet, or 8,840 metres—the highest measured elevation on the earth.

The Surveyor-General of that day proposed to the Royal Geographical Society of London to give this giant mountain the surname of his predecessor in office, Sir George Everest, to whom the great merit belonged of organising the Survey of India on a scientific basis, between the years 1823-43. A protest against this naming was raised by Mr. Brian Hodgson, on the plea that the Nepalese had already given to this mountain the name of "*Deva-dhunga*", or "God's Seat", and "*Bhairava Langur*", or "The Terrible Pass". At the meeting of the Geographical Society held on the 11th May, 1857, to discuss this objection, and at which Sir George Everest was himself present, it was shown to be doubtful whether any of the alleged native names could be really applied to this particular mountain at all. The name "Everest" therefore was given to this king of mountains, and it has appeared in the English maps ever since. On the continent, however, one of the vague Indian mythological names, obtained by H. Schlagintweit from the Hindooized Nepalese of Khatmandu, for a mountain which he supposed to be identical with the Everest of the Survey, is usually assigned to it—namely, "*Gauri-sankar*", one of the titles of the conjugal Indian god Shiva, the Destroyer, and his wife. But it is not generally known that the identity of these two mountains has been conclusively disproved by General Walker, the late Surveyor General of India, and by Colonel Tanner, his deputy. Owing to the curvature of the earth, and the interposition of other ranges, it is physically impossible to see Everest either from Khatmandu or the Kaulia or Kakani peaks, whence H. Schlagintweit believed he saw it and got his local name "Gauri-sankar". As for Kanchen-junga, which Schlagintweit says was also visible from that position, it is shown to be "fully one hundred miles *beyond the most remote* point visible from that locality." And Colonel Tanner has directly proved that the "Gauri-sankar" of Schlagintweit is certainly *not* the "Everest" of the Survey, but a much smaller and totally different mountain. He writes: "I have now before me the panoramic profiles and angular measurements of Major Wilson, for some time resident in Nepal, who observed from Sheopuri, a point on the Kaulia ridge. Schlagintweit's 'Gauri-sankar', the 'Everest' of successive (political) residents in Nepal—was pointed out to Major Wilson, and from his angular measurements I am able to identify that peak as 'No. XX', 23,447 feet, more than a mile lower than Everest, (see map on p. 349) and in point of distance very far short of it."

What then is the native name of the highest measured mountain in the world, for it is always desirable to preserve the vernacular names of great mountains? The native names which have been given to distant Himalayan peaks are misleading and confusing, and especially so are the Nepalese names. The Nepalese, who seldom themselves go near the peaks, are very loose in their nomenclature of these mountains, and the names which they apply to them generally indicate ranges and not individual mountains, except in a few instances, where the peaks, unlike Everest, are more accessible and are frequented by Hindoo devotees. Of the many natives of Eastern Nepal of whom I asked the name of Everest, not one ever called it "Deva-dunga" or "Gauri-sankar". This latter name for a hill they had never heard of, though many hills were called Deva-dunga or "God's seat". But in regard to Everest they had no specific name for it all. They simply called it, in common with all the other high snowy peaks, "The White Mountain", or *Dhaulagiri*, which is the popular generic name for all the snowy peaks: "*Himalaya*", or "The Abode of Snow", is a classic term which is unknown to the common people, and is only used by Brahmans and the learned. Nor had these men any specific name even for that striking crater-like peak "No. XIII," which towers over Eastern Nepal and which has been pointed out to Colonel Tanner by the Bhotiyas as "Khumba-lung," after the valley at its foot; although these Nepalese knew it well by headmark, and likened it, aptly enough, to a white-shrouded woman in a sitting posture. On the other hand, the Tibetans who inhabit the country around Everest and who ascend this sacred mountain for purposes of worship, as high as they dare, call it and the other neighbouring mountains by names which do not seem to have been hitherto published, or only partially or incorrectly so. The highest range of snowy peaks in this region in question, and including the Everest group, was pointed out to me by a Tibetan native of Khumbu, the province of North-Eastern Nepal bordering this range on the south, as "The Five Icy Horns of Khumbu" *(Khumbu-Gang-nga-Ra-wa)*. Whilst the highest part of this range, that is to say what we have called the "Everest group" and including "Peak No. XIII", was called by him *Lap-chi-Kang*, or "The Outer-Glacier Pass"; and the culminating peak, *i.e.* Everest, was called *Jomo-Kang-kar*, or "The Lady White Glacier". These latter two names have already been mentioned by Baboo Sarat C. Das as the cognomen of the Everest range and its highest peak. But my informant said that this range is properly the "*Lower* Lap-chi-Kang," in contradistinction to the *Upper* Lap-chi-Kang, which he said was much higher, and lay in Upper Tibet, almost due north of this Everest group, but was not visible from Khumbu or any part of Nepal.

There seems no doubt as to this nomenclature, for I have seen in Tibetan books "the *Upper* Lap-chi-Kang" noted as a high mountain, as well as the Lap-chi-Kang on the Nepalese frontier; and in the vernacular topography of Tibet, which has been partly translated by the above-named Baboo, the peak of Jomo-Kang-kar comes second in the list of the highest mountains, and is described as lying in this locality, in these words, which may be followed in my accompanying

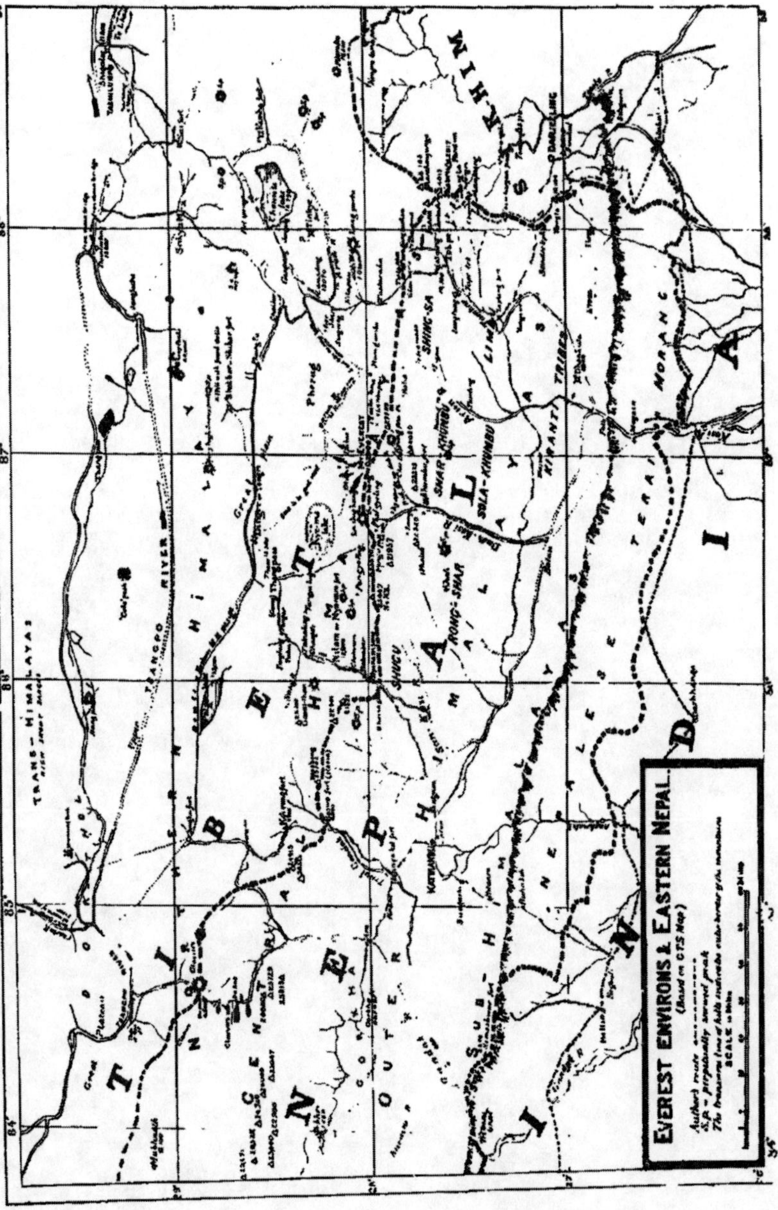

MAP OF THE ENVIRONS OF MOUNT EVEREST.

sketch-map. "To the east of the Kirong district lies Nalam, (Nyanam) in the vicinity of which are Gung Tang, the birthplace of the translator Rva; also the Toipa cave, the hermitage of saint Milarapa; and Chu-bar, the place were Milarapa died,—all these places lie on the Tibet-Nepal boundary. Close to them are the hermit-monasteries of Phel-gya-ling and Tar-gya-ling, in the neighbourhood of that grand and very lofty snowy mountain called Jomo-Kang-kar, and at the foot of Lap-chi-Kang, on the top of which dwell the five fairy sisters of long Life, the Tse-ring-chenga, the patrons of St. Milarapa. At the foot of Lap-chi-Kang, on the Tibetan side, are five glacial lakes, sacred to these five fairies, and each differs from the other in the colour of its water. To the north of these monasteries lies Kyema lake, one of the four great glacier lakes of Tibet . . . Travelling northward from Nyanam, one arrives at the foot of a lofty mountain named the Gung-Kang pass, which is guarded by the twelve she-devils called Tan-ma, who were bound by the spells of "The Lotus-born One" (the founder of Lamaism) to prevent the entry (this way) to Tibet from India of the enemies of Buddhism . . . After crossing the Gung Tang pass and going northwards, you arrive at the district of Tengri (Dingri) . . . A Chinese guard with Tibetan militia is posted at Tengri."

This description is generally confirmed and amplified by a curious Tibetan picture of this mountain, for a copy of which, as well as some notes on Everest, I am indebted to Mr. A. W. Paul, C. I. E. The Tibetans, as I some years ago noted, [51] worship Everest as the abode of the five celestial nymphs above named, who are supposed to confer long life—a cult which is also common to the Chinese and Japanese. The Tibetan pilgrims ascend its sides up to the glaciers for worship, and they also visit the tomb of the great high-priest of these deities of long-life—namely, the popular Saint Milarapa. In this picture the tomb of the saint is shown on the southern flanks of Everest, and the various temples and hermitages and shepherds' hamlets there. This bird's-eye view of the lower slopes of this little-known mountain gives interesting details of the tracks, rivers and bridges, and is inscribed with the name of the places. The summit of Everest is depicted conventionally by the Tibetan artist as ending in five snowy horns with their tips cloud-capped. In the vista to the north of this mountain is written Na-lam (a colloquial form of Nanam or Nyanam), in the top left-hand corner, and "Dingri District" in the top right-hand corner, which with several other known names fix its topographical position. [52]

Until, however, we obtain access to the Lap-chi-Kang range and directly confirm these identifications of the peaks on the spot, it would be premature to consider what should be the ultimate designation of the peak which is now known to our cartographers as "Everest"—whether or not it should be called by the hybrid term "*Kang-kar*-Everest."

The form of Everest has seldom been delineated. The reputed drawing of it by H. Schlagintweit which is treasured at the India Office was made from the peak of Tonglu, whence, as Colonel Tanner points out, this

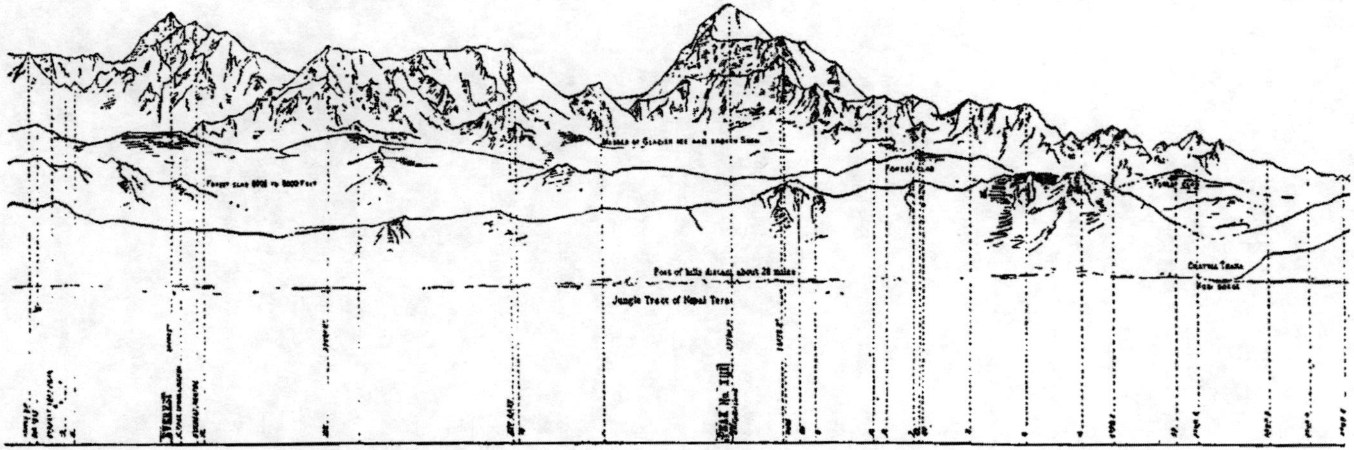

EVEREST AND "PEAK NO. XIII" from nearly due SOUTH, ON KOSI RIVER.

Lat. 26° 20' : long. 87° 5' (approx.).

(Distance of Everest about 114 miles, and "Peak XIII" about 117 miles.)

mountain is not even visible, nor is it scarcely visible from Faloot; and we have seen that the "Gauri-sankar" of the Nepalese is a different and much smaller mountain altogether. The usual authentic picture of Everest represents its peak as seen from Sandook-phu, a point from which it is 100 miles distant. This has already been shown in the preceding illustrations (pp. 331 and 342), and in the telescopic

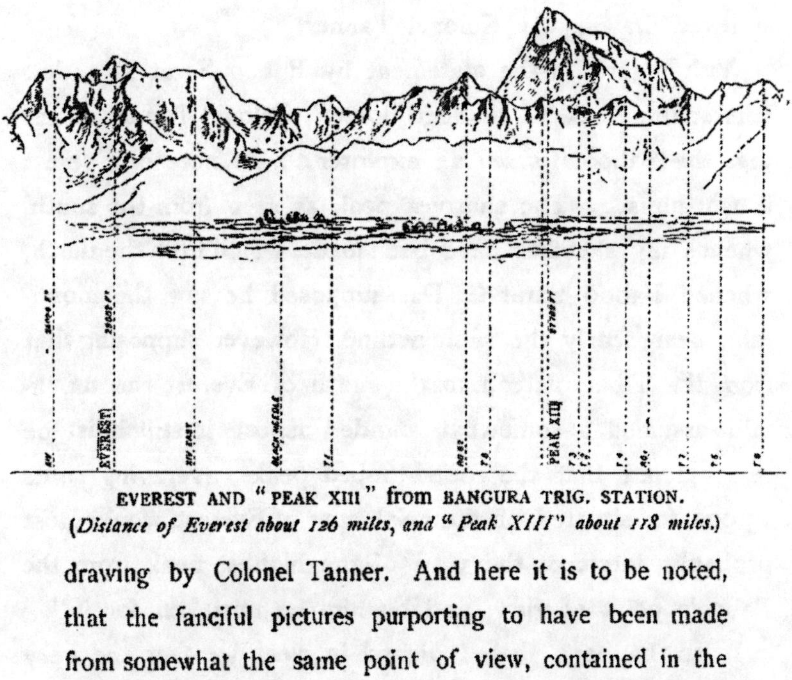

EVEREST AND "PEAK XIII" from BANGURA TRIG. STATION.
(*Distance of Everest about 126 miles, and "Peak XIII" about 118 miles.*)

drawing by Colonel Tanner. And here it is to be noted, that the fanciful pictures purporting to have been made from somewhat the same point of view, contained in the book entitled "Indian Alps", are quite unworthy of consideration, as portraits of this or any other of these peaks.

The shape of the peak of Everest, as seen from points further to the west in the Indian plains, is sharper and shows more details than from Sandook-phu. The accompanying two profiles of such views of it I reproduce from Colonel Tanner's careful telescopic sketches, as they give its outlines much more distinctly than the photographs which I took of it, when traversing that line of country at the foot of the Himalayas, from the north of Lucknow along the border of the Nepalese Terai to Sikhim. The Himalayas of Central Nepal as seen from the Someshwar range on the Gandak river are beautifully shown in the annexed drawing by Colonel Tanner.

With regard to the statement by Baboo Sarat Das, that "its summit" is "a rounded dome", Colonel Tanner writes that the Baboo "is *not* an explorer... his note on Everest is worthless... The sharpest peak as seen from the south, whence my sketches have been made, would from the north, whence Baboo Sarat C. Das supposed he saw the mountain, bear nearly the same outline. However, supposing that from the Tibet plateau to the north of Everest the mountain assumed a somewhat rounded aspect, it still must be remembered that the round-topped peaks, averaging some 25,000 ft., situated on the north spur of Everest, would most probably intercept the view of the highest peak from the Baboo's point of view, and by him be mistaken for it."

It so happens that I visited in clear weather the very spot whence the Baboo saw the view in question. His point of view was not at all north as Colonel Tanner believed, but the Semo pass, or in Lepcha "Sema-rum", to the west of the Kang La, about sixty-five miles E.S.E. of Everest, and it will be seen from the profile and description of that view,

NEPALESE CENTRAL HIMALAYAS FROM SOMESHWAR.

which I give in Chapter XI, p. 420, that the peak supposed by him to be Everest was certainly not that mountain, but the lower "Peak No. XIII." There also I give a sketch of the precipitous north-eastern face of Everest hitherto unfigured, and refer to several other, as yet unidentified, sacred mountains of Tibet, said to surpass Everest in height. Unfortunately, the travellers who have of late years visited Tibet have traversed a line of country too far to the north to throw light on this question of the mountains in this region, which are alleged to be higher than Mount Everest.

As to the possibility of anyone ever ascending Everest, a celebrated climber [53] says, "Considering how much more gradually the rarity (of the air) increases between 20,000 and 30,000 feet than it does at inferior levels, I have every confidence that the highest mountain in the world will, if Nature has not forgotten a ladder to it, be some day trodden by human foot".

CHAPTER X

THE SOUTHERN PEAKS AND GLACIERS OF THE KANCHEN-JUNGA GROUP

The frosted peaks of Chola gleamed
  Broken and bare and bold.
On the glittering crest of Kanchen' streamed
  The sunlight clear and cold.
The fleeting clouds brief shadows flung
On mighty Jannoo's brow, or hung
  On Pandim's forehead near.

C. Macaulay's *Lay of Lachen.*

THE southern glaciers of the Kanchen-junga group, and the outlying peaks of Kabru, Pandim, etc. have been approached, on the few occasions they have been visited, usually by way of the long and deep tropical valley of the Rangeet, with all its attendant discomforts of heat, bad roads, and insect-pests. I decided, therefore, to try the track along the cool ridge from Sandook-phu, as there was a good road and rest-houses for two stages beyond that point, without any dipping down into tropical forest, and only thrice apparently had part of this ridge beyond the last staging-house been traversed by Europeans, and the greater part of it not at all.

Leaving Darjeeling, on the 14th September, 1896, in a drizzle like a mild Scotch mist, that scarcely wetted us as we went, but brought the colour to our cheeks, and that cleared up every now and then to give us charming cloud effects, we found the walk through the woods to Jor-pokree and Tonglu more delightful than ever. The rich variety of dark greenery in the mossy dells and ferny grottoes under the giant moss-covered trees, luxuriant in the dripping dampness of this season, was relieved by the bright and velvety begonias, delicately pink and blue hydrangeas, orange gingers, and giant-stag moss which clambered over the bare cliffs of gneiss. We stopped often by the wayside to pick the black brambles, and higher up the red raspberries and barberries that overhung our path, keeping a sharp look-out for the leeches. And every here and there the wild cucumbers, trailing gracefully like vines, covered the shrubby undergrowth of *polygons* with a profusion of bright yellow blossoms. No less than two species of these cucumbers have been named after a former official of this district—it is something, perhaps, to be famous even from a gastronomic point of view.

It was still showery next day, and windy, as we pushed on to Sandook-phu through the rhododendron forest, which now was in seed; and we passed frequent clumps of holly, wild rose trees bearing brilliant scarlet hips, barberries blue and yellow, rowan trees with bunches of rusty red berries, and juicy red currants. And when we emerged on to the almost treeless grassy slopes of Sandook-phu we found them blue with the flowers of the deadly aconite. As we ascended this mountain, the rain stopped and gave us good views of the neighbouring hills, but no sight of the snows. In the afternoon the rain set in again, and

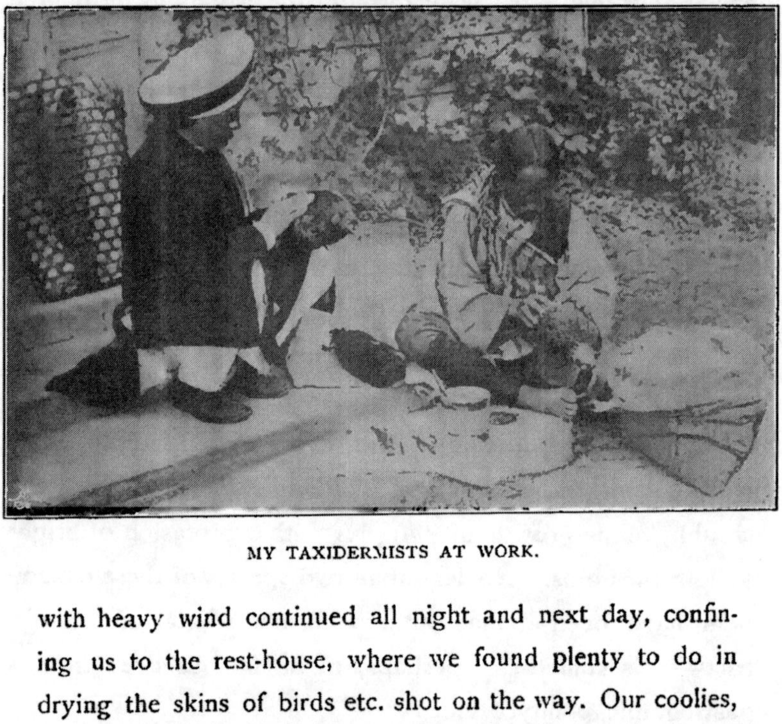

MY TAXIDERMISTS AT WORK.

with heavy wind continued all night and next day, confining us to the rest-house, where we found plenty to do in drying the skins of birds etc. shot on the way. Our coolies, mostly Tibetan Bhotiyas, amused themselves at various pastimes and games of strength, including pitching at a mark and putting the stone. At this last game, in trying to out-throw my men, I strained the muscles of my back badly, and was in agony for some hours. We were amused to find in the faces of these beardless sons of Tibet and Sikhim, despite their Mongolian cast of the eye, several absurd resemblances to Europeans. One whose features clearly suggested Lord Ripon we used to call "His Lordship"; and another, a young Lama, broad-jawed and deep-chinned, was so full of unvarying good humour and high spirits, that we involuntarily christened him "Pat".

We marched to Faloot next morning (the 18th), as the weather was clearing and giving splendidly crisp views of the snows. The following morning we witnessed at Faloot that striking aerial phenomenon, the Spectre of the Brocken. Wreaths of thin mist were rising and floating around us as we ascended the summit of this hill to see the sunrise, and a denser cloud of fog hung below us. On the surface of this last misty veil our shadows were projected by the rising sun as silhouettes, surrounded in concentric widening circles by first a dazzling white halo, then a rim of brilliant rainbow, and finally a secondary paler rainbow band. As we moved this apparition moved, and it stopped when we stopped. Altogether it seemed so supernatural that Kintoop and the other man, who was carrying my camera, threw themselves on the ground and muttered a prayer and some spells, and Kintoop declared that he had only seen it once in his life before, and that the Lamas say that it is an omen of great good fortune. I took two photographs of it, but the plates got accidentally spoiled. It lasted about half an hour, until the mist lifted. Our clothes were bedewed with the mist, and this may have contributed to the prismatic decomposition of the light. I have seen it several times when camping at the foot of the Himalayas, and in every case the sun was low, and there was a rainy mist, both between myself and the sun, and in the opposite direction, where the spectre appeared.

Beyond Faloot, the road zigzagged over the ridge down to a rocky tarn amongst the pines, where we got a bold foreground to the snowy range, and here I shot a woodcock and a solitary snipe. Thence we rose over the bare hill of Pang-ka (12,130 ft.), so called from the *Pang-ka* pasture grass which covers it.

This hill is erroneously called on the maps "Singalelah" after Hooker, who has also applied this name to the whole of this ridge that runs from Kanchen' to Darjeeling and the plains. It is always difficult to find the proper names of these uninhabited and little frequented places, as Hooker himself notes; and it is especially so when the traveller does not know the language, and the men who supply his information are not natives of the neighbourhood. The name intended by Hooker's informant, was, I fancy, "*Sing-le-lho*", or "The Slope of the Alder-tree," which is still the Lepcha name for the low-lying and insignificant part of the ridge at our next staging-house, which the Nepalese call "*Chow-banjan.*" As that, however, is a depression rather than a hill, and there is no such native name as "Singalelah," it is a pity that the latter name should be retained for this important southern offshoot of Kanchen-junga, which forms a well-defined water-parting: as the streams on its western side drain into the Ganges, and those of its eastern watershed flow into the Brahmaputra. A better name would be the "Kanchen'-Senchal" spur.

On the cold northern slopes of this grassy hill the rhododendrons creep up to the very summit in a dense tangle, through which the road descends and winds through some pine forest strewn with columnar cliffs of gneiss interspersed with bands of white quartz, like cyclopean masonry. We sighted a leopard and a wild boar, and passed the tracks of the *Serow* deer (*Nemorhædus bubalinus*) as we dipped to 10,320 ft., at the gap of Chow-banjan (the "*Chia-bhanjan*" of the maps), or "The Pass of the Edible Mushrooms", as this name means in the Nepalese. These plants are especially abundant here on the decayed trees. They are called by the Tibetans, *Shamo*, or "the hats", from their resemblance to Chinese caps. Our men gathered them in basketfuls and ate them cooked, with relish, but we found them tough and tasteless.

The wooden rest-house here was in a ruinous state, although it was relatively new, for I had seen it being built only five or six years before, and already it was tumbling to pieces in this rotting climate. By spreading the doors down over the least holey part of the rotten floor, riddled with ominous gaping holes, where previous occupants had sunk through, we managed to secure a corner for our chairs, though we had to shift these frequently to prevent them bodily disappearing with us.

A pass to Nepal leads down from here to the west, to the lower valley of Nepal, which Hooker threaded; and I was surprised to hear from some Nepalese who had been to Darjeeling on a prolonged visit, that they would each have to pay a considerable poll-tax on their return to Nepal, and have to undergo a ceremony of drinking water with an official in order to restore their caste, which they had lost by entering foreign territory: a sort of a re-initiation into their tribe.

Few Europeans have ever passed beyond this point, along the ridge; " for the road from here goes down at right angles on the Sikhim side to Pemiong-chi monastery. I felt some anxiety as to the track beyond this place, not only because Captain W. Sherwill, who in 1852 attempted to pass this way to the snows, had to turn back as he reported that his further progress was barred by a deep precipitous valley which he could not cross, but also because the existing maps were not very correct for this locality and did not show the route by which I was to go. I had got, however, for my guide the headman of the highest village in this part of Sikhim, Yampoong, who assured me that though the track was very rough and became more and more rugged as we approached the higher ranges, still it was practicable all the way up to the snows; and he added that no European had ever been over the greater part of the route by which we were going.

I pushed on from here on the morning of the 20th for the snows, in very light marching order, taking Kintoop and a few picked coolies carrying light loads slung up in blankets and waterproofs, and with two very light tents, as there are no more rest-houses nor villages.

A horribly uneven sheep-track led up the ridge, amongst shrubby rhododendrons and copses of wild rose bushes, and a few alders, which lower down are found in numbers, and give this hill-side its name of "Sing-le." It was like walking over spikes the greater part of the way, for miles; as the rugged rock here is a stratified gneiss that has been thrown up at a sharp angle of about 45°, with a dip to the N. E., and many of these knife-edges had been further sharpened by the splintering action of the frost, so that this constant stepping from knife-edges to spikes made our progress very tedious, and cut through the boots of many of our men, laming them badly.

When we had gone beyond the peak called Tim-dim-boo (11,780 ft.), with its tarns, and begun the next steep ascent, my guide, the headman, complained of giddiness and sat down, and I too was attacked. There was no headache, nor shortness of breath, but a faint feeling, and everything seemed to swim and tremble before my giddy eyes, and closing them did not relieve this sensation. It could not, I think, have been altogether due to the rarefied air, for the actual elevation was only about 12,000 feet. It was perhaps in some measure owing too ur rapid ascent, combined with the dazzling glare of the highly micaceous gneiss rock, that glanced brightly in the blazing sun. For, after a short rest and a drink of water, (as I always had a man with me carrying my water-bottle) and donning my dark goggles, a pair of which I gave to the guide, we were able to proceed.

Our toilsome progress along the narrow precipitous ridge grew monotonous, owing to the repeated stiff ascents and descents, and halts to recover breath; and the great clouds only lifted now and then to give us glimpses away down into the heart of Nepal.

The track ran along the Nepalese side of the frontier, under cliffs formed by the dip to the N. E., and past the hill of "Lambi", called on the map "Lampheram" (12,830), and, at the fourth mile, along some cliffs of gneiss with caves at the deserted grazing-station called Naya, whence the stream called the "Tawa" drains down into the Yang-wa, misnamed "Changthap" on the map. Across the Senden Pass we encamped at a rock on the southern base of Migo Hill, twelve and a half miles from Chowbanjan, by my pedometer, which was trustworthy.

On the way we met a few of that nomad tribe of Nepalese herdsmen, the Gooroongs, a shifting people, here to-day and away to-morrow, who live in rude bowers of leafy branches. I bought a sheep from them for our larder, and as it refused to come along, one of my coolies, although already heavily laden and exhausted, agreed to carry it in addition to his load; and he staggered along the precipices with it tied atop of his basket, quite happy in the prospect of receiving the lion's share of it, which had been promised to him.

We had been marching all day long, though making slow progress, till darkness set in, and with it rain, when we reached an overhanging rock in the forest, where we halted for the night. My men built up a ledge for my tent as there was no level ground, for the hillside sloped down precipitously for some thousands of feet at an angle of about 70°; and they themselves nestled under the rock. And though wet and weary by the harassing march, they all cheerfully worked away, helping one another to pitch the tent, to bring firewood and to fetch water, which last, as we were near the top of the ridge, was about half a mile down the mountain. I too had some discomforts, for my baggy tent leaked badly as it could not be pitched properly, and to keep myself dry I had to throw waterproofs over me as I reclined, and to get up now and then to shake my wraps to turn out scorpions and other insects more irritating than interesting. And more than once during the night I heard a tree blown down by the storm, with a crash like a pistol report.

In the morning it was freezing hard, and there was a glorious sunrise. Fresh snow had powdered the Dui pass, about four miles distant, and Kabru almost hid Kanchen' from sight, and the great cone of Chumo-lhari in Tibet appeared marvellously crisp and near; and lower down, I saw the monastery of Tashiding perched aloft upon the top of its isolated conical hill above the Rang-eet. Ascending the grassy hill of Migo (13,250 ft.), the view was much grander, though Everest was now completely hidden behind the crater-like Peak No. XIII. The track led down past the cliffs of Nego, a good halting-place with a small stream and splendid view. Thence obliquely down the valley, over giant flags of fine-grained gneiss like hardened slates or flags of paving-stones, lying almost flat with scarcely any dip, we descended till we struck the foaming Yang-wa; thence the path ascended a fine valley of pines, where I had a shot at a Monal pheasant, and thence up over a bleak moorland covered with dwarf juniper bushes, and dwarf

"PEAK XIII" from MIGO (13,250).

rhododendrons like bog-myrtle. Still further up a bare rocky defile, weirdly dotted with the tall cones of the giant rhubarb, we ascended to the pass of Ghara (14,000 ft.), amongst the crags of which, my guide said that he has shot the rare Himalayan giant wild sheep, the *Ovis ammon* (in Sikhimese "*Sha-pik*"), and the snow leopard, as well as musk-deer (in Sikhimese "*La-o*").

This guide is a fine, dignified, elderly man, a good specimen of the hardy Sikhimese Bhotiya. He has taken off his boots and walks barefooted on the stones. He shoots a good deal here, especially in the winter months, when the cold drives the animals down from the snowy passes, and he sends the skins and horns to Darjeeling for sale. He can shoot pretty straight too, for, yesterday, with my gun he shot two partridges and a flying squirrel on the way. He points out as we go, certain plants, and discourses on their healing virtues—one of them applied externally and internally was so valuable for broken limbs, that it was "better than all the hundred and eight great remedies put together." He gave me a large piece of turquoise-coloured stone, and asked me if I thought it was really turquoise. It was evidently quartzite covered over with a thin coating of that brilliant verdigris-coloured copper ore, "malachite." On my telling him this, he said that a great mass of this green rock towered up a hundred feet high about a mile below his village.

From this pass we continue northwards along the Sikhim side of the frontier, over open bare undulating pasture land, often without any track, until we reach "The Tiger Pass" (*Tag-La*), about 14,350 ft., with its large tarn, when we curve round to the east, immediately under the snow-covered Dui Pass, over which we now should go. But at the pressing invitation of our guide, who is the headman of this place and who says that no European has ever been to his village before, I descend to his Yak farm at Yampoong, although it is about a mile down off our route, and I am glad once more to be again amongst the yaks and their Tibetan herdsmen.

Yampoong is a summer grazing-station for yaks, and lies on the open undulating grassy slopes above the limit of trees, and considerably below the line of perpetual snow. It affords excellent pasturage and is well watered by perennial streams. It contains several marshy flats, a sort of silted up "corries." When the winter sets in the yaks are driven to warmer quarters farther down this valley of the Ringbi. The village contains only three houses, the largest of which is the headman's. It is a two-storeyed stone building with a shingle roof, and the upper storey is occupied by our host and his family. Ascending the substantial winding stair, I found a huge log fire blazing on the stone hearth in the middle of the room, and around it were the members of his family. These made way for my cook, a brother of Achoom, who quickly took up his position there, and commenced to boil some water for tea, preparatory to his culinary operations for a more substantial meal; and the best corner of the room was cleared for me. I had to sit on the floor of rough-hewn logs, as there was no chair or stool; but what I missed most was a table, it being by no means easy for a European to eat off the floor, sitting level with one's food; and the smoke of the fire caused my eyes to smart badly, as there was neither chimney nor window.

I gave the headman some of my infused tea, sweetened with sugar and tinned milk, (as the yaks were not yet milked) in an empty soup tin; and after tasting it, he handed it round the family for each member down to the lowest menial to take a sip, for these people share their little comforts freely with each other. This sweetened tea,

SHAR-PA BHOTIYAS.

which was certainly different from their own salted and buttered brick tea, was unanimously pronounced to be delicious; but a few spoonfuls of my scanty store of whiskey which I gave them, was declared to be much more so. They were eating cakes made of buckwheat, harsh and somewhat acid and bitter to the taste. I gave them a few trifling presents.

The Yak-herds are Nepalese Tibetans, that is Tibetans who have settled for some generations in Eastern Nepal, in the provinces called Shar-Kambu and Waloong, and they are known as "Shar-pa Bhotiyas." They are big, deep-voiced men like the Tibetans in general, and dress like them. Their women usually dress a little in the Nepalese style. They often wear their hair in a loose knot, and not done up into a pigtail; and their dress is a coarse woollen cloth, a kind of tartan, coloured blue, red, green and yellow.

Whilst dinner was getting ready, and as the weather was clear, I ascended the hill some distance to get a peep at the eastern slopes of the Kanchen' range, which have been visited to some extent by several travellers—whereas I was now bound for the unexplored western slopes of these snows. The mighty Kanchen', under twenty miles distant, was almost hidden from view by the bold southern end of Kabru, which rose up only about thirteen miles off, and Pandim about twelve.

These two last mountains as well as the eastern glaciers of Kanchen' can be reached from here in three to four days, *via* Jongri and the Guicha pass. Several Europeans have visited the former since Major James Sherwill's journey there in 1861, and they, like him, took the most direct road to Jongri, namely, up the hot valley of the Great Rang-eet river to its source amongst the glaciers; and this is now certainly much the best and quickest route, since a good riding-road has just been made to Pemiong-chi monastery, on this route, which enables the glaciers to be reached comfortably in five to seven days from Darjeeling. And as these glaciers lie amidst some of the grandest scenery in the whole of the Himalayas, I have no doubt that many visitors to Darjeeling will gladly visit them when they realize how accessible they now are.

Jongri (13,140 ft.), which is a small summer yak-station of two houses, like this place Yampoong, from which it is distant about eight miles N. E., was visited by Dr. Hooker, who so admirably describes both it and the journey thither from Pemiong-chi monastery. He likens the view of Kanchen' from thereabouts to the view of Mt. Blanc from Chamonix, but he was prevented ascending beyond Jongri by the snow in the depth of winter. Major *James* Sherwill (not *W.* S. who attempted the other route) was the first traveller to visit and describe the glaciers of this valley. [55] He visited them in November, and says that the path led through the grandest scenery up the river (Praig) to the glaciers of Kabru at the grazing-station of Aluktang, which the Lamas visit in the rains to worship Mt. Kanchen': "The grandeur of the surrounding snow-clad mountains and the wildness of the scenery of the valley of the Ratong (Praig) surpasses anything of the kind I have elsewhere witnessed in the Himalayas. On looking directly north up the valley, Kanchen-junga rose majestically above everything else. Between us and it, thrown completely across the valley and only two miles distant, was seen a stupendous moraine, a thousand feet high, which forms the conspicuous object seen from Darjeeling. Immediately on our right, rose a long range of perpetually snow-clad mountains, running parallel with the valley, culminating in the glacier-flaked peaks of Kabui Kang (19,450 ft.), and to the north Ting-ching-Kang, to the west of which rose the formidable peak of Pandim, 22,015 ft. in height, at the base of which rests the glacier above alluded to, and many other masses of debris washed down from above, in wild confusion. To our rear, winding its course down the broad

PANDIM
from Tong-Shyong-Tam.

valley, the hills on either side covered with dense fir forests, was the noisy foaming Ratong."

Pandim proved too formidable for Mr. Graham and his two trained Swiss guides. He says that they purposed "to attack it from the north, but, on reconnoitring, we found it quite impracticable. I do not know of any more formidable peak. On the west side it drops sheer, while the other three are guarded by the most extraordinary overhanging glaciers, which quite forbid any attempt.... the same applies to Narsing ('The Uplifted Nose')." The name "Pandim" or "Panden" means in Lepcha, "The King's Minister", as it is considered to be an attendant on the King of mountains, Kanchen'.

To resume the ascent to the Guicha pass, Major Sherwill goes on to say: "Having ascended the immense mass of debris forming the moraine, probably at an elevation of 15,000 ft., we found ourselves, to our great surprise, standing on the top of a stupendous glacier. This huge mass of ice and debris descending from the Pandim mountain extends nearly across the valley, where it is met by, and abuts upon, another glacier equally vast in its dimensions, and formed at the base of (Kabru and) the other snow-clad mountains on the western side of the valley, the two together forming a complete barrier across the valley and choking it up to the height of a thousand feet or more. The moraine forming the retaining wall to this mass of moving ice and debris is composed of rounded and angular blocks of highly contorted gneiss, intermixed with pieces of syenite, micaceous schist, coarse granite quartz with

GLACIER AT THE GUICHA PASS.

tourmaline crystals, white and pink quartz often containing veins of crystallized felspar, and coarse gravel and debris.

Proceeding onwards, the glacier presented a perfect wilderness of blocks of ice invariably covered with the stones and debris brought down from the mountain above by avalanches, with deep crevasses through which the sound of running water was heard. A little way up the valley, beyond where the glaciers meet, we observed a small lake. Although the surrounding hills were literally covered with glaciers of all sizes, and the valleys overhung with masses of ice and snow, we observed only one avalanche, but frequent loud cracking of the ice during the hottest part of the day.... Mounting over the two glaciers and proceeding by the lake 500 yards long by 100 broad, we ascended another immense moraine, which confined a third glacier on the west side of the valley descending from Kochirang-Kang, on the south-eastern shoulder of Kabru (24,015 ft.). This one appeared to begin nearly on a level with the top of the mountain range, at probably 20,000 feet, then descending by the mountain side, came sweeping along the valley in a curve about a mile in length, the more elevated portion being formed of masses of ice covered with snow, rising in steps one above the other, and the lower portion presenting a sea of broken masses of ice covered with snow and debris. A more stupendous mass of ice and snow it is scarcely possible to conceive. Descending from the glacier, we proceeded for a mile, occasionally along the dry smooth bed of the Ratong, (past a silted-up lake, Chemtang, 15,250 ft.,) and over frozen snow, when we arrived at the fourth and last great glacier, equal in extent to the others." On reaching the northern extremity of this glacier, he arrived at the *Guicha*, or "The Locked pass"—so called, as the legend has it, because it was locked against man by the spells of a saintly Lama.

The view from this Guicha pass is thus described by Major Sherwill. "We found ourselves standing on the watershed between Kanchen' and the Pandim, Kabroo, and Junnoo ranges to the south and west. We were at an elevation of about 18,500 ft. (? 16,430), and had we proceeded farther, we should have had to descend into what appeared to us a perpetually snow-covered valley. Kanchen' stood apart, unconnected with any of the high mountain ranges to the south. The nearest spot not covered with snow in its southernmost spur was probably not more than a mile and a half or two miles distant, the stratification of which was clearly visible. Its formation is probably of gneiss, not of a contorted type, and which has a dip of 20° to 25° to the east. Others may determine the interesting point of its geological structure, but this important fact was elicited—namely, that Kanchen' is detached from the other mountains forming the Kanchen' group, and that none of its waters find their way into the Great Rang-eet," as Hooker supposed.

The south-eastern glacier of Kanchen' to the north of this pass was visited by Mr. W. Graham on March 31st, 1883. He writes: — "We crossed the pass, rather over 16,000 feet, and descended first to a level bit of grass land

KANCHEN-JUNGA: SOUTH-EAST FACE
from Tong-Shyong (17,000 feet).

containing five small tarns, and then a further descent to the great glacier, which flows almost due east from Kanchen'. Right above us rose the towering crags of Siniolchum (?Simvovonchum), behind us lay Kabru and Pandim, so that we were absolutely surrounded by the snowy giants."

EASTERN GLACIER OF KANCHEN-JUNGA
from Tong-Shyong (17,000 feet).

The stupendous glittering spire of the south-eastern face of Kanchen' as seen to the north of this pass, is beautifully shown on page 381 from a photograph by Mr. White, who also took the other fine photographs here reproduced to illustrate this region. Its south-eastern glacier is also seen. These photographs show that the great precipice below this southern pinnacle of Kanchen' (27,820 ft.) is likely to prove an insuperable obstacle to any attempted ascent from the south; but the north-eastern slopes by way of the Zemu glacier or across the "Gap, 19,300 feet", look more hopeful; and in the opinion of Mr. Freshfield these photographs show that there is here possibly a route not steeper than that up Mont Blanc from Chamonix. Here, too, there is obviously a "Grand Plateau" at the base of the final crest.

Mr. Graham, describing Kanchen' from a climber's point of view, says, "I do not call it impossible, but improbable in the highest degree. The peak runs east and west like a wall, the two *arêtes* being the most frightful imaginable. From the south nothing but a fly could make the ascent, as it is overhung in two or three places. From the north it is one continuous slope of rock and ice at a mean angle of 50 and more than 15,000 ft. of rise".

The north-eastern glacier of Kanchen' which descends the Zemu valley already referred to, is about sixteen miles long, which is the longest in Sikhim.

The geological position of Kanchen' is obviously in the main axis of the Himalayas, although that mountain lies considerably to the south of the line of water-parting between the Tibetan plateau and India, and on a spur which runs at right angles to this line, so that even the drainage of its *northern* slopes flows directly down into the Indian plains. Still Kanchen', nevertheless, may be regarded as lying upon, and forming part of, the true main axis or back-bone of the Himalayas, and its position to the south of the present water-parting may be accounted for by its northern drainage finding its way through a gap in the main axis, left by interruptions of the force which elevated the Himalayas; while the basin to the north has become further deepened by erosion of the Tibetan plateau. Thus several of the great Tibetan rivers, such as the Gandak, Kosi and Arun, appear to pierce the main chain of the Himalayas (*vide* my map on p. 349), and even the Tsang-po itself and the Indus turn round the ends of the range to escape into the Indian Ocean.

In the upheaval of the Himalayas there appear to be three main lines of elevation running more or less parallel. The middle of these lines or axes, the so-called "*Central* Himalayas", contains the highest peaks, and runs through Kanchen' by Jannu to Everest etc. The line of the "*Northern* Himalayas" bounds the southern side of the Tsang-po and Upper Indus valleys—immediately north of which the ranges have been named the "*Trans*-Himalayas" (see p. 349). The line running through Tonglu, including Senchal and Darjeeling, Tendong, Lingtu etc., forms the "*Southern* or Outer Himalayas". And the small outlying detached range of sandstone hills, the "*Siwaliks*", running from Dehra Doon by Someshwar to Sookna, have been called the "*Sub*-Himalayas". Such nomenclature should be remembered in referring to the different portions of these enormous ranges of mountains which collectively go by the name of the Himalayas, if we would avoid unnecessary confusion or ambiguity.

The rocky structure or formation of the back-bone of

the Himalayas, as seen in Kanchen', seems to consist mainly of white granitic rock and quartz in the loftier crests, and of crystalline schists in the lower, through which latter numerous veins and sheets of molten granite and gneiss have been extruded. Some of the peaks, such as "No. XIII and D[1]", are suggestively like extinct craters, and the numerous hot springs in the higher ranges attest the present existence of latent volcanic activity in these regions. The highest peak of Kanchen-junga and the true summit, (28,150 ft.) is called by the Tibetans "The Repository of Gold." This name, it seems to me, has arisen from the interpretation of the popular name of this mountain in too literal and mythological a manner. The name Kanchen-junga is Tibetan and means, literally, "The Five Repositories of the Great Glaciers," and it is physically descriptive of its five peaks. When, however, the patron saint of Sikhim wrote the manual of worship for this mountain-god he converted these five "repositories" into real storehouses of the god's treasure, and the god himself was represented as a form of the Buddhist God-of-Wealth, as is figured at page 217. In this way the loftiest crest, which was most conspicuously gilded by the rising and setting sun, was made the treasury of gold; the southern peak which remained in cold grey shade till it whitened in the rising sunlight was made the treasury of silver, and the remaining peaks were made respectively the treasuries of gems, grain and holy books—the chief objects worth treasuring, in the opinion of the religious Tibetans.

The worship of this mountain-god, which dates back to

long before the Buddhist period, is celebrated with great pomp every year throughout Sikhim. It is of the devil-dancing or Shamanist kind. The Lamas dress themselves in the costumes of the pre-Buddhist Tibetan religion, the so called "*Bon*", and carry out the ritual of the devil-dancers, as seen in the accompanying photograph, where

WORSHIP OF THE GOD OF KANCHEN-JUNGA.

our friend, the young Lama of Phodang who so hospitably entertained us, is seated in state to receive the offerings from the people, of money, jewellery etc., to defray the cost of these ceremonies.

The Lepcha name of this mountain is *Kong-lo-chu*, or "The Highest Screen or Curtain of the Snows."

It was from Jongri, too, that Mr. W. Graham made his famous ascent of the peak which he believed to be Kabru, and also of the Kang-La pass. Leaving Darjeeling on the 23rd March, 1883, with a Swiss guide, he reached Jongri on the 29th, and calculated that in that distance of forty-two miles, as the crow flies, the road ascended 23,000 ft. and descended some 16,000 feet in vertical height to reach Jongri (13,140 ft.).

In the second visit in September he climbed Jubonu (21,400 ft.). Of this he writes:—"Early on the 30th September, 1883, we started for Jubonu, which lies immediately east of our camp. At 2 p.m. we had reached a suitable place, well above snow-line, and camped there. Height by aneroid was 18,300, and though absolute reliance cannot be placed on such uncorrected observations, I think that at least 18,000 may be taken as correct. We got off at earliest dawn the next day, *i.e.* at 4-30, and settled down to our work at once, leaving the coolies behind. The snow was in good order, and Kauffmann led the way at a great pace. He is, I believe, generally admitted to be the fastest step-cutter living, and this day and afterwards he fairly surpassed himself. The glacier was crowned with steep rocks which formed the edge of a noble amphitheatre formed by Jubonu and Nursing. We were now on the peak itself, and proceeded to cut up a steep snow *couloir.* This gradually got steeper, till we were forced to take to the rocks. With the exception of one place, which greatly resembled the celebrated Chimney on the Matterhorn, we got along very well till we reached the final crags, which rose some 300 feet above us. We now turned northwards along the slopes of the glacier which swept down from the rocks. Fortunately there was an incipient *bergschrund*, and we passed along in this to the north side, whence a short but exceedingly steep slope of *névé* led us to the summit, which we reached at 11 a.m., without a halt. This was incomparably the hardest ascent we had in the Himalaya, owing to the great steepness of the glacier work." [56]

His celebrated ascent of the peak, which he believed to be Kabru, 24,015 feet—the ascent of which, if proved, would be the highest point hitherto reached by any mountaineer—has been disbelieved by the Indian surveyors. His ascent is thus described by himself: "On the third of October we examined carefully the east of Kabru, and made all preparations for an assault. On the 6th we finally started, and made our way up the eastern glacier of Kabru. On its banks we met with immense quantities of Edelweiss, the climber's flower, and success was prophesied accordingly. Up the highest moraine I have seen, fully 800 ft., brought us right under the east cliff of Kabru. There was only one route to the higher slopes, and that we could not find in the mist. Heavy snow fell, and we camped where we were. Next day we found our opening, and worked up it. We three went on ahead, and pushed straight up the face of the ridge, intending, if possible, to camp on the summit. This we reached at midday, but found that we were cut off from the true peak by a chasm in the *arête*, so that we were on a detached buttress. We descended, met the coolies ascending, and turned north along the steep snow slope, finding at last a small ledge just big enough to accommodate the Whymper tent.

"This was, I think, the highest camp we had, being certainly 18,500 ft. The night, however, was mild, and the coolies, who were very tired, preferred to stay up, instead of descending as before. We were off next morning at 4-30, and found at once all our work cut out for us. The very first thing was the worst. A long *couloir* like a half-funnel, crowded with rocks, had to be passed. The snow was lying loose, just ready to slide, and the greatest possible care had to be taken to avoid an avalanche. Then a steep ice slope led us to a snow incline, and so to the foot of the true peak. Here we had nearly 1,000 ft. of most delightful rockwork, forming a perfect staircase. At ten we were at the top of this, and not more than 1,000 ft. above was the eastern summit. A short snack, and then came the tug of war. All this last slope is pure ice, at an angle of 45 deg. to nearly 60 deg. Owing to the heavy snow and the subsequent frost, it was coated three or four inches deep with frozen snow, and up this coating we cut. I am perfectly aware that it was a most hazardous proceeding, and in cold blood I should not try it again, but only in this state would the ascent have been possible in the time. Kauffman led all the way, and at 12-15 we reached the lower summit of Kabru, at least 23,700 ft. above sea-level.

"The glories of the view were beyond all compare.

North-west, less than seventy miles, lay Mount Everest, and I pointed it out to Boss, who had never seen it, as the highest mountain in the world. 'That it cannot be,' he replied; 'those are higher'—pointing to two peaks which towered far above the second and more distant range, and showed over the northern slope of Everest. I was astonished, but we were all agreed that in our judgment, the unknown peaks, one rock and one snow, were loftier. Of course, such an idea rests purely on eyesight; but looking from such a height, objects appear in their true proportions, and we could distinguish perfectly between the peaks of known measurements, however slight the differences. However, we had a short view, for the actual summit was connected with ours by a short *arête*, and rose about 300 ft., of the steepest ice I have seen. We went at it, and after an hour and a half we reached our goal. The summit was cleft by three gashes, and into one of these we got. The absolute summit was little more than a pillar of ice, and rose some thirty of forty feet above us still, but, independently of the extreme difficulty and danger of attempting it, we had no time. A bottle was left at our highest point, and we descended. The descent was worse than the ascent, and we had to proceed backwards, as the snow might give way at any moment. At last we reached the rocks and there fixed a huge Bhotiya flag, and finally turned into camp at ten. The ascent was dangerous rather than difficult, but without the new snow the difficulties would have been enormously increased."

Commenting on this ascent, Sir Martin Conway writes to me:—"The question of Mr. Graham's ascent of a big mountain in Sikhim is a very difficult one. His recorded sensations, and those of his companion, are not compatible with his having reached an altitude exceeding 20,000 ft. It was the unanimous opinion of the Indian officers and members of the Survey with whom he conversed shortly after his ascent, that his observations were not consistent with an ascent of Kabru. The natives who saw him on the mountain said that it was not Kabru he climbed, but another and much lower peak. I believe he stated that his aneroid read about 24,000 feet on the top. Knowing as we now do, and as at that time was not known, how aneroids behave at high altitudes, this is a further proof that his peak must have been many thousand feet less than 24,000 feet in height.. All this implies no attack upon Mr. Graham's veracity. He carried no instruments, and made no observations for position. He merely believed that the peak climbed was Kabru. Nothing is easier than to make a mistake in such a case. It is only when an observer's position is determined and confirmed by a series of observations, and his altitude measured either by trigonometrical measurement or observations with a mercurial barometer, that it is possible to be sure where he has been. Mr. Graham doubtless climbed a difficult and high peak, but it cannot, in my opinion, have been Kabru or anything like the altitude of Kabru. Your suggestion that it may have been Kang-tsen (a ridge of Kabru, 2,000 ft. less in height) is well worthy of consideration."

Colonel Tanner, who has specially studied the forms of the higher peaks of the Himalayas, says, "Your Kang-tsen appears to have the sharp knife-edge crest demanded by Graham's account, and I think it very probable in the light thrown on the neighbouring topography by your photograph, that Kang-tsen is what he ascended. He would never have omitted to describe the wonderful table-land which occupies the summit of Kabru, had he ascended that position after the fearful climb necessary for surmounting its awful sides." This table-land on the top of Kabru is seen in Colonel Tanner's drawing at p. 395; and, curiously, this characteristic feature is, I find, denoted in the Lepcha name for "Kabru", which means "The Straight Snow-level" (*Nan-tam-chu*).

This point is further referred to in connection with my visit to Kang-la Pass and Kang-tsen, in the next chapter.

CHAPTER XI

TO KANG PASS FOR THE WESTERN GLACIERS OF KANCHEN-JUNGA AND FOR JANNU—NEPALESE JEALOUS EXCLUSIVENESS

WHILST something is thus known of the general features of the eastern peaks and glaciers of the Kanchen-junga group, almost nothing practically is known of the western, as these lie within the jealously guarded territory of Nepal, which has not been visited by Europeans. For Hooker, the only European who has travelled in Eastern Nepal, passed somewhat too low down to see them, and Mr. Graham, whose claims to have scaled Kabru are disputed, has recorded only the brief and general note above quoted.

In my attempt to see a little of this western side of the peaks,—the distant telescopic profile of which, by Colonel Tanner, is given on page 395—I experienced much difficulty in getting a guide to show me over the pass to the Nepalese side of the range, as the natives of these parts dread the pains and penalties that the Nepalese rulers inflict on all who impart information, or assist Europeans in gaining information, concerning the country or the people. Ultimately, however, a Tibetan trader from Waloong (the Walloon-choon of Hooker) in Nepal, who chanced to be at Yampoong, and who knew the tracks well, was prevailed on by Kintoop, for a small present, to guide us

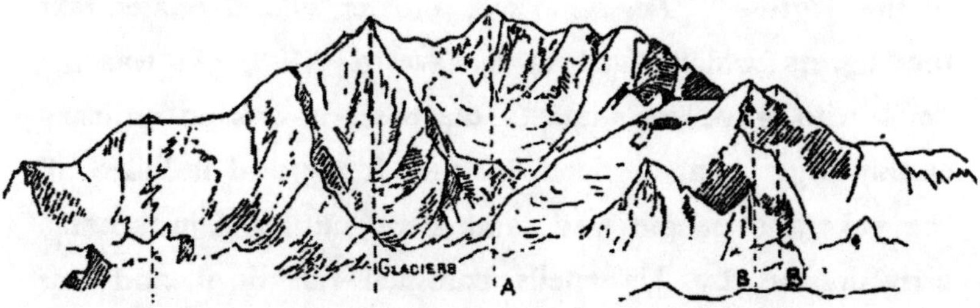

KANCHEN-JUNGA FROM THE WEST.
A. Highest crest of Kanchen'. B, B[1]. Kabru.

over, and keep above the inhabited part of the Nepalese valleys.

On the 22nd September, 1896, I set out from Yampoong in company with this guide—who was rugged and hard, like his own rugged hills,—and the headman of that village, seven coolies under Kintoop, and three yaks, of which two were for the baggage or riding, and one as meat for the camp.

The ascent of about two miles to the bare rocky "Pass of the Devil" (*Dui-La*) was easy walking, over great sheets of gneiss like paving-stones, as this stratified rock was almost horizontal here. We passed on the way a rude trap for a snow-leopard. It was baited with the leg of a yak, and constructed of the large stone-flags of the place, on the principle of a school-boy's box-trap of bricks and slate for catching birds. Only here, the falling door was a massive paving-stone, weighing about a quarter of a ton, and intended to crush the beast to death.

Just below the pass was a rocky tarn called "The Lake of the Tigress" (*Tag-mo Tso*); and its legend related that the tigress which lived in a cave on its banks was the devil who gave its name to the pass. It was no ordinary earthly tiger, but a fiend in that form; and it killed all the yaks and people who came here, until a saintly Lama arrived, and by his spells banished this devil, and now every passer-by puts a stone on the cairn in the pass, to commemorate this happy event.

On penetrating the pass (14,900 ft.), our track wound past several plants of the giant rhubarb and the woolly aromatic balls of *Saussurea,* along the eastern shoulder of the ridge for about 1½ miles, over flags of gneiss permeated by veins of quartz, amongst blocks of coarse crystalline grey granite, and under an overhanging cliff called "The Falling Rock" (*Dang-bya'bir*), which was a favourite haunt of wild sheep, according to my guide. Here I went off the track to see on the left a wild tarn, nearly a mile in length, called "The Loch of Everlasting Life" (*Tse' pag-med Tso*), and reputed to contain fabulous gems; the Nepalese call it "The Lake of Good Luck" (*Luckee-pokree*).

Rounding a corner to the north, at the Oma Pass

(15,320 ft.), we came suddenly into snow, and a magnificent view of the Kanchen' range burst on our eyes. Kanchen' with Kabru seemed quite near, the top of the latter was within twelve miles' distance; but they were fast clouding over ere I got my camera ready, for I had sprained my ankle slightly, and was riding on the spare yak. Still I

CROSSING OMA PASS ON A YAK.

secured the accompanying photograph of the Kang pass. A steep descent of about 3,000 feet in three miles, led down through a gloomy gorge lined with landslips, to the deserted yak-station of Gamo-tang.

This precipitous gorge was infested a few years ago by a gang of Tibetan brigands. They murdered and robbed the traders and others who laboriously threaded the narrow neck of this gorge—by rolling down rocks upon them, and then rushing out and despatching any still left alive. They had emissaries resident at Darjeeling who kept them advised not only of the traders' movements, but also of the police who were sent on their track; and it required the conjoint efforts of the military police of Nepal and Darjeeling for some years to disperse them. Only a few were captured, and these were hanged. I myself had seen the tree on the Nepal frontier where one of them was hanged about a year before, little thinking that I should ever visit the scene of their exploits. Several of the band were still at liberty, and the headman of Yampoong, who pointed out their former eyrie, high up on the crags, and the places of their ambuscade, said that travel hereabouts was still unsafe on this account, and that when he and others had to go this way, they armed themselves and formed a big party.

From this dark defile of the brigands we emerged on to a pretty mountain-girt dell, Ġamo-tang, or "The Level Mead" (12,550 ft.), through which the crystal water of the little Rathong river rushed noisily over a pebbly bed, fringed with trailing willows and sedges. I pitched my tent on the bank of the stream, near the deserted hut of the yak-herdsmen, of which latter my men took possession. This small meadow was a charming spot in the bright sunshine. On all sides bold rugged cliffs rose above the pine woods, up to snow-tipped peaks. Below these patches of snow, the face of the dripping rocks, wet with the melting snow, glittered and gleamed like mirrors in the sunlight. And a curious wintry effect was produced by several cascades that slid and tumbled down the white quartz and granite cliffs, forming broad white streaks, beyond the dark pines, a thousand feet in length.

This pretty meadow, now so desolate, was once a thriving settlement; and my friend of Yampoong pointed out traces of the fields of buckwheat which had flourished here in his grandfather's day, but now were overgrown by the young pine woods. The prosperity of the place, said he, was owing to a holy milk-white bull-yak that had miraculously appeared and roamed over these hillsides. It was reputed to be an incarnation of the mountain-god Kanchen' himself, and it acted as a luck-commanding talisman, like the Mascotte. When this lucky yak deserted these haunts all sorts of disaster followed. The Nepalese invaded Sikhim. Then a deadly pestilence broke out amongst the yaks, and all the people who ate the flesh of the dead beasts, and they comprised nearly everyone in the village, died. Thereupon the survivors fled, in the belief that a malignant devil had taken possession of the place. No one returned for many years, and even now the spot is only occupied as a grazing-station for a few weeks in the summer time.

I went after some partridges and pheasants that I heard calling in the thick cover, and got one partridge. During my absence the young yak had been killed, and amongst the portions reserved for me, were the tongue and the heart, which are esteemed especial delicacies.

At night the fear of the brigands weighed heavily on our little camp. All lights and cooking fires were put out at dusk, so as not to reveal our position, and Kintoop came to my small tent with two trustworthy men as sentries. They mounted guard with their knives, at the door *inside* the tent, as the temperature outside was below the freezing point. In this rough exposed life, it is needless to say that I had for some days given up the vulgar habit of undressing before retiring for the night. My bed consisted of a blanket spread over springy pine-branches, and under my pillow and alongside me were laid my revolver and gun. But when Kintoop drew his ugly knife and laid it down beside him on a corner of my couch, I felt some misgivings lest he should, in a night-mare, mistake me in the dark for one of the dreaded robbers. The night, however, passed without mishap. I slept soundly, fatigued by the day's marching, and was only awoke once or twice by the high wind shaking the tent.

At daybreak the temperature registered 3° Fahr. of frost, slight snow had fallen, and the tent was frozen stiff as cardboard. So cold was the wind that a young eagle fell dead a few yards from my tent, the shaggy coats of our yaks glistened with a thick coating of ice spangles, and one of our men seemed to have caught acute inflammation of the lungs; he was delirious with high fever. I gave him some medicine, and Kintoop had to leave one of our already small party to look after him, or as Kintoop grimly put it: "to feed him and sacrifice to the devils for him, and if he died to bury him."

Fording the stream on boulders and following it up towards its source at the Chabab pass, over which we had to cross into Nepal, we rose, in about a mile and a half, up out of the region of trees, through stunted bushes of juniper to the deserted yak-hut of Bogto (13,350 ft.). The grassy shoulder on which it lay, about 600 feet above the river, was somewhat suggestive of an old moraine, though no glaciers now existed in this valley; nor did the stream evidently contain any glacier water from sources higher up.

In this lonely hut of Bogto, I was told, the young daughter of a wealthy Sikhimese, with her maid, had halted about sixteen years ago on their way to Tibet, about a month later in the season than we had come. A heavy snow-storm not only prevented them from proceeding, but cut off their retreat as well, and the unfortunate damsels died here of starvation. Some of their bones were still strewn about the place, and their skulls had been made, by my guide, into drums for summoning the devils.

Pursuing our track up the valley, we flushed several *Monal* pheasants, which characteristically flew downwards, as we passed through the stunted junipers, pruned low by the cutting wind, and we emerged on the bleak uplands. Here bears were to be found, it was said, but few or no wild sheep, on account of some poisonous grass that grew there. We passed several tempest-swept tarns variously coloured red, black, and green, and named accordingly. They were the reputed abode of Caliban-like spirits. Near these bare lochs a few butterflies still hovered over the last few flowers of summer, at an elevation of over 14,000 feet. The most numerous were the silvery spotted "Queen of Spain" (Fritillary).

The opposite side of the valley, rising steeply with its knife-edge ridge, was called "The Black Tiger Hill" (*Tak-ri-nag-po*), and certainly its long undulating outline and its crest picked out with snow did suggest a reclining tiger. The body of the beast was formed by the black lichen-covered granitic gneiss, which was broadly striped with the white veins of granite and by the shoots of the disintegrating granite crags above. And a columnar formation of the rock outlined the shoulder, haunches and paws.

The valley suddenly opened out, about four miles above Bogto, into a broad rounded rocky basin, evidently of glacial formation, and surrounded by an amphitheatre of rugged snow-streaked peaks; on the one side the Kanchen' Senchal ridge, pierced by the Chabab pass about 2 miles off, and on the other a spur of Kang-La and Kabru, which latter peak towered close above us, on our right.

This bleak rocky basin was strewn with great white blocks of quartz and light grey granite, the white patches of which, uncovered by bronzing lichens, must give this landscape a snowy wintry aspect even in summer.

A weird lake lay in this wild setting, under the white horn of the Kang-La snows to our right. It was called "The Enchanted Lake of the Peacock's Tail" (*Tso Dom-dong-ma*); and from its blue transparent depths there gleamed several large spots of brilliant turquoise. This peculiar appearance, which gave the lake its name, was due to the great blocks of dazzling white quartz which studded its dark-blue bed. It was evidently a "Corrie", or a lake formed in the dammed-up end of the latest moraine of a glacier

"THE ENCHANTED LAKE OF THE PEACOCK'S TAIL"
(TSO DOM-DONG-MA.)

which had come down from the Kang-La peaks, but which had now disappeared. The evidence of glacial action here was such as is rarely met with in the Himalayas. The smooth face of the projecting cliff to our left, which had abutted into the glacier, was scooped out, scratched and scored in characteristic fashion for a considerable distance, about twenty feet above the present level.

The spirits of this haunted lake were, of course, worshipped by my men. These spirits, said they, were dragons who occasionally appeared to men in the form of furious bull-yaks, or as mild mermaids who siren-like allured the lonely traveller to a cruel death. So whilst my men were praying to the deities of the lake and the mountain, I tasted the sweet crystal water. The loch is 14,600 ft. above the sea, about half a mile in length, somewhat triangular in shape, and into its further narrow northern end fall several thin cascades from the melting snows overhead. Edelweiss and other allied woolly flowers bloomed on its bleak banks.

The pass (15,950 ft.) was reached by a stiffish climb for about a mile, over great masses of sharp splintered rocks; yet none of us suffered here the slightest inconvenience from the rarefied air, although the altitude was considerably more than that of Momay below the Dong-kia pass, which had tried us all so much. The view from the cairn at the top was not very extensive owing to the clouds that were drifting over us. The summit was a rugged knife-edge, with the most precipitous fall to the western or Nepalese side; and this also was the character of the peaks and ridges both north and south of the pass. The weathering rocks of the uplifted crest fell away abruptly on the Nepalese side, leaving jagged columns and towering pinnacles that looked like castellated battlements and needle-shaped spires.

Thin snow lay for over a hundred yards down the Nepalese side, in the cold northern shade. Thence we descended the precipitous slope, picking our way over about a mile of massive blocks of sharp splintered rocks. Here it was marvellous to see how the laden yaks lumbered along over these rocks, and skirted precipices that were formidable enough for the unladen human pedestrian. The yak frequently had to spring up on to ledges, like a goat, and poise itself with arched body, and all its four feet close together, before taking another spring; and at other times the patient beast circumvented sharp curves by a series of wriggles. In deep snow, such as is said to lie here from November to April, this passage must be much more difficult on account of the steepness of some of the slopes of crumbling loose rock; but the story of the glaciers and crevasses which had been reported here by the Indian traveller Baboo Sarat C. Das is unfounded.

From the western foot of this rocky pass the view up towards the Kang-La was grand. Several huge needles traced with snow, soared into the air like cathedral spires; and between these, several long shoots of stones from the splintering granite and quartz rocks of the ridge above swept down for full two thousand feet or more.

We crossed a short distance below the bottom of these stone-shoots (14,650 ft.) to the other side of the valley, and thence, after five weary miles round a spur, we gained the valley of the Yaloong river, and then commanded extensive views down into Eastern Nepal, which spread out before us like a map, in that remarkably clear atmosphere.

The Everest group, with its most prominent peak "No. XIII", stood up boldly about sixty miles away, though in the distant perspective from our elevated point of view these peaks seemed to be far below us. And through the deep cleft of the Arun river, I could see to the north of the Everest group some other snowy peaks further in the interior of Tibet, including some which were alleged to be higher than Everest. And it was now evident that the Everest range, like that of Kanchen-junga, seemed off the main axis of the Himalayas and the margin of the great Tibetan plateau, and appeared as a spur running south, and at right angles to that axis. At the northern end of this spur where it adjoins the Tibetan plateau of Dingri is the Tang-La, or "Terrible pass" (Bhairav-Langur), which Hodgson identified with Everest, which, however, is fifty miles farther to the S. E.

This upper part of Nepal of which we got such extensive views is so little known, even in regard to its broad territorial and tribal divisions, that I have embodied in the sketch-map on page 349 some of the brief information supplied by my guide. The upland tract to the south of Everest, lying between the Arun river and the glacial "milky" Kosi (*Doodh*-Kosi, a corruption of the Tibetan *Dud-tsi*) river, is called Khoomboo or Khumbu, and its inhabitants are Bhotiyas, that is of Tibetan stock. The purest of these occupy the northern half, which is called "*Shar*-Khumbu". The southern half or "*Solo*-Khumbu" is peopled by the "*Shar-pa*" or "*Sher-pa*" tribe, whom we have already seen, and who are slightly Hindooized by contact with the Kiranti tribe of the lower ranges and with their Nepalese neighbours, but they still retain their Tibetan dress. The Bhotiyas on the west bank of the Doodh-Kosi and between the San-Kosi, in the lower ravines of *Rong-Shar* also seem to be called "Shar-pa". The approximate distribution of the other Bhotiya tribes I have also indicated, namely, the Shugu-pa, Shing-sa-pa, Tok-be-pa, Waloong-pa, as well as the Kiranti and Limboo countries.

In regard to the adjoining part of Tibet to the north, I also got from my guide some interesting geological scraps of information, as he had resided near Tinki fortress and travelled much thereabouts. Fossils, so rare on the southern slopes of the Himalayas, are not uncommon on the northern. A short distance north of Tinki, across the Arun (there called the "*Ya-ru*"), is a great deal of chalky fossiliferous limestone, and also beds of yellow and red ochre, which the people use for decorating their houses. Also, still further north beyond Sakya, or "The Yellow Clay", at Jang-lache on the south bank of the Tsang-po, garnets are found embedded in a chalky formation, and rock-crystal, of which he had some specimens in his amulet-box. And close to the north of fort Shikar (Shel-kar), between and to the west of the two sites above mentioned, are very large fossil shells. This is interesting with reference to the Eocene nummulitic limestone found by Hooker on the margin of the Tibetan plateau above the Dongkia pass, and evidently a deposit similar to those found in Ladak, so that this land would appear to have been raised in very early times, and the nummulitic sea which seems to have run as a gulf up the Indus valley to Ladak, as Godwin-Austen has showed, probably extended thus far southwards, with open ocean to the east. As to the gold mines, my guide, like most superstitious Tibetans, was very reticent in giving information as to these supposed treasure-houses of the malignant earth-spirits. He had been near some of these on the borders of the snows, and said they were strongly guarded by troops, and the miners only occasionally worked. They offered sacrifices to the spirits and then rushed to the lodes, and after a few hours rushed back again laden with their treasures. Mica (Tibetan *Nam-do*, *i.e.* "sky-stone") is quarried in considerable quantities near Tinki, about six or seven miles below the line of perpetual snow. The Tibetan rock-salt which forms such a large trade with Nepal and Sikhim, is got directly from the great lakes. The ordinary rusty sort is gathered on the shores of the lakes, whilst the purer kind is picked up in large crystals on the wet margin of the water.

We then turned northwards, down into a sort of "devils' punch-bowl", and passing above the very small tarn in its bottom, called "The Spoonful of Water" (*Choo-lok-nyo*), at an elevation of 14,100 feet, we entered a gloomy valley of rocks, over which we clambered for about a mile, till we reached a point at which the small stream that flowed under the rocks shewed itself on the surface for a few yards; and here we encamped under a great boulder about

40 feet high, that had fallen from the ridge above. The wildness of this scene was forbidding. The valley for miles around seemed a vast quarry of stones hurled down pell-mell. And overhead, the snowy peak of Kang-La sent down a bitter blast of icy-cold glacier air on us, which our scant shelter and poor fire of faggots did little to relieve. This place was the source of the Nepalese river called the "*Cho-Gan-ga*", a branch of the Tambra or Tamru.

Yet, even so desolate a region as this, is guarded by the jealous Nepalese. So far, we had escaped encountering their patrols, but these latter captured the King of Sikhim not far from here when he tried to flee to Tibet in 1892—for since our last reference to him, on the occasion of our visit to the Jelep pass, several political developments have occurred.

The King, brooding over his fancied wrongs, fled from Sikhim in 1892, and tried to reach Tibet by this track we are following; but was captured by the Nepalese and handed over to the Indian Government. Then, after having been kept a State-prisoner in Darjeeling district for about three years, he was restored this year (1896) to his throne, and returned to the new capital at Gantok, which has grown to a considerable-sized village. His son and heir, however, still remains without any education worthy of the name.

Meanwhile the "Sikhim-Tibet Convention" to facilitate trade with Tibet and to demarcate the boundary, a Convention of which such great things were expected, has ended, like most of our other arrangements with China, in a fiasco. The boundary pillars were not allowed to be set up, and the opening of a nominal trade mart at Yatoong below the Jelep pass was discounted by the fact that no Tibetan trader was allowed to settle there, and still more vexatious restrictions were imposed on traders than before the war. For this block of Tibetan trade and this policy of an exclusion more rigorous than ever, the Chinese excuse themselves by alleging that it is all the doing of the Lama-priests of Lhasa. But it is the Chinese themselves undoubtedly who are at the bottom of it all, and they merely make a cat's-paw of the Lamas. The Tibetans are not unfriendly to Europeans, and the Lamas least of all wish the trade to be tied up, as they themselves are the chief traders of the country. China, on the other hand, wishes to keep the Tibetan markets to itself, as well as to consolidate its political power there, and its sinister influence at Lhasa in instigating the Tibetans against us on every opportunity has been clearly manifest from the time of Huc onwards.

So evident, indeed, was this influence in regard to this Sikhim-Tibet question that a casual visitor to Darjeeling, Count d'Alviella, remarked it many years ago. He wrote: "On sait que, d'après les Autorités du Thibet la fermeture "de cette province aux étrangers est due exclusivement à "des ordres envoyés de Pékin par le Gouvernement Chinois. "A Pékin, au contraire, on repond aux Anglais que c'est "uniquement le fait des Lamas et des fonctionnaires Thi-"betains;" and he quotes a letter that the Chinese resident

ANGLO-TIBETAN BOUNDARY COMMISSIONERS.

at Lhasa sent to the king of Sikhim in 1873, and which fell into our hands. In this letter the Chinese said: "Your "state of Sikhim borders on Tibet. You know our "wishes and our policy. You are bound to prevent the "English from crossing our frontier. Yet it is entirely your "fault—thanks to the roads which you have made for "them in Sikhim—that they have conceived this project. "If you continue to act thus, it will not be good for you. "Henceforth you must fulfil your obligations, and obey "the commands of Grand Lama Rimboche and those of the "twelfth Emperor of China."

Yet notwithstanding this recognised deceit of China, diplomacy was again tried with it over this very question, and under cover of their old excuse—blaming the Lamas for everything—the Chinese, without suffering any sacrifice themselves, have obtained important concessions, considerably strengthened their grip and prestige over Tibet, prevented us obtaining any solid recompense for the great cost of the late war, and have postponed more distantly than ever the opening up of that country to Europeans, and the development of its undoubted trade possibilities in the export of gold, wool, etc. in exchange for British and Indian goods. The situation, however, must eventually become critical again, and in that event it would be far better to throw over China altogether with its deceit and false promises, and deal directly with the Tibetans.

A "national party" is arising in Tibet in rebellion against the grinding yoke of the Chinese. I had the pleasure of meeting one of the leading spirits in this movement which has the moral and political progress of their country at heart. This gentleman came to Darjeeling in the train of the Chinese Commissioners, on the boundary question, and he is now the chief lay-Governor at Lhasa.

THE LAY-GOVERNOR OF LHASA, AND SUITE.

It was he who stopped M. Bonvalot and Prince Henry of Orleans on their way towards Lhasa, and at a point fully a *week's* journey from that city instead of the one day's journey as claimed by them.

In talking of the Chinese, when I mentioned that our troops had held Pekin, he treated the matter as a joke, like the official whom Mr. Blanford met, and exclaimed

"Perhaps your general reported that he had occupied Pekin, but he certainly never got there, for such a thing was quite impossible!"—so successfully have the Chinese concealed their indignity from the Tibetans.

But I cannot here refer to the many interesting conversations that I had with this enlightened, kindly man, who seems destined, if he lives, to play an important part in the history of Tibet.

As we came along this desolate track towards Tibet by which the unfortunate King of Sikhim had fled, my men had been keeping an outlook for a box of precious jewels which, according to a bazaar report, had been lost here by the king in his flight.

Morning broke fiercely cold with 5° Fah. of frost, and a keen wind raged. I was up two hours before daylight to see the sunrise from the western side of the peaks. The traders' trail to the north led over a pass bearing the characteristic name of "The Cold Pass" (Se-mo La), or Semarum as the Lepchas call it, at an elevation of 15,370 ft. At the summit I was again disappointed to find absolutely no trace of the glaciers and crevasses reported here by Baboo Sarat C. Das. There was at this season not only no snow in this pass, but none visible from it except the tips of the Everest group, which showed over the ranges to the west, and the distant snow-streaked ranges of Kambachen. To the north and east all the snowy peaks of the Kanchen' range, including the Kang-La, were hidden from view by a precipitous ridge which rose about 300 ft.

above the north side of the pass. This point, which had not been reached by the Baboo, I hurriedly scaled, with Kintoop and two of my men, as the sun was just rising, and I then got a magnificent view, not marred by a single cloud.

The wildness and majesty of this panorama was awful. The western side of the Kang-La, or "Pass of the Glaciers" rose up about two miles away in cold grey shade, and I could see lying within it, its snowfields and glaciers with their ice-falls, and the outflowing milky grey streams that ploughed down the bare grey granite valley, over 4,000 feet

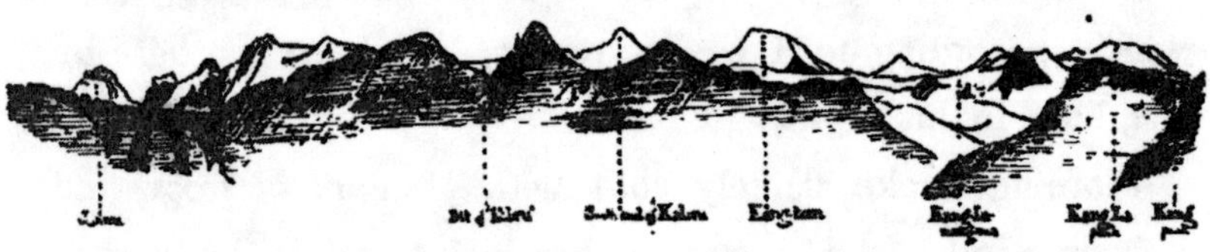

PROFILE OF KABRU, JANNU ETC. FROM SEMO PASS.

almost sheer below me, for I was on the knife-edge ridge of the shivered cliff. From this giddy height I saw, above and to the north of the tooth-rocks of the pass, the Kang-La Nang-ma, or "The Interior of the Pass of the Glaciers", which is not a pass at all as has hitherto been stated, but is only, according to my guides, a *cul-de-sac* or basin of snow and *névé*, where no traffic ever goes.

Above this, rose the knife-edge peak of Kang-tsen on the southern base of Kabru, which, for the reasons already stated, I believe to be the peak which Mr. Graham ascended in mistake for Kabru. And certainly it appeared from here to be the most prominent peak; for the long ridge of

KANG-LA PASS FROM THE WEST.

"Kabru" (properly "Kaboor") fell away lower in the perspective, over the bare cliffy shoulder of the opposite side of the valley, which latter also unfortunately blocked out from my view, not only the bases of Kabru and Jannu, but also the peaks of Kanchen-junga itself.

The tip of the tremendous southern cliff of Jannu, or "Juona", which Hooker, who had a near view of it, estimated at 9,000 feet and in appearance like that of Mont Cervin from the Riffel, gleamed with its warty knobs in the rising sunlight, over the dark ridge. My men called it Kanchen-Jo, or "The Lord of the Great Glaciers", apparently because it was the most dominant peak visible. As to the possibility of climbing it, Mr. Graham, who saw it from the east, says: "I think it is possible from the east, but there is an enormous glacier at least twenty miles long to be traversed before reaching the *arête*, and even when there it would be very difficult. From west and south the peak is obviously impassable."

West of Jannu, a sharply serrated snowy peak like a lion's tooth was called to me "The Glacial Goddess of Medicine", (*Man-lha-L'a-mo Kang*) and is an object of worship. It seems to be the "Choonjerma" of Hooker. Whilst, behind it, showed up the snowy tip of a higher peak, which was called Tang-tong-Kang, apparently the "Nango" of Hooker. Further west, beyond this, were the snows of Yangma and Tashi-raka, bounding Tibet; and still further west were the tips of the Khoombu and Everest group of peaks. The northern cliffy face of Everest was very bold and precipitous, as shown in the accompanying sketch; but the rounded northern spur seen by Colonel Tanner from Sandook-phu and estimated at about 25,000 feet high, was not visible, it must have been hidden by the rocky ranges in my middle distance. The compass-bearings of these peaks are detailed in the appendix.[57]

Kang-La, or "The Pass of the Glaciers", is perpetually

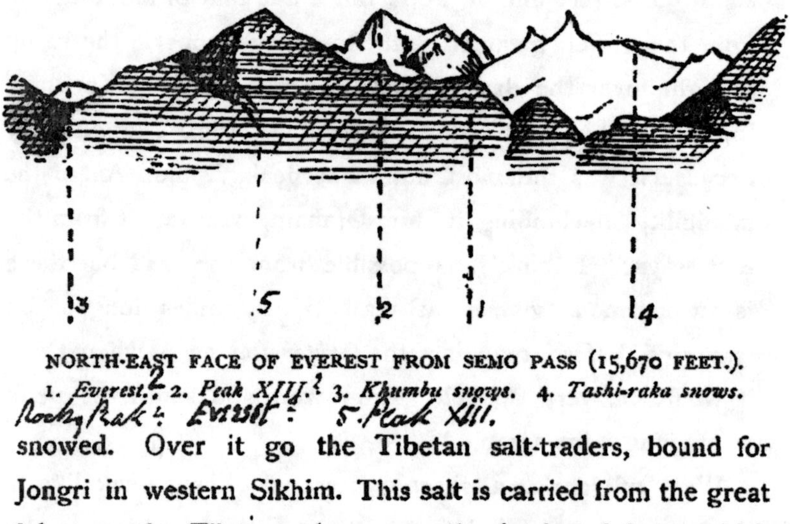

NORTH-EAST FACE OF EVEREST FROM SEMO PASS (15,670 FEET.).
1. *Everest.* 2. *Peak XIII.* 3. *Khumbu snows.* 4. *Tashi-raka snows.*

snowed. Over it go the Tibetan salt-traders, bound for Jongri in western Sikhim. This salt is carried from the great lakes on the Tibetan plateau on the backs of sheep, which are driven up the valley, beneath us, and over this pass in summer. A little also comes in November, after the October snows have hardened sufficiently to bear the weight of pedestrians and the salt-laden sheep. The salt is bartered for rice, *Murwa*, maize, bundles of madder dye-stuff, etc. Mr. Graham crossed this pass from Jongri, and his description of it, which has an important bearing on his ascent of the peak which he believed to be Kabru, will now be more intelligible from my foregoing photograph on p. 417 and the key to it on p. 416. He wrote:

"The next day (30th March, 1883,) we took the three best men and proceeded west to the foot of the Kangla pass, which leads into Nepal. The summit of the pass is some 17,000 ft., and is crowned by a noble saddle glacier, whilst *on either side rises a sharp rock-tooth some 1,500 ft. higher. We turned to the right, to the foot of the glacier,* which flows in a beautiful stream south-west from Kanchenjunga. Here we encamped on the moraine in one of the grandest amphitheatres imaginable. *Due east rose Kabru, 24,015 ft., its western face almost like a wall,* corniced with hugh masses of glacier and snow, from which thundered an incessant volley of avalanches. North-east rose Kanchen', its grey precipices even now but lightly touched with snow. North, Jannu showed its awful southern cliff, while west, rose a great peak of snow and rock, great actually, though small and easy as compared with its neighbours. The night was the coldest we experienced in the Himalayas—8° (?) Fahr. being the minimum reading of the thermometer. Early next morning Imboden and I started to ascend the peak on our west. It was a hard and interesting scramble of some five hours and a half, rock and snow alternately. Only one place offered any serious difficulty, and at 10.15 we were at the summit. Though the western view was clouded, we had a noble view of the north-west of Kanchen'. Both by aneroid and by comparison with surrounding peaks, we estimated the height at rather over 20,000 ft."

The foregoing sentences which I have placed in italics, taken in connection with Mr. Graham's description of the peak which he ascended in the belief that it was Kabru appear to indicate *Kang-tsen* both in direction and physical aspect, rather than Kabru.

Mr. Graham is not the only one who has claimed to have ascended Kabru. The patron saint of Sikhim, Latsun Chembo, is said to have miraculously reached that peak over two centuries ago. And the wild bare rocky gorge beneath us bears the ironical name of "The Pleasant Garden" (*Nam-gah-tsal*), because, says the legend, that saint lived "happily" in a hermitage here, when he was composing the ritual for the worship of Kanchen'. He is said to have dwelt under this western side of the pass in a cave called *Kam-pa Kha-brag*, and near the "Monkey's-back Rock" (*Preu-gyab-tak*), so named with reference to its outline, as suggesting a sitting monkey.

My panorama also included some ominous smoke from the village of Tseram in the deep valley below, where a Nepalese guard was stationed. I had hoped to have been able to reach the upper glacier valley of Yaloong, and so right up to the great western glacier of Kanchen', without sighting any Nepalese villages; but now, I found that, in order to get round the opposite spur, I must descend quite close to the guard-post of Tseram, where there was a strong probability of my getting discovered; and the political complications certain to ensue in such an event were more than I, as a Government official, could risk. It was exasperating, after undergoing so many hardships in reaching thus far, and penetrating for more than thirty miles over a track not previously traversed by any European, to be stopped within one and a half day's journey, from what must be one of the grandest bits of the Himalayas, namely, the south-western glacier of Kanchen-junga within its amphitheatre of magnificent peaks, ranging from the precipitous Jannu (25,300 ft.), round by Kamba-chen (25,780 ft.) and the curving crests of Kanchen' (28,153 ft.) to Kabru (24,015 ft.).

It is to be hoped that the existing prohibition to travel in these grand regions may soon be relaxed, as so many interesting geographical and geological problems there await solution; and especially so as the country that is thus closed against Europeans more absolutely than any other in the world, except Tibet, is yet within our "sphere of influence", and its Government is on the friendliest terms politically with the British.

Until I commenced to descend from the sharp crest of this tremendous precipice on which we had been clinging, I had not realised how insecure our pinnacle had been. It was such a knife-edge that I had to be held by my men when I stretched out to take the photographs; but it was only when about to descend that the rottenness of the rocks was so apparent. These latter were so deeply gashed and fissured by the shivering action of the hot sun on the frozen granite, as to be almost a wall of loose splinters. As we descended, some pieces broke off and fell into the yawning abyss below. In fact not a single bit of this rock could be trusted. Before leaving the summit, the young Lama—who with Kintoop had built a tiny cairn on the topmost pinnacle and decorated it with rags torn from their dress; for, said they, no human being had likely ever been there before—stopped behind to blow a farewell blast on a human thigh-bone to the spirit of that monarch of mountains, Kanchen-Junga.

As we retraced our steps down the Semo pass, several of the beautiful Tibetan snow-cocks (*Hrak-pa*, so named after their cry) were calling amongst the rocks of grey granite and quartz on our left. Lower down, we came on a covey of blood-pheasants (*Ithagenes cruentes*), of which I shot a brace as they scampered upwards over the stones. Their bright coloured plumage, mottled crimson and green, is admirably adapted to conceal them amongst the green and crimson lichen-covered rocks in their bare mountain home. On returning to our bivouac of the previous night, my collector brought me a splendidly plumaged *Monal* pheasant in one hand, and the shattered fragments of his gun in the other, and dolefully explained that as he fired his gun it had burst. He was relieved when, instead of receiving the expected scolding, I congratulated him on his escape. These men cram so much powder and shot into their rusty old muzzle-loading guns, that the wonder is that fatal accidents are not more frequent.

Slight snow then began to fall from the murky clouds that were quickly banking up overhead, so that we decided to push quickly over the Cha-bab pass that day, in case a heavy snowfall might cut off our retreat in that direction. But the baggage-yak was nowhere to be found; these beasts when unloaded are turned loose to forage for their food in the scanty tufts of grass and herbage amongst the rocks. The yak-herd after looking high and low for it, to see whether it had not fallen over a precipice in the neighbourhood, decided that it probably had gone back to seek its companion who had been left behind at the Cha-bab pass, where it had been lamed by the sharp rocks; and sure enough this had happened, for as we approached that pass we heard through the snowy fog the musical tinkle of their bells, and found them quietly herding together near the foot of the pass, much to the joy of the yak-herd who had himself been carrying most of the absent beast's burden.

The pass was now powdered with freshly fallen snow for about a mile from the top; a little, too, had fallen on the other side, as far as the weird lake of "The Peacock's Tail". It was dark ere we reached the verdant dell of Gamotang, embowered in wooded hills, and presenting such a grateful contrast to the bleak regions from which we had come. Here we were pleased to find a blazing fire in the herdsman's hut, and a large heap of firewood collected by our two coolies who had been left behind, of whom the sick one was now recovering.

In the morning, which rose bright and sunny, I went after some pheasants that were calling in the woodlands, and I got two fine *Monal* cocks and four partridges as the morning's bag. These gorgeously plumaged *Monal*, which are so abundant in the mountains hereabouts, are snared and slaughtered wholesale by the natives, for the sake of their skins, which are sent down to Calcutta for export. In the latter place as many as a thousand skins are offered for sale at one time.

My men were delighted at the prospect of returning homewards from these wild regions, and started up hill with light hearts,—and lighter loads as we had eaten up almost all our stores. And as we re-crossed "The Pass of the Devil", where the white snow among the black cliffs was weeping away in tears, the young Lama collected bunches of juniper and the aromatic rhododendron leaves to burn as incense before the altar of the great Buddha, as a thanksgiving offering for our safe return.

Some zest was added to our threading of the track down the lower slopes on the Nepalese side of the ridge, when we saw in the places where we crossed the thawing mud, between the rocks, the fresh footprints of a bear who also was evidently going along this track, a short way ahead of us; but after about a mile they disappeared amongst the rhododendrons, whence the brute doubtless had a peep at us as we passed.

We spent the night in the shallow cave of Nego (13,170 ft.). It was little more than an overhanging ledge of rock, and could have afforded scant shelter from rain; but the night fortunately was dry, with little wind, though very cold. From my corner of the cave, the figures of my men seemed

BIVOUAC IN CAVE.

weird and spectral-like as they flitted about in the gloom, or crouched over the camp-fire which lit up their features with its lurid glare. It is only by being placed in such close relations to these natives that one fully realizes their many good traits, and how very human they are after all. Their hearty good humour under hardships, their willing and untiring energy when work is heaviest, their good comradeship, and generous sharing of their few comforts with each other, all this redeems them from much of what they lack in civilization.

The next day brought us through fine forests and mountains, back to our larger tents and a fresh store of much needed provisions; and in this free open-air life amidst magnificent scenery, we go on gathering fresh trophies and quaint experiences, till our tents are struck for the last time, and we return to the tyranny and comforts of civilization.

And as we bid farewell to our trusty Tartar servants—our genial fellow-travellers—and our train races us down from Darjeeling, and the silver vision of Kanchen-junga recedes from our view, we regretfully realize that these wanderings have become a memory of the past.

APPENDIX

NOTES TO THE TEXT

1. Dr. Hooker was the first European to explore and survey Sikhim and the Eastern border of Nepal scientifically, and he did this work with such fulness of knowledge that his book [*Himalayan Journals* by (Sir) Joseph D. Hooker, M.D., 2 Vols., 1854,] must always remain the leading authority on the botanical and physical history of these regions. Of other books referring to parts of these regions, the *Gazetteer of Sikhim* is restricted to that portion of Sikhim which still remains under native rule, and it consists of detached official reports upon a few topics, the greater portion being my contributions on the religion of one of the tribes, and on the birds of this section of the Himalayas. Dr. Buchanan-Hamilton's *Account of Nepal* (1820) and Brian Hodgson's *Essays* contain miscellaneous notes of interest to students of ethnology: Sir William Hunter's *Imperial Gazetteer*, and *Account of Bengal* embody some statistical information in regard to Sikhim; and Sir Clement Markham's *Tibet* and Mr. Saunders' compilation on the Himalayas refer incidentally to a few of the passes and general physical features of the mountain ranges thereabouts. Colonel Gawler published in 1873 a few notes on his military expedition to Sikhim in 1871; and "A Lady Pioneer" gives in her *Indian Alps* a vague account of a short ramble in the outer ranges of the same country. The political reports on Sikhim by Messrs. Edgar and Macaulay, containing some observations of general interest, were not made public.

2. Whilst generally following the current map-forms of the names, I have spelt some of the chief names nearer the vernacular form, yet in a way to be pronounceable by English readers, and recognizable by the natives themselves, which many of the current forms are not. Thus "*Kanchen-junga*" for "Kinchinjinga" "*Rang-eet*" for "Ranjeet", "*Choong-tang*" for "Cheungtong", "*Sandook-phu*" for "Sundakfu" etc.

3. W. T. Blanford, F.R.S., in *Bengal Asiatic Socy. Jour.* 1871, p. 393.

4. The name of this place, "Siligoori", I find, means in the patois of the native Koch tribe "The Stony Site", for it is the outermost point at which pebbles from the Himalayas appear upon the surface of the muddy Delta of Bengal.

5. These are the Hindooized aboriginal *Chandals*, and those members of this tribe who have been proselytized to Mohammedanism, the *Nashyas.* There are also some Mongoloid Koch, and in the recesses of the forest on the bank of the Mech river are to be found a few survivors of those semi-aborigines who have given their name to this river, which divides the Terai or Morang of Sikhim from that of Nepal.

6. This, I think, is the etymology of the Nepalese name for this country (namely "Sik*h*im" and not "Sik*k*im" as it is sometimes misspelt in English books). The word seems to me to be derived from the Nepalese or Parbatiya *Sikhin*, "The Crested", which well denotes the leading feature of the country as seen from Nepal, where its mountain ridges running transversely to those of Eastern Nepal seem to form a bristling series of *crests.* The aborigines, the Lepchas, however, call it *Nelyang* or "The Place of Caves", while the Tibetans call it *Den-jong* or *Demo-jong*, or "The Country of Rice and Fruit", as it is a granary for bleak Tibet.

7. Sir Edwin Arnold's *Light of Asia*, II, 42—43.

8. Colonel Everest, after whom the great mountain was named, when organising the Trigonometrical Survey of India, recognised the disturbing influence of the local attraction exercised by the Himalayas, and endeavoured to minimize it by placing the northernmost station for the observation of his great Indian arc of meridian at Kaliana, over sixty miles from the Himalayas. Still he found a discrepancy existed between the length of the arc as measured and as astronometrically observed. Archdeacon Pratt, who took up this question about 1852, showed that the disturbing effect of the Himalayas was much greater than had been supposed, and he attempted to estimate the amount of this local attraction, and published his results in the *Transactions of the Royal Society* for 1860—62.

9. *Proceedings Royal Geographical Society*, 1884, pp. 429 etc.

10. "Twenty Years' Climbing and Hunting in the Himalayas" in *Alpine Journal* about 1880.

11. 1889.

12. *Eleusinæ crocana.*

13. For geological notes on this part of Sikhim see Mallet's paper in the Indian Geological Survey Reports. He calls these slates and schists, the "Daling" series, after a place of that name in the east of the Darjeeling district.

14. This custom, as I have shown elsewhere (*Jour. Bengal Asiatic Soc.*, III, 1898), seems a survival of the matriarchy or mothership of the clan, which appears to have been prevalent in this tribe.

15. The less-known Hindoo title of *Pati* or "Master" was used in the ballad.

16. The proper form of this Nepalese name for them is "*Lap-che*", which I find means the "vile speakers"; for the Lepchas, unlike their Nepalese neighbours, adhered to their own vernacular and did not adopt the fashionable Hindoo dialect of the Goorkhas as did the Nepalese, and hence these latter applied this contemptuous name to them. This tribal name is curiously paralleled in the case of the "Welsh". According to Canon Taylor (*Words and Places*, p. 67) this is a similar derisive term applied by the neighbouring Saxons and meaning the "Jabberers".

17. The other *Kazis* in addition to this one of Lasso, are Yangthang, Gangtok, Rhenok, Dallom, Barmiak, Tashiting, Song, Living, Maling, Simik, and Pendom. The word *Kazi* seems to me to be borrowed through the Nepalese from the Mahomedan rulers of India, and to be the Persian word *Kazi* or *Kadi*, a magistrate, a name familiar to the readers of the "*Arabian Nights*". Other titles thus adopted by the Nepalese are *Subah*, a governor; and *Jung Bahadur* ("Brave Warrior"). These *Kazis* are called by the Bhotiyas *L'ünpo*, or "Ministers", and by the Lepchas *Puno-Sadam-bo*, or "King's Chiefs". The subordinate officials in order of precedence are the military officer, the *Ding-pön* or *Mak-pön*; the larger village headman, *Gyu-mi* in (Lepcha *Ta-so* or *Atyak-bo*); and the smaller village headman, *Gya-pön* or *Pi-pen*.

18. J. W. Edgar's *Report on a Visit to Sikhim and the Tibetan Frontier*. Calcutta. 1874.

19. In the *Pioneer* of March 7th. 1895.

20. The description of this new species, named after me by Mr. W. Ogilvie Grant of the British Museum, is thus given in the *Bulletin of the British Ornithological Club* and reprinted in the *Ibis* 1894, p. 424:—"Like *G. pectoralis*, but with the rufous collar almost obselete; the superciliary stripe grey, not white; ear coverts pale buff, with blackish shaft-stripes instead of black, or black streaked with white; and the tail rather narrowly tipped with ashy; whereas in *G. pectoralis* it is

broadly tipped with white. Habitat.—Rungeet (Rangit) Sikhim. 4,000 feet." The type specimen is in the British Museum, and three other skins (*Vide* G. pectoralis sp. "*Gazetteer of Sikhim*", p. 231.) are in my large collection in the Hunterian Museum of Glasgow University.

21. *Malay Archipelago*, 204 (5th edition. 130) with figure.

22. Major Sherwill has described the mechanism of these bridges in the *Journal* of the Bengal Asiatic Society, also Hooker.

23. Details of his dynasty are given in my "*Buddhism of Tibet*" and in the *Gazetteer of Sikhim*, p. 24 etc.

24. This expedition was under Colonel Gawler who details it in his booklet afore-cited.

25. In Tibetan *Dorje-pag-mo.*

26. W. T. Blanford's *Mammalia of British India.* W. B. Tegetmeier in *Field*, September 4th, 1897.

27. *Ceremonial Institutions.*

28. In Tibetan *Sang-nag cho-zin.*

29. Hooker's *Journals*, II, p. 48. An eye-sketch of the plant was figured by Captn. W. S. Sherwill in *Journ. Bengal Asiatic Society*, 1853, p. 618.

30. The water blackened a silver coin in three minutes and was faintly alkaline to litmus paper. And I found on analysing a sample that it had the following chemical composition:—Total solid matter including

free Sulphur, Iron, Lime and Silica . . .	16·38	grains	per	gallon.
Calcium carbonate	2·08	"	"	"
Chlorine	0·14	"	"	"
Ammonia, free	0·0014	"	"	"
do. albuminoid.	0·0008	"	"	"
Nitrates and Sulphates	traces.			

31. *Himal. Journals*, II. p. 116.

32. *Jo-dud-tse*, which may also mean "the honourable ambrosia".

33. On the origin of the Flora of the European Alps by J. Ball, *Proc. Royal Geographical Society*, I. (1879), pp. 564—588. A. Wallace in *Darwinism*, p. 401, and Thistleton Dyer in *Trans. Linnean Socy.* July 1896. p. 121.

34. *Proc.* Roy. Geog. Socy., 1884, p. 416.

35. *Jour.* Bengal Asiatic Society, 1871, p. 407.

36. *Sil-bo* is the written form.

37. A great cattle epidemic was reported from Upper Tibet under the name of "Chunneah", also foot-and-mouth disease (*Khucha*), as detailed in the report of the Indian Cattle Plague of 1871.

38. Published in the *Indian Daily News*, 1891, and reproduced in part in the *Proc.* Roy. Geog. Society for Sept. 1892, p. 613, etc.

39. Report on Locusts by E. Cotes, in *India Museum Notes*, from which also the illustration is derived.

40. The remarkable local differencies in the rainfall in this portion of the Himalayas, due to the intervention of elevated mountain ridges precipitating the rain-clouds, are detailed in the following table, for the data of which I am indebted to the Meteorological Reporter of the Government of Bengal.

Rainfall in Sikhim Himalayas and Chumbi Valley of Tibet.

	January	February	March	April	May	June	July	August	September	October	November	December	Yearly Total
1. Siligoori .	0·60	0·54	1·22	4·21	10·15	25·49	32·29	25·37	17·90	5·04	0·37	0·09	123·27
2. Kurseong .	0 74	1·60	1·47	6·08	12·41	28·30	49·26	36·32	23·46	5·46	0·39	0·26	165·75
3. Darjeeling	0·67	0·95	1·65	4·61	8·50	23·69	32·45	25·61	17·31	5·83	0·20	0·22	121·69
4. Pedong . .	1·07	1·08	2·82	5·31	9·92	16·83	25·56	22·02	14·34	3·33	0·32	0.38	102·98
5. Gantok. . .	0·65	1·91	4·52	10·14	28·46	21.46	21·82	24·96	22·75	7·79	1·33	0·57	146·36
6. Yatung Chumbi.	0·41	0·60	3·94	5·69	4·91	6·72	7·95	9·77	12·96	3·70	0.31	0·05	57·01

The above average rainfall has been computed from the rainfall recorded during a period of over ten years in the case of Darjeeling, Siligoori Pedong, 7 years for Kurseong, and 4 and 3 years respectively for Gantok and Yatung. The rainfall at the latter place in a valley of Tibet was registered by Mr. Hobson of the Imperial Chinese Customs Service.

41. For further details of the etymology of the Mountain, River, and Place Names of these Himalayas see my article *Jour. Bengal Asiatic Socy.*, 1891, pp. 53—79.

42. These "*Dooars*" are usually estimated at 18 in number, of which 11 lie on the frontier of Bengal, where this Dooar of Daling and that of Buxar are the chief. The other seven are on the corresponding frontier of Asam.

43. This is a literal translation of the tribal prefix "*Motanchi*' and seems to me to be a vestige of the former matriarchal organisation of this tribe (see my articles in the Berlin Ethnological Journal, 1898, and Bengal Asiatic Socy. Journal, part III, 1898).

44. See map on p. 349. Their eponymous patron saint is Goorkha-nath, a form of the Indian god Shiva, the Destroyer.

45. For further instances of their valour, see a paper by Captain E. Vansittart in *Jour. Bengal Asiatic Socy.*, 1895.

46. Detailed in my paper on "Frog Worship" in *Indian Antiquary*, 1893.

47. Yule's *Marco Polo*, I. 220. "On the road from Kashmir towards Tibet", writes Ferishta (Brigg. IV. 449), "there is a plain on which no other vegetable grows but a poisonous grass that destroys all the cattle that taste it, and therefore no horsemen venture to travel that route." In the North-Western Himalayas the plant *Andromeda ovalifolia* is notorious for poisoning sheep and goats, while those living in the locality are exempt (H. Cleghorn, Jour. Indian Agricult. Socy., XVI, 4). And in regard to a plant of the same order (*Ericacea*) Mr. Marsh "Man and Nature", 40, attests the like fact regarding the *Kalmia angustifolia* of New England. Some of the Himalayan rhododendrons affiliated to the Ericacea are also poisonous.

48. My Monograph "Are Venomous Snakes Auto-toxic?" Calcutta 1887—which anticipated the line of enquiry followed by Calmette and Frazer in regard to "Antivenene".

49. Seven species are found in the Himalayas, of which at least four occur in Sikhim. The most deadly, *A. ferox* was described by Dr. Buchanan-Hamilton in his "Nepal". *A. uncinatum* is confined to Sikhim and is very rare, its stems turn. *A. luridum* is found at a higher elevation, about 14,000 feet, and has dull *red* flowers. *A. palmatum* has kidney-shaped leaves and greenish-blue flowers and grows at elevations of 8—10,000 feet. The two species *hetero-phyllum* and *lycoctonum* are confined to the Western Himalayas. The former yields the "*atees*" drug of the Indian bazaars.

50. This sketch-map gives a correction in detail to the larger map (appearing on p. 349) and is derived from Native Explorer M.H.'s report which was not available when the original map was prepared. This explorer also reports that the track from Dingri passes to the south of the Palgo lake. See also note No. 52.

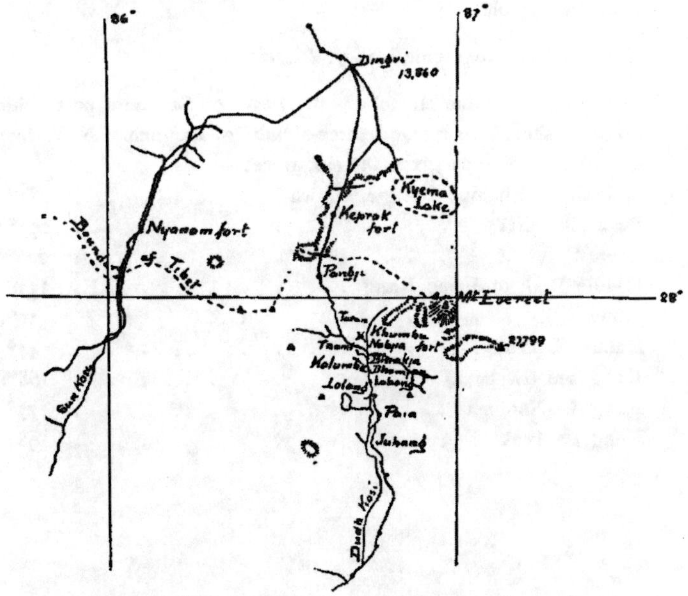

51. My *Buddhism of Tibet.* pp. 67, 370, 371, 382 f.n., 430.

52. The chief pass in this picture appears to be the "Pangu" pass (see Map in preceding note No. 50 where this name is spelt "Pangji") traversed by Native Explorer M.H. in passing from Nepal to Tibet in 1885—86, of whose report no full details seem to have been published. He mentions that he saw from this pass, a high black rock with the outline of a horse crowning an inaccessible spur, also ice-tables, and masses of rock piled up in the form of pillars 20 to 30 feet high and standing on solid beds of ice.

53. D. Freshfield, "Geograph. Jour." *loc. cit.*

54. The only Europeans who seem to have passed along part of this ridge beyond this point are Captn. W. Sherwill, Messrs. White and G. Gammie

and possibly "A Lady Pioneer". Baboo P. N. Bose accompanied Mr. White as geologist (*Records Geological Survey India*, XXIV. p. 46 etc.)

55. In *Jour. Bengal Asiatic Socy.*, 1862, p. 457 etc. The words and sentences in brackets have been added by me, in order to render the narrative more intelligible.

56. In Jour. Royal Geographical Socy. *loc. cit.*

57. The bearings from the cliff above the Semo or Semarum pass, which on my map should be marked three-eighths of an inch N.N.W. from the end of my route as given therein, were:—

S. Peak of Khumbu Kang-nga-rawa	282°	W.
Peak No. XIII	293°	„
Everest	296°	„
Middle Peak of Lamo Kang	353°	„
Jannu	10°.5	E.
Kabur, S. Peak	47°	„
Kang-tsen (N. Peak)	68°.5	„
Kang La-Nangma	77°	„
Kang La Peak	98°	„

INDEX

INDEX

A

B

C

D

E

F

G

H

I

J

K

L

M

N

O

P

Q

R

S

T

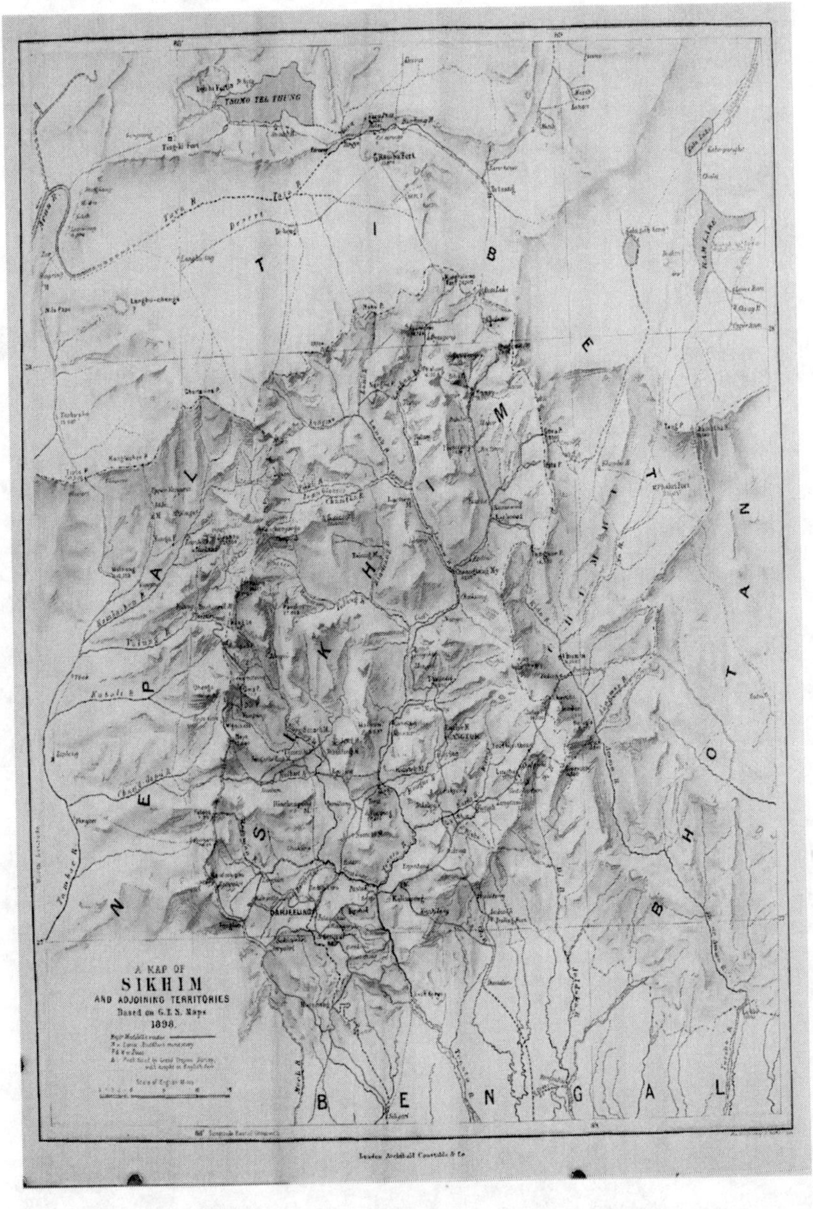

London: Archibald Constable & Co

Published by

Facsimile Publisher
Ashok Vihar, Delhi-110052 (India)
Website: www.facsimilepublisher.com

Distributed by

Gyan Books Pvt. Ltd.
5, Ansari Road, Daryaganj, New Delhi-110002 (India)
E-mail: books@gyanbooks.com, Website: www.gyanbooks.com

2 222000 005542